Color Atlas of
Liver
Disease

Second Edition

Dame Sheila Sherlock

DBE, MD, DSc(NY)(Hon), FRCP, FRCP(E), FRCCP(Hon),
FRCP(I)(Hon), FACP(Hon)

Professor of Medicine in the
University of London at the
Royal Free Hospital School of Medicine
London, England

John A. Summerfield

MD, FRCP

Reader in Medicine in the
University of London at
St Mary's Hospital Medical School,
Imperial College of Science, Technology and Medicine,
England

Mosby
Year Book

St. Louis   Baltimore   Boston   Chicago   London   Philadelphia   Sydney   Toronto

Mosby Year Book

Dedicated to Publishing Excellence

Published in 1991 with rights in the USA, Canada and Puerto Rico by Mosby–Year Book Inc
Second Edition Copyright © 1991 Wolfe Publishing Ltd
English second edition first published by Wolfe Publishing Ltd, 1991
Printed in The Netherlands
ISBN 0 8151 7658 9
First English edition published in 1979, Paperback edition in 1988

Library of Congress Cataloging-in-Publication Data

Sherlock, Sheila, Dame.
    A colour atlas of liver disease/Sheila Sherlock, J. Summerfield.
  —2nd ed.
        p.   cm.
    ISBN 0-8151-6634-6
    1. Liver—Diseases—Atlases.   I. Summerfield, John A.   II.
Title.
    [DNLM: 1. Liver Diseases—atlases.   WI 17 S552c]
    RC845.S51918   1991
    616.3'62'070222—dc20
    DNLM/DLC
for Library of Congress   91-19645
                                                              CIP

Contents

Preface to the Second Edition

When this Atlas was first published twelve years ago our hope was that the collection of colour pictures of the physical signs, pathology and investigations of liver disease would withstand the barriers of language and time. However, the pace of change in hepatology has been so great that to bring this second edition up to date has required a major revision – about half the book has changed. More than 70 pictures have been removed, either because of quality or because the investigations illustrated are now redundant, and 150 new pictures have been added. Existing chapters have been updated and there are new chapters on AIDS and the liver, liver transplantation, and trauma. We hope that this second edition will prove to be a comprehensive collection of pictures of liver disease for the 1990s and beyond.

For the new material in this edition we wish to express our gratitude to Dr Rob Goldin, Dr Mary Crofton, Dr W. Gedroyc, Mr Michael Thick, Dr N. Frances, Dr Carol Seymour, Mr Steve Pollard, Dr L. Berger, Dr Henri Bismuth, Dr Robert Dick, Dr G. Dusheiko, Dr R. de Francis, Dr L. Gayotto, Mr N. Habib, Professor K.E.F. Hobbs, Dr M.S. Khuroo, Dr C.C. Kibbler, Dr Kishore Reddy, Professor P.J. Scheuer, Dr E.R. Schiff, and Dr A.T. Tavill.

Preface to the First Edition

Recent advances in hepatology have made it even more essential to be familiar with the clinical signs and pathology of liver disease. The correct management of patients is becoming increasingly dependent on a precise diagnosis. Our aim in this Atlas has been to compile an up-to-date and comprehensive collection of the physical signs, pathology and investigations of liver disease. This format has permitted the collection of a much larger number of high quality colour photographs than is normally possible in standard textbooks. However, the Atlas should be used as a companion to the standard textbooks on the subject. For this reason the legends to the pictures have been ruthlessly pruned to keep them short; the pictures should speak for themselves. The book begins with a general chapter on the examination of the liver and the signs of liver disease. Subsequent chapters deal with the major groups of diseases affecting the liver, with their special signs.

We hope that clinical medical students and candidates for higher examinations, both medical and surgical, will find the Atlas a useful adjunct to their studies. General physicians, surgeons and gastroenterologists will find a comprehensive survey of the signs of hepatology, including rare conditions that they will only occasionally encounter.

For systematic accounts, in particular of disease mechanisms and treatment, readers are recommended to consult the standard texts on liver disease, including Sherlock, S., *Diseases of the Liver and Biliary System,* Eighth Edition 1989, Blackwell Scientific Publications; Schiff, L. and Schiff, E.R., *Diseases of the Liver,* Sixth Edition 1987, Lippincott; Scheuer, P.J., *Liver Biopsy Interpretation,* Fourth Edition 1988, Baillière Tindall.

It is hoped that this book will withstand the barriers of language and time. The message should be understood by those whose first language is not English and after many current theories of disease and methods of investigation and treatment have been long forgotten.

Acknowledgements

We are deeply indebted to Dr R. Dick (Consultant Radiologist) and Professor P.J. Scheuer (Professor of Histopathology), at the Royal Free Hospital, for their help and advice. In addition, Dr R. Dick provided many of the radiological illustrations and Professor P.J. Scheuer much of the histological material. We are very grateful for the many pictures provided by Mr J. Agnew and Mr J. Wood (Senior Physicists), Dr L. Berger (Consultant Radiologist) and Professor K.E.F. Hobbs (Professor of Surgery).

We also thank our past and present colleagues at the Royal Postgraduate Medical School and the Royal Free Hospital, including Dr Bengt Arborgh, Dr G. Chadwick, Dr J. Dooley, Dr E. Elias, Miss Phyllis George, Dr Angela Gorman, Dr R. Hunt, Dr D. Jewell, Dr A.P. Kirk, Dr T. Lyssiotis, Dr N. McIntyre, Mr S. Parbhoo and Dr G. Smith-Laing.

This Atlas could not have been compiled without the generous help of many other friends and colleagues, including Dr June Almeida, Wellcome Research Laboratories, Kent, Dr S. Bender, Dr K. Hübner and Dr P. Rottger, Frankfurt, Germany, Professor M.J. Clarkson, Liverpool School of Tropical Medicine, Liverpool, Major-General J.C. Crook, Ministry of Defence, London, Professor G.M. Edington and Dr Y.M. Fakunle, Zaria, Nigeria, Dr S.V. Feinman, Toronto, Canada, Dr J. Galambos and Dr Hersh, Atlanta, USA, Mr B. Hawkes, Sittingbourne, Kent, Professor M.S.R. Hutt, St Thomas's Hospital, London, Professor Prayat Laksanaphuk, Bangkok, Thailand, Dr F. Margolin and Dr J. Bennington, San Francisco, USA, Professor G.A. Martini, Marburg, Germany, Professor W. Peters, Liverpool School of Tropical Medicine, Liverpool, Dr W. Pipatnagul, Bangkok, Thailand, Dr M.F. Sorrell, Omaha, USA, Dr G. Whelan, Melbourne, Australia, Dr E. Williams, Pembrokeshire, Wales and Professor A.W. Woodruff, London School of Tropical Medicine and Hygiene, London.

Finally, we thank Mr Cedric C. Gilson (Director) and his colleagues, Mrs Ruth M. Eastwood, Mr Michael J. Graham, Miss Julie M. Phipps, Mr Jozef Pollak and Mrs Ann K. Sym of the Department of Medical Illustration at the Royal Free Hospital for the excellent photographic work, Miss Janice Cox for the artwork and Mrs Jean Fulcher for typing the manuscript.

1. Clinical examination of the liver and biliary system

Examination of the liver

1 Functional anatomy of the liver.
Three main hepatic veins divide the liver into four sectors, each of them receiving a portal pedicle. Hepatic veins and portal veins are intertwined as the fingers of two hands. Each segment (roman numerals) has its own major blood supply. This concept is very important when hepatic resections are performed.

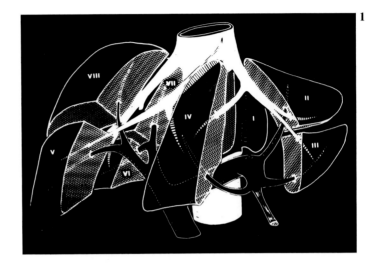

2 The normal liver, the largest organ in the body, weighs about 1.5kg. The upper border is at the level of the fifth rib, the lower border lies under the costal margin on the right. The lower edge is usually palpable in deep inspiration when the liver moves downwards. The upper border is defined by heavy percussion. Light percussion together with palpation will identify the lower border. An estimate of liver size can be obtained from the vertical length of dullness to percussion in the right mid clavicular line (usually 12–15cm). It is reduced in cirrhosis and fulminant hepatitis and is important in monitoring progress. Routine examination of the liver must include auscultation for friction rubs. These may be due to a recent liver biopsy or to a tumour. Arterial bruits may be related to acute alcoholic hepatitis or to primary liver cell cancer. Venous hums can be due to portal hypertension. The spleen is rarely palpable in health.

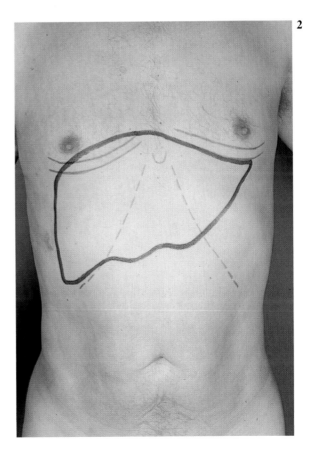

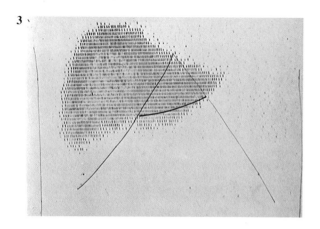

3 Isotope scan of the liver. An intravenous injection of the gamma-emitting isotope ^{99}technetium is taken up by the reticulo-endothelial cells of the liver. The normal scan shows a uniform distribution of the isotope throughout the liver; no isotope uptake is seen in the spleen. Filling defects larger than about 2cm will be shown. In special circumstances other isotopes are employed. ^{67}Gallium citrate is taken up by primary liver cell cancers and granulocytes in the walls of abscesses. These lesions give filling defects with a ^{99}technetium scan.

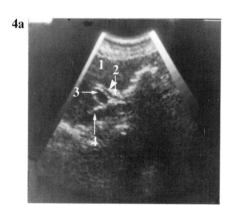

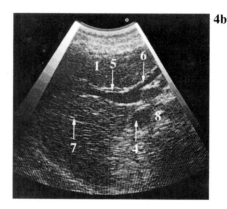

4 Ultrasonography reveals the liver as a large trans-sonic area (1). The longitudinal scan (A) shows the common bile duct (2), portal vein (3) and inferior vena cava (4). The transverse scan (B) shows an intrahepatic bile duct (5), the left branch of the portal vein (6), intrahepatic portal tracts (7), the inferior vena cava (4) and aorta (8). This non-invasive technique can also be used to study the pancreas.

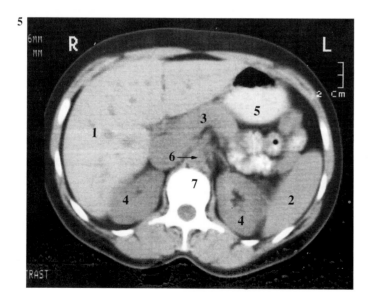

5 Computerized tomography (CT) of the liver shows the liver (1), spleen (2), pancreas (3), kidneys (4), stomach (5), aorta (6) and a vertebral body (7). CT scans may be enhanced by radio-opaque contrast media. Oral contrast media are given to enhance the stomach and gastrointestinal tract, and intravenous contrast media are given to enhance contrast in the liver. Intravenous contrast enhancement is used to detect small lesions in the liver.

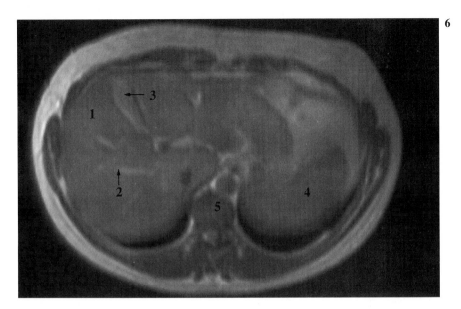

6 Magnetic resonance imaging (MRI) is another powerful and non-invasive tool for imaging the liver. This scan of a normal subject shows the liver (1), intrahepatic blood vessels (2), gall bladder (3), spleen (4) and a vertebral body (5).

7 Riedel's lobe. The right lobe of the liver is enlarged by a tongue-like extension. This anatomical variation is more common in women and is of no consequence. It may be mistaken for a liver tumour or an enlarged right kidney.

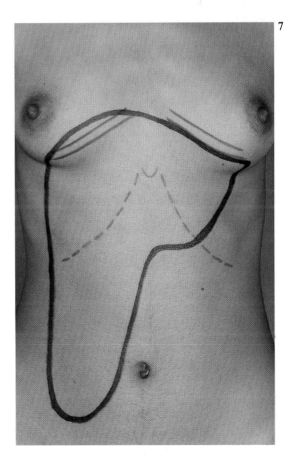

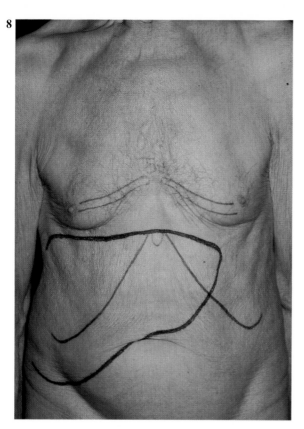

8 The liver in emphysema. Diseases such as emphysema, which increase the volume of the chest may displace the liver downwards so that its lower edge is easily palpable. Percussion of the upper border of the liver will reveal that the liver is not enlarged. Late in the course of emphysema hepatomegaly is common, due to right heart failure.

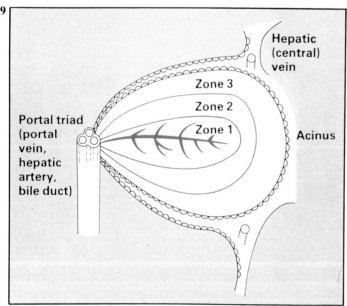

9 Zonal anatomy. The liver has an acinar structure and can be divided into functional zones. Zone 1 (formerly termed portal) is adjacent to the portal venous inflow. Zone 3 (formerly termed central) adjoins the terminal hepatic venous outflow from the liver. Hepatocytes in zone 3 are most at risk from damage from almost any cause, such as anoxia, viruses or drugs.

10 Liver biopsy. The normal liver consists of sheets of hepatocytes, supported by a reticulin framework, separating hepatic veins in zone 3 from portal tracts in zone 1. The *Haematoxylin and Eosin (H.&E.)* stain *(×40)* shows the relationship between the hepatic veins (1) and portal tracts (2).

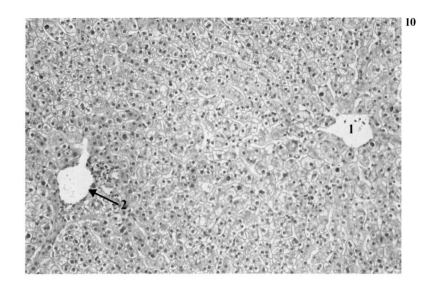

11 Hepatic veins (1) drain the sinusoids (2) which perfuse the sheets of hepatocytes. *(H.&E. ×140)*

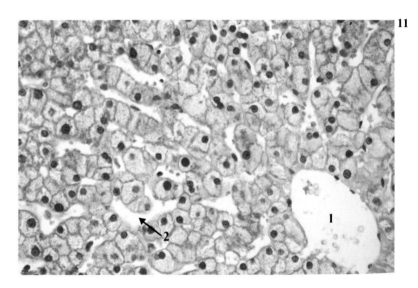

12 Portal tract contains a portal vein radicle (1) and hepatic arteriole (2), which supply the hepatic sinusoids, and a small bile duct (3) draining the biliary canaliculi which traverse the surface of each hepatocyte. *(H.&E.×160)*

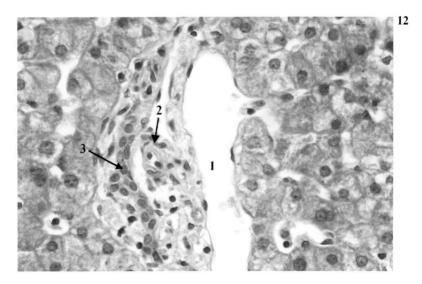

Jaundice

13 Mild jaundice (serum bilirubin 3mg/100ml; 51 μmol/l). Jaundice is due to staining of the tissues with bilirubin and possibly other pigments such as biliverdin. It is first detected in the sclera of the eye where it is strongly bound by the abundant elastic tissue. Accumulation of bilirubin may result from either overproduction (haemolytic anaemias) or reduced excretion (liver cell or biliary disease). This patient had a cancer of the common hepatic duct.

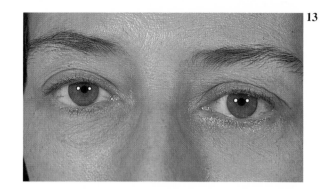

14 Severe jaundice (serum bilirubin 16mg/100ml; 272 μmol/l). As jaundice deepens the skin becomes progressively more pigmented, although paralysed and oedematous areas are usually spared. In severe jaundice all tissues except the brain become pigmented and bilirubin appears in the urine, sweat, semen and tears. Rarely in severe jaundice bilirubin in the eye results in yellow vision (xanthopsia). In the newborn unconjugated bilirubin may enter the central nervous system and accumulate in the basal ganglia (kernicterus). Jaundice may be classified into three main groups: haemolytic, hepatocellular (hepatitic) and cholestatic (biliary obstruction). This patient had primary biliary cirrhosis where the jaundice is of predominantly cholestatic (biliary obstructive) type. The colour of the jaundice differs in the three types.

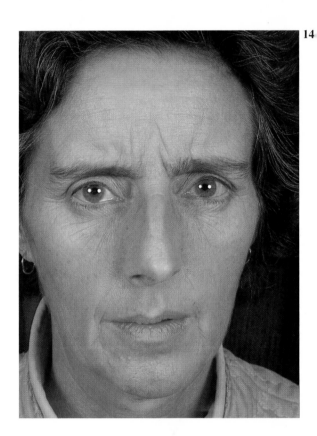

15 Haemolytic jaundice (serum bilirubin 4mg/100ml; 68 μmol/l) in a young woman with auto-immune haemolytic anaemia. Haemolytic jaundice has a light lemon yellow colour and is due to overproduction of bilirubin. The serum total bilirubin level rarely exceeds 5mg/100ml (85 μmol/l) and the circulating bilirubin is mainly unconjugated (non-esterified).

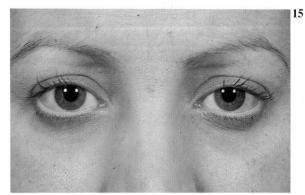

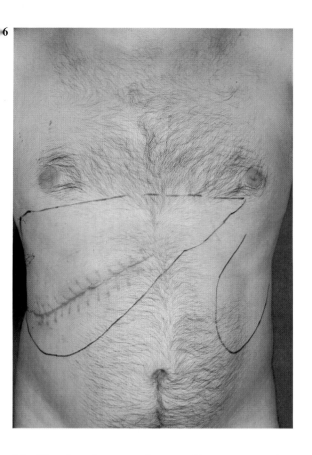

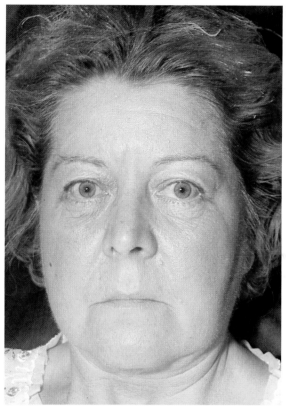

16 Hepato-splenomegaly usually accompanies haemolytic jaundice. This man, with chronic auto-immune haemolytic anaemia, had previously had his gall bladder removed because it contained pigment gallstones.

17 Hepatitic jaundice is usually of orange-yellow colour as shown in this patient with a drug-induced hepatitis due to isoniazid; the total serum bilirubin was 18mg/100ml (306 μmol/l). The liver was not enlarged.

18 Alcoholic hepatitis. The orange-yellow colour of hepatitic jaundice is also evident in this patient with alcoholic hepatitis. The serum total bilirubin concentration was 22mg/100ml (374 μmol/l). The liver was enlarged due to infiltration with fat. In addition histology showed liver cell necrosis and cellular infiltration, typical of alcoholic hepatitis.

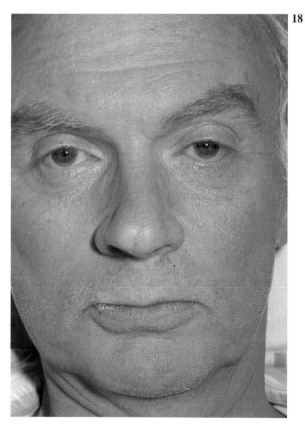

19 Urine in jaundice. In jaundiced patients the normal urine (1) is darkened by the renal excretion of bile pigments. In cholestasis conjugated bilirubin in urine confers a greeny-yellow colour (2). In haemolysis and cirrhosis (3) the urine is a warm orange colour due to urobilin. The excretion of bile pigment falls with recovery or the onset of renal failure.

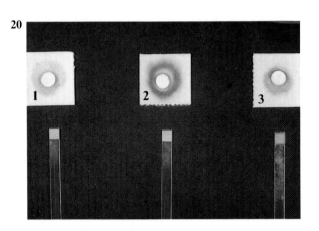

20 Urine testing in jaundice should include examination for conjugated bilirubin (by Ictotest) and urobilinogen (by Urobilistix or Ehrlich's aldehyde reagent). Normal urine (1) contains neither pigment. Cholestatic urine (2) contains conjugated bilirubin, shown by the purple ring around the Ictotest tablet, but no urobilinogen because bilirubin is not present in the gut contents. In haemolysis or cirrhosis (3) there is no bilirubin, but an excess amount of urobilinogen, indicated by the brown colour of the Urobilistix, because bilirubin is excreted into the gut and is converted into urobilinogen, which is reabsorbed. In haemolysis the excess urobilinogenuria is due to increased production in the gut. In cirrhosis it is caused by failure of the liver to excrete the normal load of reabsorbed urobilinogen.

21 The stools in jaundice are pale because there is obstruction to the biliary excretion of bilirubin pigments. The degree of pallor depends on the severity of biliary obstruction, being most marked in cholestatic jaundice. These are the faeces of a patient with complete bile duct obstruction due to a bile duct carcinoma. Cancers of the ampulla of Vater give a 'silver' stool due to the presence of blood in addition to lack of bile pigments. In haemolysis the stools are darker than normal due to increased red-cell destruction and bilirubin formation.

22 Carotinaemia. Every day this 47-year-old woman consumed tomatoes and carrots in large quantities. Her palms and soles became yellow, but her sclerae were white. Serum bilirubin was normal, but serum carotene was markedly increased. Yellow palms are shown on the right with a normal hand on the left.

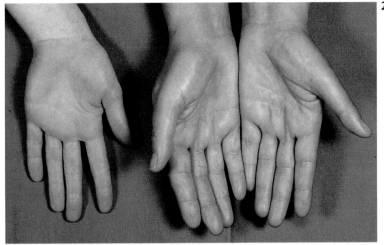

Signs in liver disease

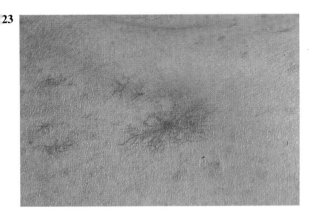

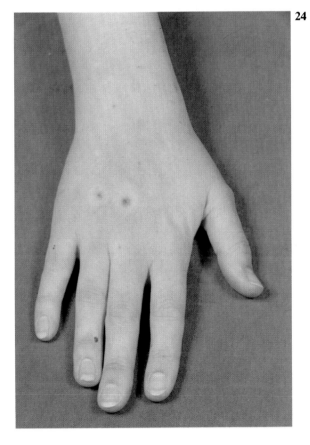

23 Spider naevi (vascular spiders) are vascular skin lesions. These are supplied by a central arteriole and they blanch if it is occluded with a pinhead. Palpation of larger spiders may reveal pulsation due to the arteriolar dilatation.

24 Spider naevi are characteristically surrounded by a pale area or white spot (see also **28**). The pale areas are clearly seen on the hand of this young girl with chronic active hepatitis. Spider naevi occur in the distribution of the superior vena cava, the chest above the nipples, face, arms and hands.

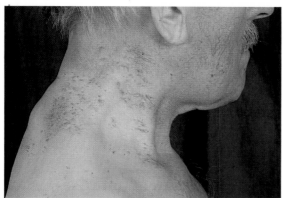

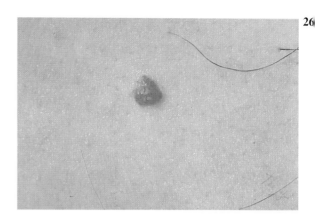

25 Spider naevi. One or two spider naevi may be found in health, especially during pregnancy or in childhood. The later appearance of such lesions and their increase in size indicates chronic liver disease, as on the neck of this patient with alcoholic cirrhosis.

26 Campbell de Morgan spots must be distinguished from spider naevi. These bright-red discrete punctate spots are 1–2mm in diameter. Campbell de Morgan spots are found mainly on the chest and abdomen, especially as age advances. They are of no significance.

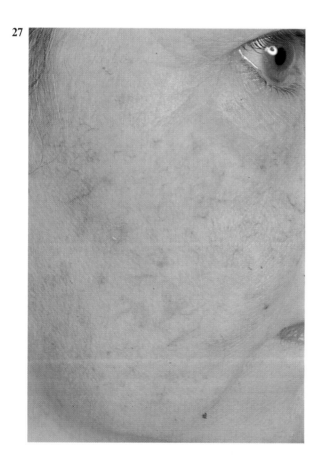

27 Paper money skin describes the random distribution of fine threadlike blood vessels just under the skin, seen here on the face of a patient with alcoholic hepatitis. Paper money skin occurs in the same distribution as spider naevi and indicates chronic liver disease. It is named after the silk threads in American dollar bills.

28 White spots develop on the arms, buttocks and legs in patients with chronic liver disease, especially when the skin is cold. In the centre of each white spot is an arteriole which later develops into a spider naevus. This patient had chronic active hepatitis. White spots are also seen in pregnancy.

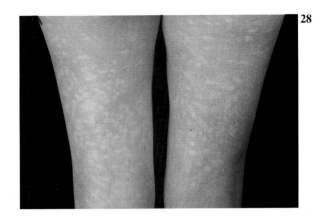

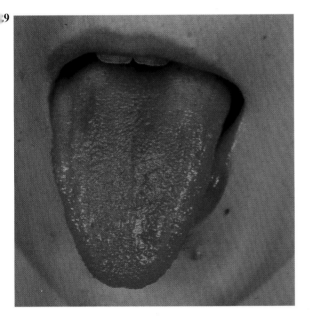

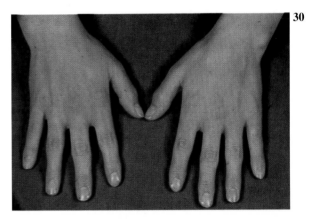

29,30 Central cyanosis is due to vasodilatation and arteriovenous shunting in the lungs. It may be demonstrated in decompensated cirrhosis. An extreme example is shown in this young woman in the late stages of chronic active hepatitis. Her hands (**30**) are also cyanosed. The chronic cyanosis has resulted in clubbing of her fingers.

31 Palmar erythema, an exaggerated red flushing of the palms, affects especially the thenar and hypothenar eminences and the bases of the fingers. It fades on pressure. Although a useful sign of chronic liver disease, it is also seen in pregnancy, thyrotoxicosis, bronchial carcinoma and as a genetically determined abnormality.

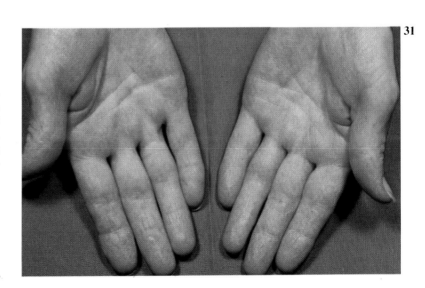

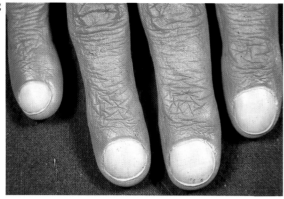

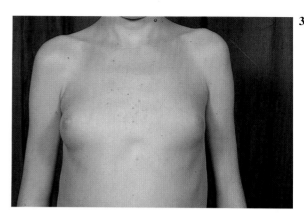

32 White nails are present in most patients with cirrhosis. The tip of the nail remains pink and in severe cases, such as this patient with primary biliary cirrhosis, the lunula of the nail disappears. Clubbing of the fingers in this patient is also seen in chronic cholestasis.

33 Gynaecomastia or enlargement of the breasts is sometimes seen in males with cirrhosis. The diagnosis can only be made if there is palpable enlargement of breast tissue. The breasts may be tender and the areolar pigmented. There is usually associated diminished libido and testicular atrophy. Gynaecomastia is common in alcoholic cirrhosis, but is also found in men with chronic active hepatitis. Note the absence of body hair, and the jaundice and spider naevi in this young man with chronic active hepatitis. Spironolactone therapy is a very frequent cause of gynaecomastia in male patients with cirrhosis and ascites. In women with chronic liver disease, breast atrophy and amenorrhoea occur.

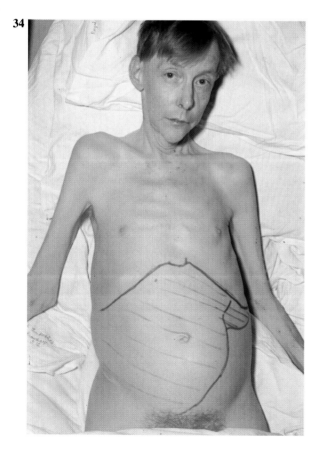

34 Weight loss is a feature of advanced chronic liver disease. Severe weight loss with an enlarged, hard, irregular liver suggests a malignant tumour in the liver, as illustrated by this patient who suffered from primary liver cell cancer. More common causes of secondary deposits in the liver are metastases from cancer of the breast, bronchus, stomach, pancreas, colon or thyroid. In the patient illustrated note the cachectic facies and profound loss of muscle bulk.

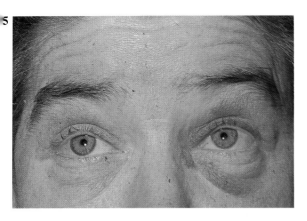

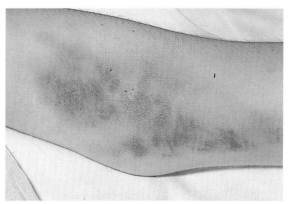

35 Spontaneous bruising around the eye of this cirrhotic patient is caused by a clotting defect due to the failure of hepatic synthesis of clotting factors.

36 Venepuncture sites. Excessive bruising around venepuncture sites is another important sign of a clotting disorder in liver disease. This patient had fulminant hepatitis and a prothrombin time prolonged more than 10 seconds over control values after intramuscular vitamin K therapy.

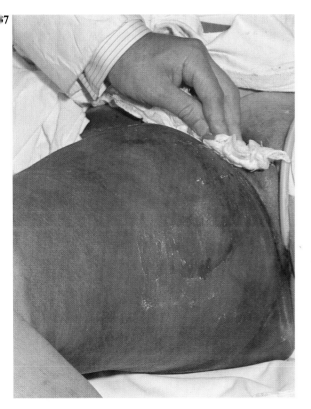

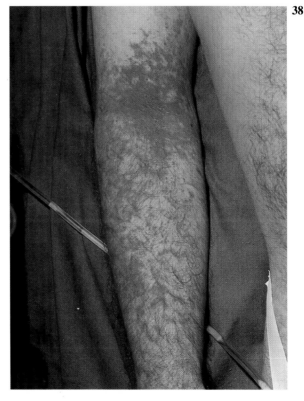

37 Arterial puncture in this patient with fulminant hepatic failure has resulted in massive extravasation of blood, despite prolonged pressure over the puncture site. This is due to the profound clotting disorder following failure to synthesize clotting factors.

38 Spontaneous ecchymoses become widespread late in the course of hepatic failure and this is a poor prognostic sign. This man with fulminant viral hepatitis died three hours later.

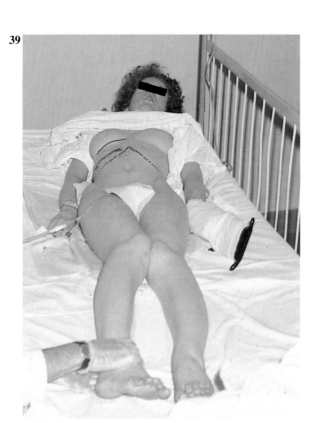

39 **Hepatic coma** is a late stage of acute hepatic failure and of chronic liver disease. Personality changes, sleepiness and a day–night reversal of sleep patterns are early features. Mania and violent screaming attacks are common 'in children. Other signs include fetor, a coarse, flapping tremor and increased tendon reflexes with upgoing plantar responses. Hepatic coma is easily confused with encephalitis and other metabolic causes. This young girl is in hepatic coma due to fulminant type B viral hepatitis. Stimulation of her achilles tendon has resulted in the posture of decerebrate rigidity. The arms are internally rotated at the shoulders and extended at the elbows. The legs are extended and adducted. This is usually a poor prognostic sign appearing late in the course of acute hepatic coma.

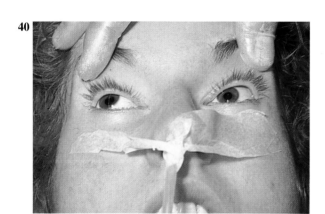

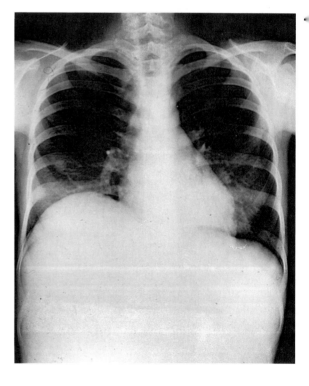

40 **'Doll's eye' movement,** another grave sign of brain stem dysfunction, is present in the patient shown in **39**. The eyes remain fixed as the head is moved. However, these signs, severe as they are, are not always incompatible with survival. This patient recovered completely after careful supportive management.

41 **Chest x-ray** is an essential part of the investigation of a patient with liver disease. An enlarged liver elevates the right hemidiaphragm in this patient with primary liver cell cancer. A metastasis is present in the right lower zone of the lung.

Signs in cholestatic (biliary obstructive) liver disease

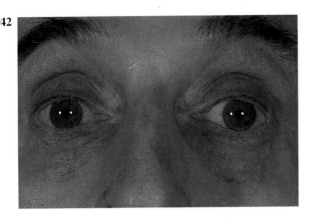

42 Cholestatic jaundice has a greenish-yellow colour. The patient had a carcinoma of the head of the pancreas which resulted in obstruction of the common bile duct. The serum total bilirubin level was l5mg/100ml (255 μmol/l).

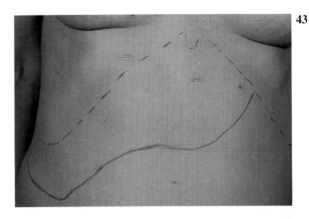

43 Hepatomegaly is an important sign of cholestasis due to obstructed bile ducts. Scratch marks were seen on the abdominal wall due to pruritus (itching).

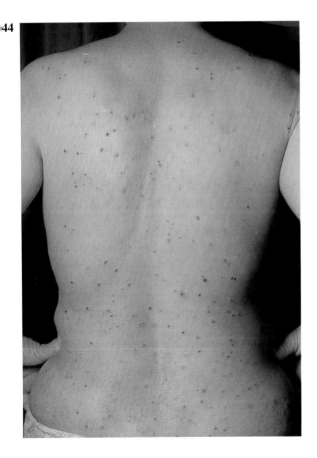

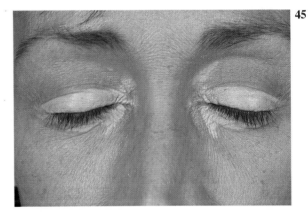

44 Pruritus occurs in cholestatic liver disease. Although usually generalized, the palms and soles are most affected. The symptom may become intolerable in chronic cholestasis, such as this patient with primary biliary cirrhosis, resulting in severe excoriations.

45 Xanthomas develop in prolonged cholestasis. These consist histologically of foamy cells full of cholesterol. They are associated with an elevated serum cholesterol concentration. Xanthomas first develop around the eye (xanthelasma), starting at the inner canthus and spreading laterally. Later xanthomas appear on extensor surfaces, particularly elbows, buttocks, palms, neck, chest and back.

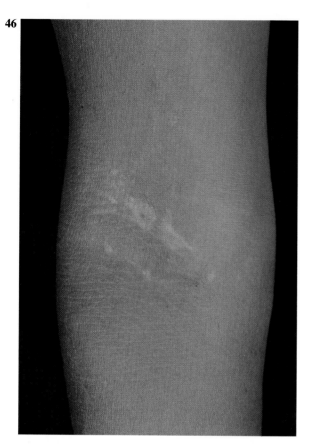

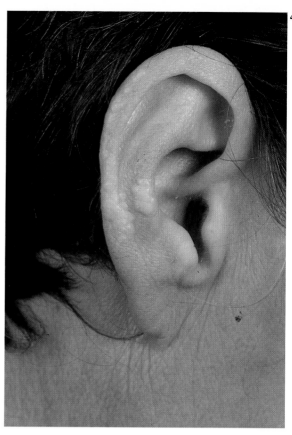

46 Thickened skin (lichenification) results from prolonged scratching in patients with chronic cholestasis. Note the xanthomas in the antecubital fossa. They mark the sites of past venepunctures. This patient had primary biliary cirrhosis.

47 Xanthomas. Later in the course of a chronic cholestasis, tuberous xanthomas may appear. Typically they develop on the extensor surfaces, pressure areas and in scars. The xanthomas on the ear of this patient with primary biliary cirrhosis are related to pressure on the ear lobe when she lies down.

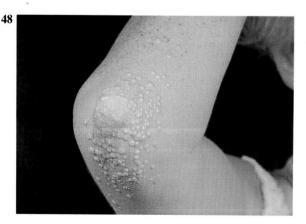

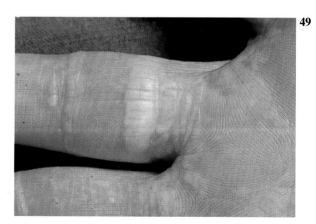

48 Xanthomas. The extensor surfaces of the elbows are a common site for the development of tuberous xanthomas. This patient had primary biliary cirrhosis.

49 Xanthomas. Pressure from a tight-fitting ring caused the circular xanthoma on this finger.

50 Xanthomas commonly develop
on the palms. The palmar creases
are affected first. Later tuberous
xanthomas appear on the fingers.
In very severe cases, such as in
this patient with primary biliary
cirrhosis, finger movements are
limited by the xanthomas. In
cholestasis tendon sheath xanthomas are rare.

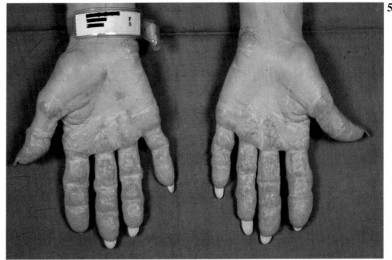

51 Xanthomas. The dorsal surface of the hands of the patient
shown in **50** are also covered with
large tuberous xanthomas. The
fingers are clubbed.

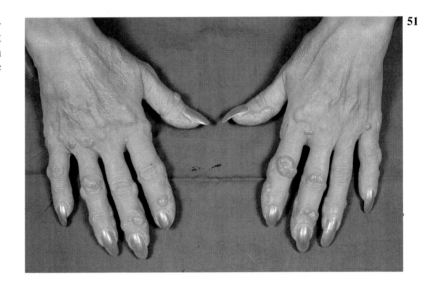

52 Xanthomas. Tuberous xanthomas may develop on the
buttocks following constant pressure in this area. This patient had
primary biliary cirrhosis.

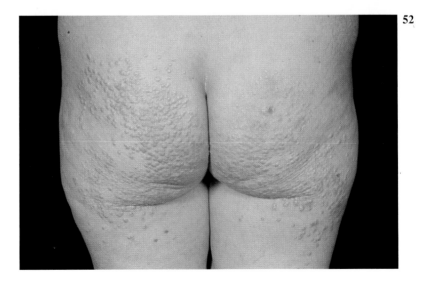

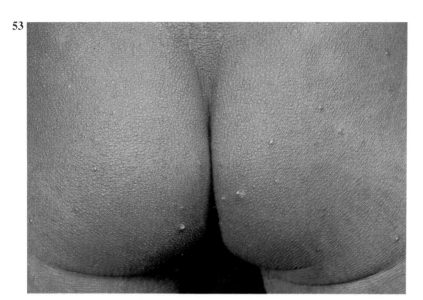

53 Xanthomas. In black patients the bright yellow colour of the xanthoma may be obscured by skin pigmentation. This patient had secondary biliary cirrhosis following a traumatic bile duct stricture. The xanthomas appear as hard raised papules on his buttocks.

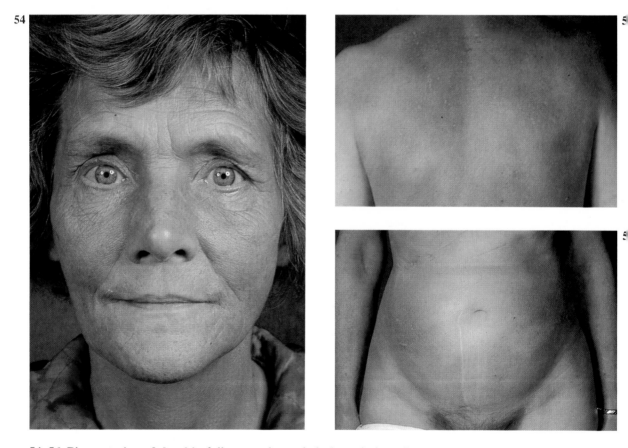

54–56 Pigmentation of the skin follows prolonged cholestatic jaundice. The grey or brown pigmentation is due to melanin in the skin. This European patient had long-standing cholestasis due to primary biliary cirrhosis. Careful camouflage make-up is necessary to hide the progressive pigmentation. On the back (**55**) an area in a butterfly distribution may escape pigmentation. This butterfly sign is attributed to the patient being unable to scratch that area. Pigmentation of the skin in chronic cholestasis is found all over the body. This patient's abdomen is heavily pigmented, but old scars are spared (**56**).

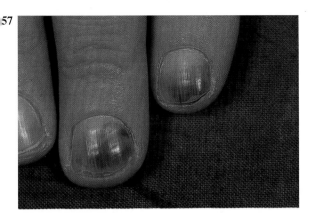

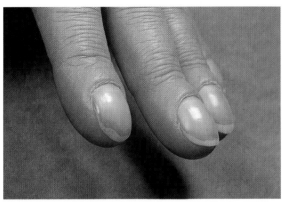

57 Pigmentation of the nails in cholestasis is due to staining with bile pigments. This patient developed nail pigmentation during attacks of benign recurrent intrahepatic cholestasis.

58 Finger clubbing is a feature of chronic cholestasis. This patient has primary biliary cirrhosis.

59 Bruising around venepuncture sites is caused by a clotting disorder in cholestasis. The clotting disorder is due to reduced intestinal absorption of vitamin K. This patient had a carcinoma of the bile duct. The prothrombin time was prolonged eight seconds over the control value but returned to normal after vitamin K injections.

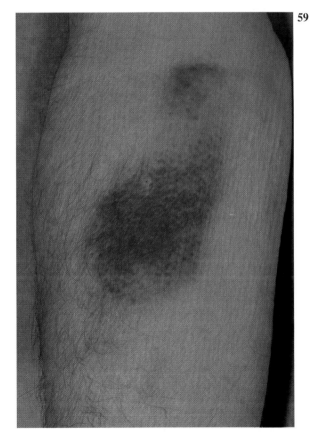

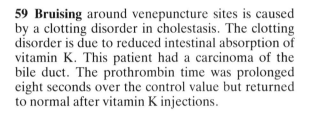

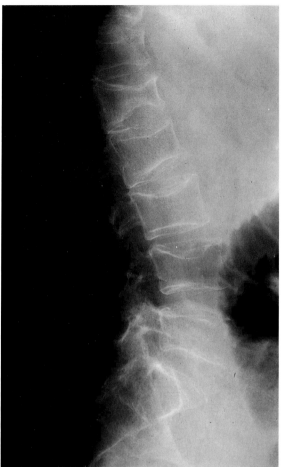

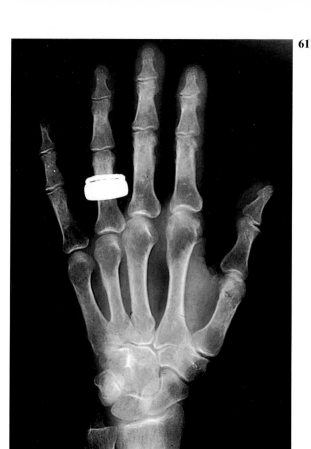

61 Osteomalacia. The hands of the patient in **60** show grossly demineralized bones as a result of osteomalacia. Bony erosions are sometimes present, caused by bone xanthomas.

60 Osteomalacia develops in chronic cholestasis due to abnormal calcium and vitamin D metabolism. Demineralization of the bones has led to crushed and wedge-shaped vertebral bodies in this patient. She had been jaundiced for five years following a benign bile duct stricture. Secondary biliary cirrhosis had developed. Back pain is a prominent complaint. Osteoporosis may also contribute to the bone thinning. Severe osteoporosis develops in cholestatic patients given prednisolone.

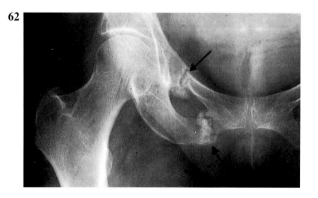

62 Looser's zones are a sign of osteomalacia. This patient with primary biliary cirrhosis suddenly developed pelvic girdle pain without previous trauma. An x-ray of the pelvis shows bands of decalcification (arrowed) in the superior and inferior pubic rami. On either side of the decalcified band are denser shadows of callus. Looser's zones tend to be symmetrical and are also found on the axillary border of the scapula.

63 Osteomalacia in chronic cholestasis may lead to loosening of the teeth which then fall out. There is resorption of bone around the tooth and the lamina dura disappears. These changes are present in the x-ray (1) from a patient with primary biliary cirrhosis. The adjacent x-ray (2) shows the normal appearance.

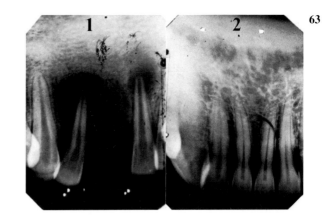

64 Hypertrophic osteoarthropathy may develop in cholestasis, causing painful swelling of the wrists and ankles. Hypertrophic osteoarthropathy is responsible for the ankle swelling in this patient with primary biliary cirrhosis.

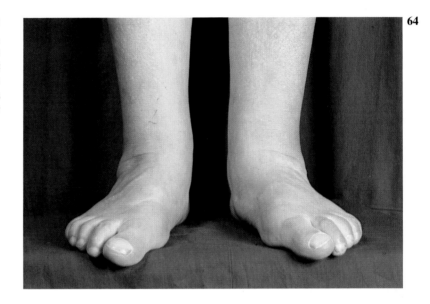

65 Hypertrophic osteoarthropathy. An x-ray of the ankles of the patient shown in **64** reveals a ring of new subperiostial bone at the lower end of the tibia ('onion skin' appearance).

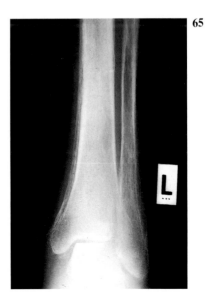

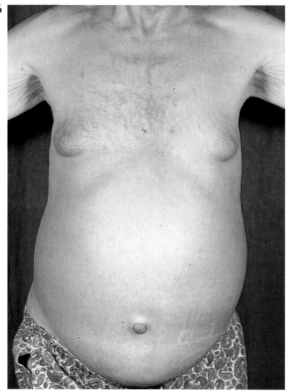

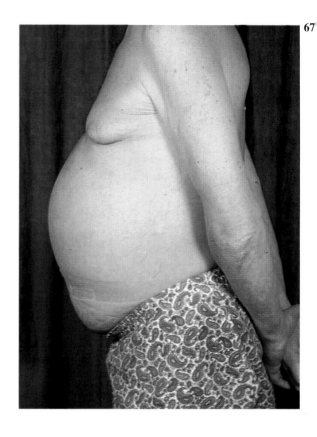

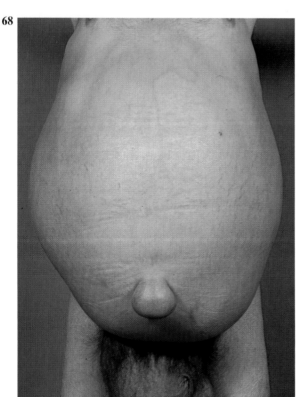

66 Ascites represents the accumulation of fluid in the abdomen. When due to liver disease the cause is either local, such as a tumour, or liver cell failure with portal hypertension. This patient with decompensated alcoholic cirrhosis has moderate ascites. The abdomen is distended, especially in the flanks. The distance between the umbilicus and the symphysis pubis appears diminished and the umbilicus is everted.

67 Ascites. The lateral view of this patient shows that the maximum circumference of the abdomen is above the umbilicus, which is everted. Dullness to percussion is maximal in the flanks but shifts on movement. There is marked muscle wasting and gynaecomastia.

68 Gross ascites in a Persian man with cirrhosis due to chronic viral hepatitis (type B). The umbilicus has herniated and the scrotum is distended with fluid. The veins on his upper abdomen and chest represent portal-systemic venous collaterals and signify portal hypertension.

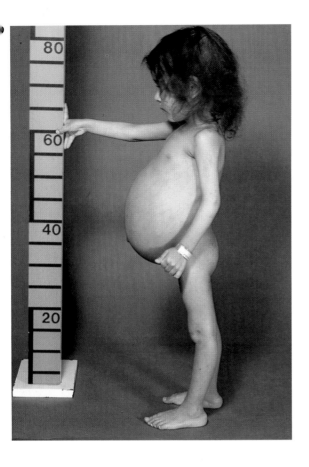

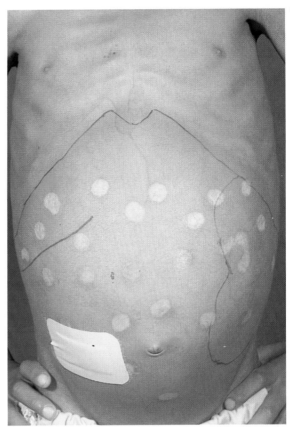

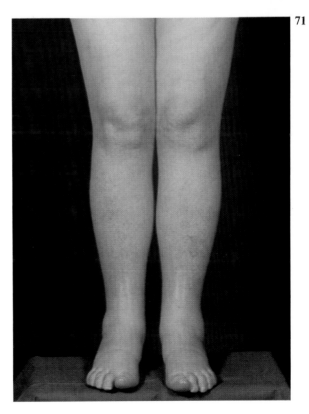
71

69 Ascites in a child with cirrhosis. The profound muscle wasting is apparent in the limbs and buttocks. Growth in this four-year-old child is retarded.

70 Ascites. This child with cirrhosis shows wasting of the chest muscles, an enlarged spleen and superficial abdominal veins due to portal hypertension. A dressing covers the site of a diagnostic tap of the peritoneal cavity. The circular white scars on the abdomen of this Arab child result from native treatment.

71 Peripheral oedema usually appears at the same time as ascites, causing tense, shiny, swollen legs which pit on pressure, as in this cirrhotic woman.

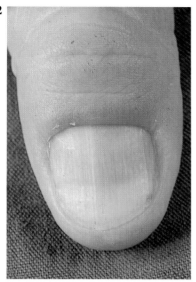

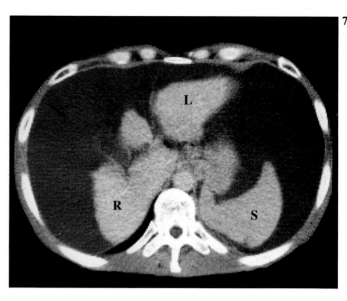

72 Hypoalbuminaemia in cirrhosis may result in these horizontal white bands across the distal part of the finger nails.

73 Cirrhosis with ascites. CT scan shows massive ascites (arrowed). The liver is very small (R is the right lobe; L is the left). The spleen (S) is normal size.

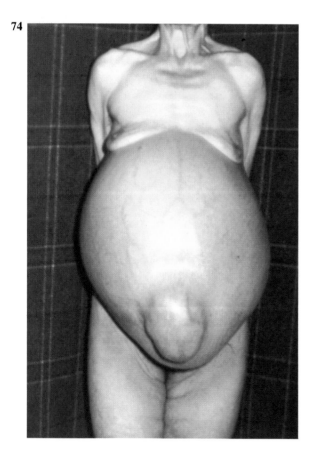

74 Ovarian cysts when very large may be confused with ascites. However, with an ovarian cyst the maximal dullness is in the centre of the abdomen and not in the flanks, and the maximum circumference of the abdomen is below the umbilicus.

75 Ascitic fluid. A diagnostic tap (50ml) should be performed on every patient with ascites. This normally results in a clear, straw-coloured fluid with a low protein concentration (10–20g/l) and containing up to 200 cells/mm^3, which are mainly endothelial.

76 Infected ascites. In cirrhosis occult ascitic infections are important causes of general deterioration, often with few if any abnormal signs. The fluid is usually turbid and contains over 300 cells/mm^3, mainly polymorphonuclear leucocytes. Enteric bacteria are commonly cultured, but tuberculous peritonitis must always be considered.

77 Malignant ascites is often bloodstained with a high protein concentration (above 30g/l) and cytology may reveal malignant cells.

78 Chylous ascites is a milky fluid containing chylomicrons and is due to lymphatic obstruction, usually by a tumour. The lipid concentration of the ascites is usually twice that of plasma. Ascites containing a lower concentration of lipid (similar to plasma) is known as pseudochylous ascites and may be a complication of cirrhosis.

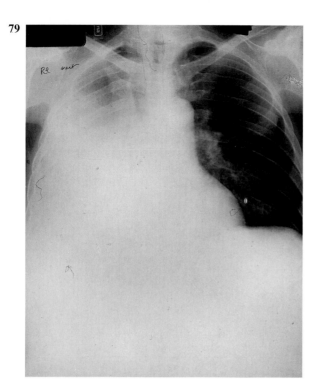

79 Hydrothorax. A pleural effusion is occasionally found in association with ascites. It is usually right-sided and arises by the passage of ascites through defects in the diaphragm into the pleural cavity.

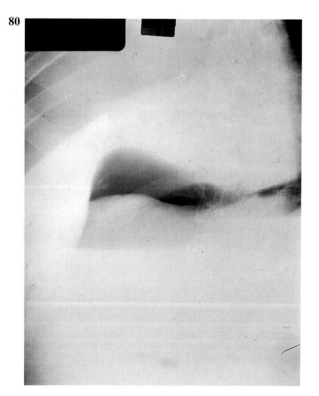

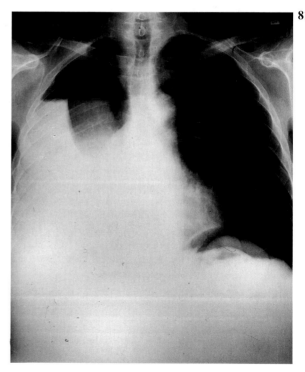

80,81 Hydrothorax. The diaphragmatic defect can be demonstrated by introducing air into the peritoneal cavity (**80**), when it is later found above the pleural effusion (**81**).

2. Hepatitis

Viral hepatitis

Currently five hepatitis viruses have been identified. Hepatitis A virus is an RNA containing *Picornavirus*. Hepatitis A virus causes an acute hepatitis but does not cause chronic liver disease. Hepatitis B virus, a DNA virus of the *Hepadna* group, causes both acute and chronic hepatitis. The delta virus (hepatitis D) is an RNA containing *Satellite* virus which can only infect patients carrying hepatitis B. Delta virus requires hepatitis B surface antigen for its coat protein. Patients infected with hepatitis B virus who acquire delta virus have more aggressive liver disease. The diagnosis of non-A, non-B hepatitis is made after exclusion of hepatitis A and B infections by specific serological tests. One cause of non-A, non-B hepatitis is hepatitis C virus, which is an RNA containing *Flavivirus* that causes acute and chronic hepatitis. Another cause of non-A, non-B hepatitis is hepatitis E virus, an RNA containing *Calicivirus*, which causes an acute hepatitis, like hepatitis A. Hepatitis viruses B and C are important causes of cirrhosis and primary liver cancer.

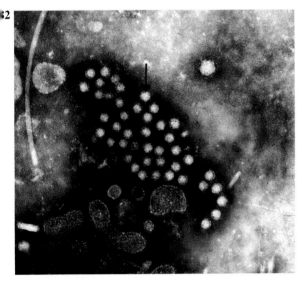

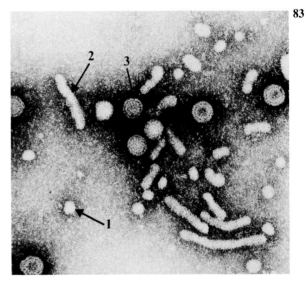

82 Hepatitis A virus is an RNA containing *Picornavirus* (diameter 27nm) and can be identified by immune electron microscopy in liver and faeces. This virus causes acute hepatitis usually in children and young adults. The virus is excreted in the faeces for two weeks prior to the onset of jaundice and is spread by faecal oral contamination. When jaundiced the patient is usually no longer infectious. Type A hepatitis occurs throughout the world with the highest incidence in countries with low standards of public health.

83 Hepatitis B virus is a DNA virus of the *Hepadna* group. Electron microscopy shows three components: small spheres (1, diameter 28nm), tubules (2), which are groups of small spheres, and Dane particles (3, 42nm), which are probably the infective virions. The small spheres and tubules, viral coat lipoproteins, are the hepatitis B surface antigen (HBsAg). This virus causes both acute and chronic hepatitis. Type B hepatitis is distributed throughout the world, being especially prevalent in the tropics where it is a major cause of chronic liver disease (chronic hepatitis and cirrhosis) and primary liver cancer.

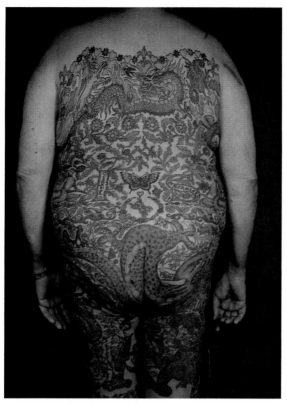

84 Tattooing with needles that are used repeatedly in poor hygienic conditions carries the risk of transmitting hepatitis B, delta virus and hepatitis C. This 57-year-old man was extensively tattooed as a young man and now has decompensated cirrhosis following type B hepatitis.

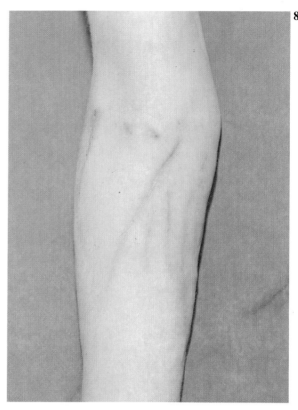

85 Drug addicts who abuse intravenous drugs often share syringes and needles which transmit hepatitis B, delta virus and hepatitis C. The superficial thrombophlebitis in this young addict reveals the source of his acute hepatitis.

Acute viral hepatitis

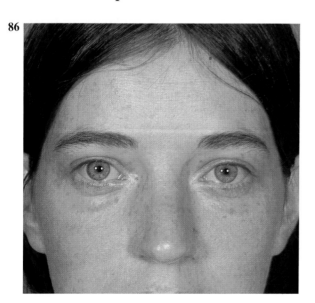

86 Acute hepatitis. The clinical picture is identical in type A, type B and type C hepatitis. However, clinical hepatitis with jaundice occurs in only a small proportion of patients infected with these viruses. Anorexia is usual a few days before the appearance of jaundice, and smoking and alcohol are avoided. Malaise, nausea, vomiting and discomfort or pain under the right costal margin may be prominent. Transient rashes and arthralgia also occur. Shortly before the appearance of jaundice the urine becomes dark and the stools pale. The liver is usually slightly enlarged with a smooth tender edge. The illness lasts between two and six weeks. This patient had acute type A hepatitis (the serum bilirubin level was 16mg/100ml; 272 μmol/l).

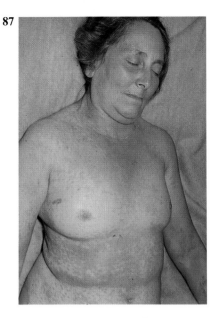

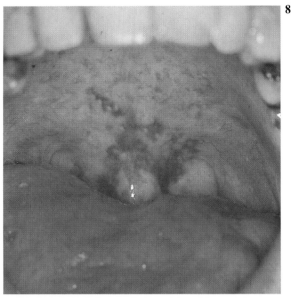

87 Thrombocytopenia is a part of the pancytopenia which occurs in viral hepatitis. Occasionally, in severe hepatitis, the thrombocytopenia is sufficient to result in generalized purpura, as in this patient with type A hepatitis.

88 Purpura is also present on the palate of this patient.

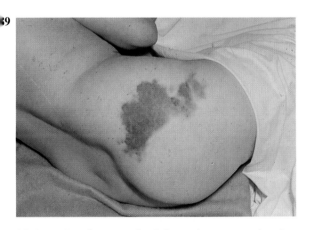

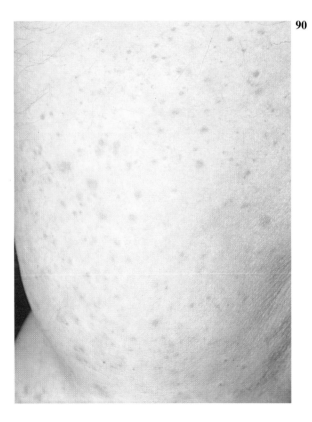

89 Bruising has resulted from intramuscular injections in this patient. This reflects the clotting disorder in acute hepatitis.

90 Vasculitis, another feature of viral hepatitis, is the cause of this rash. This allergic vasculitis is more common in type B hepatitis and may be severe, resulting in polyarteritis nodosa with glomerulonephritis and renal failure.

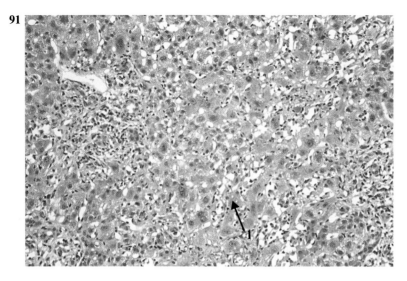

91 Liver biopsy appearances are similar in both type A and type B hepatitis. The whole liver is involved. Liver cell necrosis is most marked in the centres of the lobules (zone 3). This biopsy shows a large area around the central hepatic vein (1) devoid of liver cells. Only cell debris and acute inflammatory cells remain. *(H.&E.×40)*

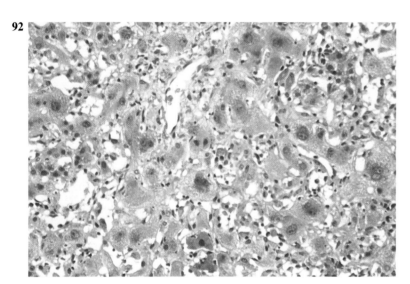

92 Liver biopsy at higher magnification shows prominent swollen cells, mitoses and eosinophilic changes in the cytoplasm of some cells (acidophilic or councilman bodies). *(H.&E.×63)*

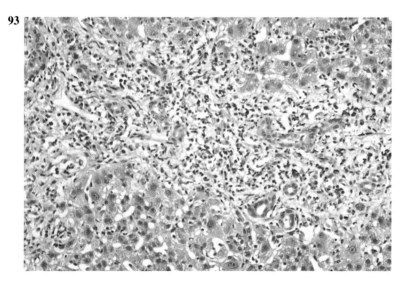

93 Portal tracts are expanded by infiltration with acute inflammatory cells, mainly leucocytes and histiocytes. Fatty infiltration is noticeably absent. The reticulin is usually well preserved and acts as a framework for the new liver cells during recovery. *(H.&E.×50)*

94 Resolving viral hepatitis. A biopsy late in the course of viral hepatitis shows focal areas of 'spotty' necrosis (1) scattered throughout the lobule. Mild portal tract inflammation (2) is also present. (*Diastase periodic acid Schiff×40*)

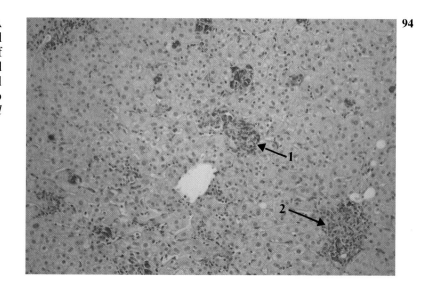

95 Resolving viral hepatitis. The biopsy shown in **94** has been stained for iron. During recovery iron is found in the Kupffer cells (1). This reflects the increased reticulo-endothelial activity in the liver during recovery from viral hepatitis. (*Perls×40*)

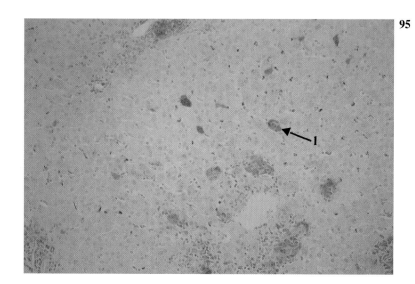

96 Fulminant hepatitis may result from type A, type B and type C hepatitis. This most severe form of viral hepatitis often develops suddenly, before the patient is very jaundiced. The prodroma of persistent vomiting, nightmares and confusion rapidly develop into drowsiness and coma. Prognosis is related to the depth of coma and also to liver size. The liver of this patient with fulminant type B hepatitis is typically small and daily measurement of the lower border of liver dullness by percussion shows it to be shrinking, which is a bad sign.

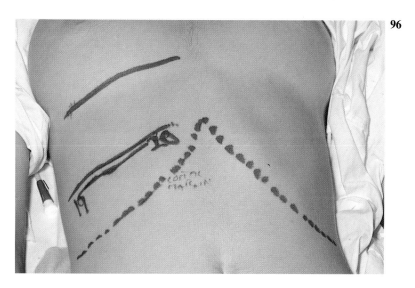

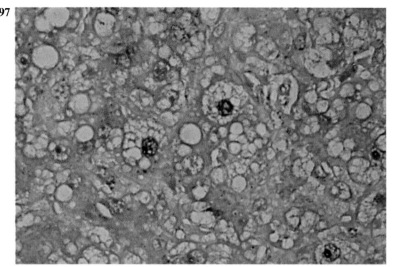

97 Fulminant acute delta virus hepatitis (Labrea hepatitis). Severe delta virus infection has been reported to cause epidemics in the Amazon Basin and in Central Africa. This three-year-old girl from northern Brazil, a hepatitis B carrier, died with fulminant hepatitis after three days' symptoms. An autopsy liver sample shows microvesicular fatty change in large hepatocytes with central nuclei (morula or vegetable-type cells). The nuclei stained brown contain delta antigen. (*Immunoperoxidase×500*)

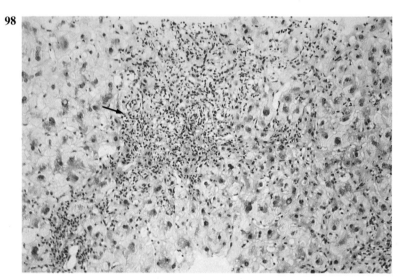

98 Hepatitis E. This faecal waterborne virus disease clinically resembles hepatitis A. It is very fatal in pregnant women. It has caused epidemics in India, Pakistan, Mexico, USSR, Africa and the Middle East. This 18-year-old Pakistani girl was 22 weeks pregnant when she developed features of severe acute virus hepatitis. She ultimately recovered after a fulminant course complicated by hepatic encephalopathy. Liver biopsy shows an intense portal (zone 1) inflammatory, largely mononuclear cell infiltrate (arrowed). Adjacent liver cells show necrosis and some are ballooned. *(H.&E.×40)*

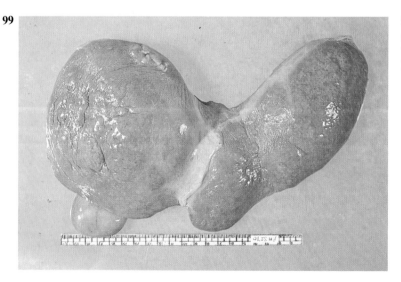

99 Liver in fulminant hepatitis is small and flaccid and the capsule is wrinkled. The left lobe is particularly shrunken.

100 Liver in fulminant hepatitis.
The cut surface shows a mottled appearance with yellow areas of necrosis adjacent to red areas of haemorrhage. Histologically there is massive hepatic necrosis with loss of the normal lobular structure due to collapse of the reticulin.

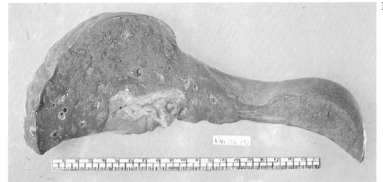

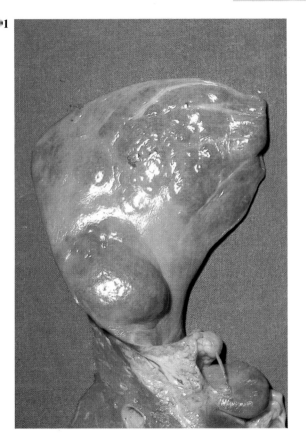

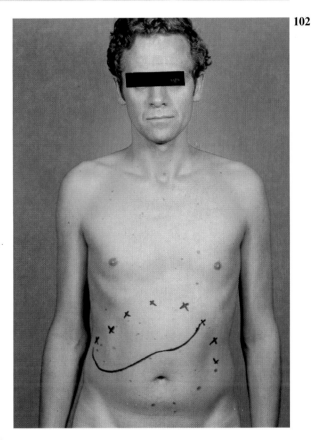

101 Regenerating nodules of normal liver are present in patients dying more than two weeks after the onset of acute hepatic failure due to hepatitis.

102 Cholestatic viral hepatitis, usually associated with hepatitis A virus, is seen in some patients with acute viral hepatitis. Following the normal prodromal phase of acute viral hepatitis, a deep green-yellow jaundice and marked itching develop. The liver is enlarged. The serum bilirubin in this patient was 30mg/100ml (510 μmol/l). The cholestatic phase usually disappears in two months, but may last up to one year. The patient feels well. The ultimate prognosis is excellent. Cholestatic viral hepatitis must be distinguished from other causes of cholestasis, particularly extrahepatic biliary obstruction and drug-related cholestasis.

Chronic viral hepatitis

Type A hepatitis is self limiting and does not cause chronic liver disease. In contrast, type B hepatitis may pursue several courses. The virus may cause asymptomatic or symptomatic acute hepatitis and then be cleared from the body. Occasionally the patient becomes a chronic carrier of the B virus. Some carriers have histologically normal livers ('healthy carriers') while others develop chronic liver disease . Chronic type B hepatitis is more common in males. Patients infected with hepatitis B virus who acquire delta virus tend to have a more aggressive chronic hepatitis. Hepatitis C virus infection is frequently followed by chronic hepatitis.

The pathological course of chronic type B hepatitis

This is usually assessed by liver biopsy, performed when the acute changes have subsided.

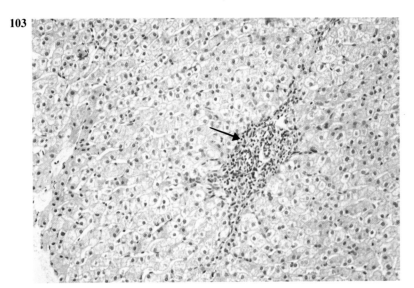

103 Chronic persistent hepatitis is found following acute hepatitis and in healthy carriers. This biopsy comes from a fit young man found to be HBsAg positive at a blood donor session. The portal tract is expanded with mononuclear cells, but the limiting plate of hepatocytes is intact (arrowed) and there is no piecemeal necrosis of liver cells. The reticulin framework is normal. This picture may persist for years, but the prognosis is good. *(H.&E. ×50)*

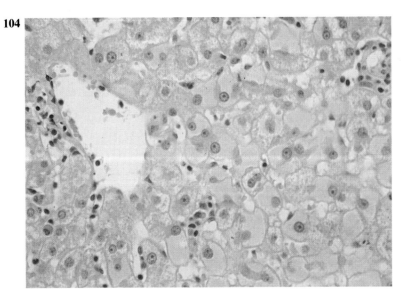

104 HBsAg containing hepatocytes are present in the biopsies of chronic carriers. This biopsy is full of large cells with pale pink 'ground glass' cytoplasm. This represents a hypertrophic endoplasmic reticulum containing HBsAg. *(H.&E. ×100)*

105 Orcein stain shows the liver cells that contain HBsAg more clearly as groups of dark pink staining cells. (×*100*)

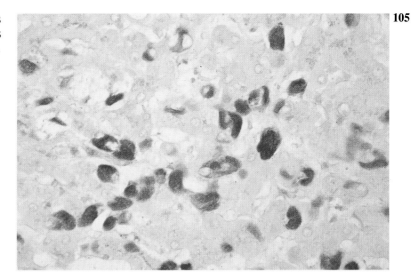

106 Peroxidase–antiperoxidase coupled with HBsAb specifically stains those cells which contain HBsAg a yellow-brown colour. (×*100*)

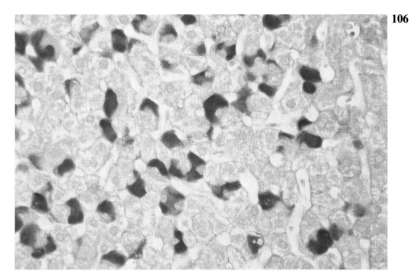

107 Hepatitis B. In this liver biopsy from a patient with chronic hepatitis due to the hepatitis B virus, hepatitis B core antigen has been stained by immunoperoxidase. Core antigen is shown in the nuclei of the hepatocytes. (×*100*)

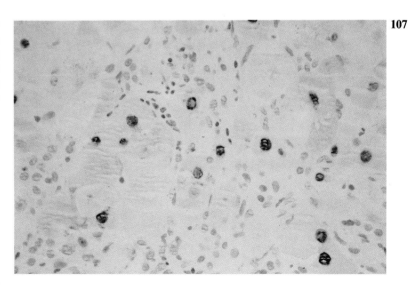

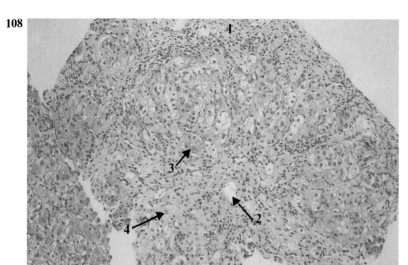

108 Chronic active hepatitis, formerly called chronic aggressive hepatitis, is the pathological description of this very active liver lesion. The portal tracts are enlarged with a heavy infiltrate of chronic inflammatory cells, mainly plasma cells and lymphocytes (1). From the portal tracts, active fibrous septa extend to the central veins (2) isolating groups of ballooned hepatocytes to form rosettes (3). The limiting plate of liver cells around the portal tract is no longer distinct but eroded by piecemeal necrosis and fibrosis. Bridging hepatic necrosis (4) has developed. *(H.&E.×40)*

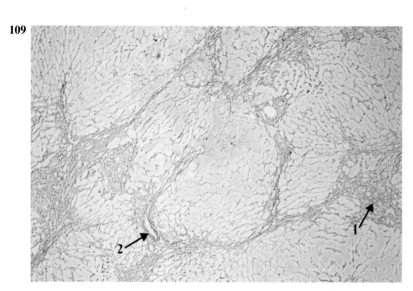

109 Bridging necrosis accompanies chronic active hepatitis, when liver cell necrosis is followed by fibrosis. The fibrosis links portal tracts (1) to hepatic veins (2) disrupting the normal lobular architecture (reticulin×24). These active fibrous septa may be the precursors of cirrhosis.

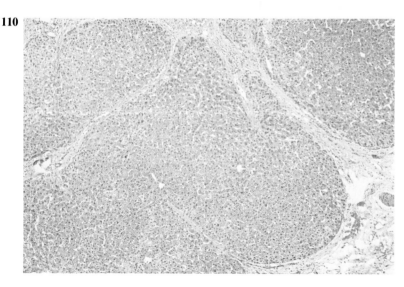

110 Inactive macronodular cirrhosis may be the end result of chronic active hepatitis due to type B hepatitis. Following extensive liver cell necrosis and reticulin collapse, some liver cells regenerate to form nodules of various sizes separated by septa of inactive fibrous tissue. The normal lobular architecture of the liver is lost. *(H.&E.×10)*

111 Primary liver cancer is the final complication of chronic type B hepatitis. It is usually seen in patients with established cirrhosis and is often heralded by sudden deterioration of liver cell function and ascites. In many patients α fetoprotein appears in the blood. Occasionally, a small primary liver cancer is an incidental finding at autopsy, as in this patient with inactive cirrhosis who died from liver failure. (*Martius-Scarlet-Blue ×10*)

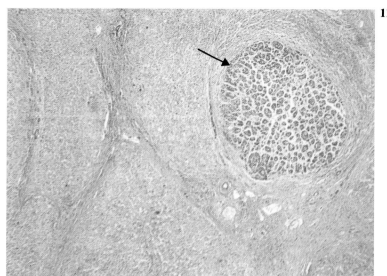

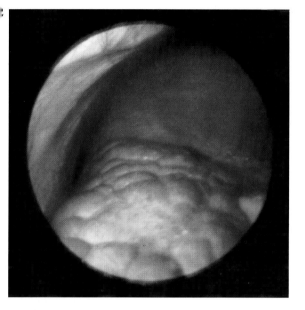

112 Laparoscopy is valuable in chronic hepatitis to establish whether cirrhosis is present. The transition of chronic active hepatitis to cirrhosis may not be visible in a small liver biopsy specimen. However, the nodularity of the liver surface characteristic of cirrhosis is easily seen at laparoscopy. In this patient, who is HBsAg positive, the shrunken, nodular liver clearly indicates cirrhosis.

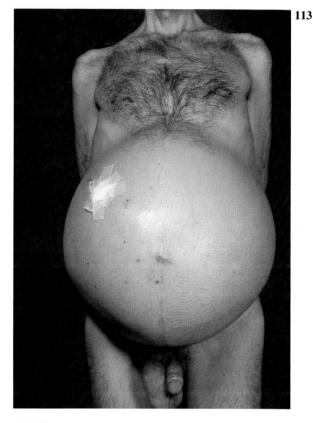

113 Decompensated cirrhosis with portal hypertension and ascites eventually develops in many patients with cirrhosis due to type B hepatitis. This cirrhotic patient first presented when ascites appeared. The dressing covers the site of a diagnostic peritoneal tap performed to exclude ascitic infection.

Hepatitis C

Hepatitis C causes one type of non-A, non-B hepatitis. It is related to blood transfusions from carrier donors but may be sporadic. It is frequently followed by chronic hepatitis which can develop into cirrhosis. It is marked by a long rather benign course with fluctuating transaminases and very suggestive liver biopsy appearances of portal (zone 1) lymphoid aggregates with damaged bile ducts, fatty change, acidophil bodies and sinusoidal cell infiltration.

114 Post-transfusion hepatitis C. This patient developed acute hepatitis six weeks after a blood transfusion. Serum alanine aminotransferase (ALT) rose and then fluctuated as chronic liver disease developed (YoYo transaminases). Hepatitis C virus RNA (HCV RNA) was present from the onset. The serum antibody to hepatitis C (anti-HCV) appeared 20 weeks after exposure.

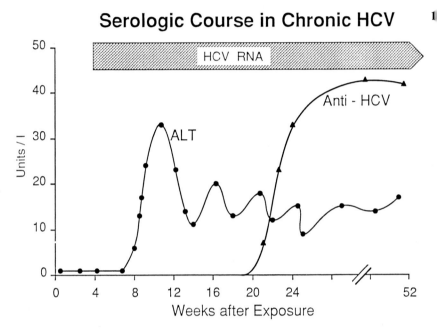

115 Chronic hepatitis C. Liver biopsy from the patient shown in **114** showed a well-preserved hepatic anatomy with portal (zone 1) areas (P) bearing a normal relationship to central (zone 3) areas (C). The portal zone is expanded. *(H.&E. ×40)*

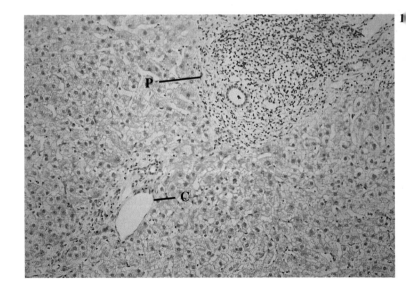

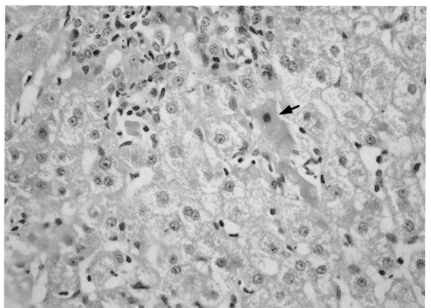

116 Hepatitis C. A higher magnification of the biopsy shown in **115** shows marked infiltration of the sinusoids with inflammatory, largely mononuclear cells. A rhomboid acidophilic hepatocyte can be seen (arrowed). There is mild fatty change. *(H.&E.×100)*

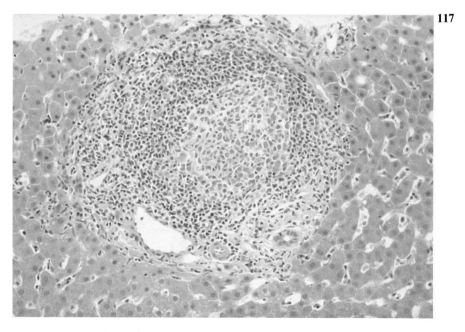

117 Hepatitis C. A portal (zone 1) area from the liver biopsy shown in **115** showed a lymphoid aggregate with damaged bile ducts. *(H.&E.×80)*

Lupoid hepatitis (autoimmune chronic active hepatitis)

This chronic hepatitis affects women predominantly (75%), usually young adults but also women around the menopause. The aetiology is unknown and tests for hepatitis B and C are always negative. Immunological changes include the presence in the blood of anti-nuclear factor in about 50% of cases, smooth muscle antibody in about 66%, and a very high serum gammaglobulin (particularly the IgG fraction). Other diseases are frequently associated, including diabetes mellitus, thyroiditis, fibrosing alveolitis, pericarditis and myocarditis, renal tubular acidosis, ulcerative colitis, autoimmune haemolytic anaemia and vasculitis. The illness may start as acute viral hepatitis. However, the onset is usually insidious with a mild fluctuating jaundice, fevers, malaise and tiredness. Untreated, lupoid hepatitis progresses to cirrhosis. Portal hypertension and portal systemic encephalopathy are late features. Spider naevi are usually present and moderate hepato-splenomegaly is usual.

118

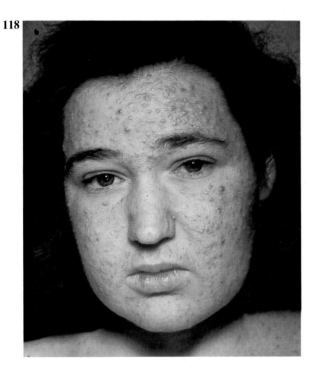

118 Acne vulgaris and a moon-shaped facies are common at the presentation of lupoid hepatitis, even before prednisolone treatment.

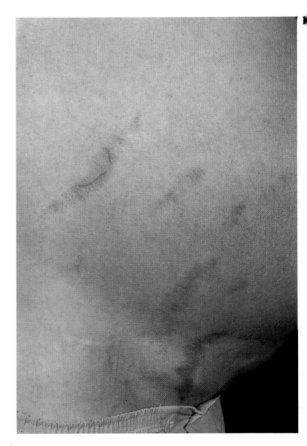

119 Striae develop on the abdomen, buttocks, thighs and upper arms. This sign, together with the acne and a moon face, sometimes leads to lupoid hepatitis being confused with Cushing's syndrome.

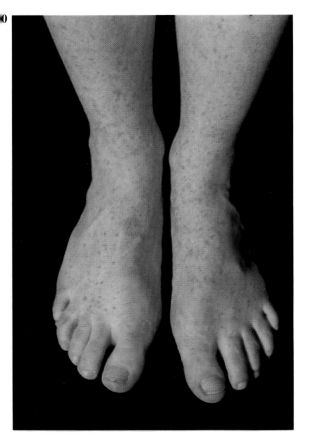

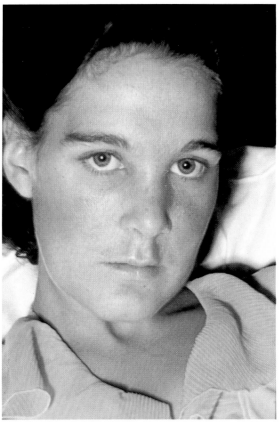

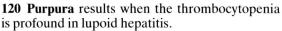

120 Purpura results when the thrombocytopenia is profound in lupoid hepatitis.

121 Butterfly rash may be seen in non-B (lup-oid) chronic active hepatitis. This erythematous rash on the cheeks and the bridge of the nose is similar to that seen in systemic lupus erythema-tosus. Despite the occasional finding of L.E. cells in the blood (in about 15% of patients), the full syndrome of systemic lupus erythematosus does not occur.

122 Vitiligo is shown as patchy depigmentation and hyperpigmentation and is present in some patients with lupoid hepatitis.

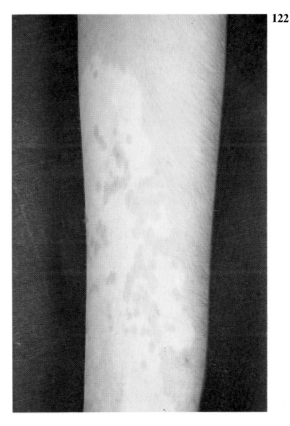

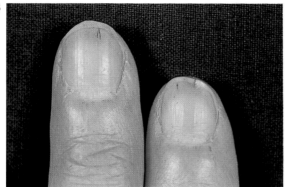

123 Splinter haemorrhages in the nails of this patient with lupoid hepatitis are a sign of a widespread vasculitis.

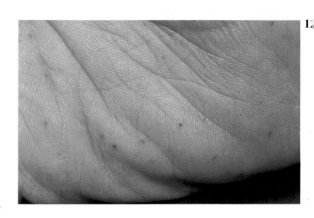

124. Vasculitis has resulted in these dark pinhead lesions on the hand of a patient with lupoid hepatitis. Later, the lesions may undergo necrosis and ulcerate.

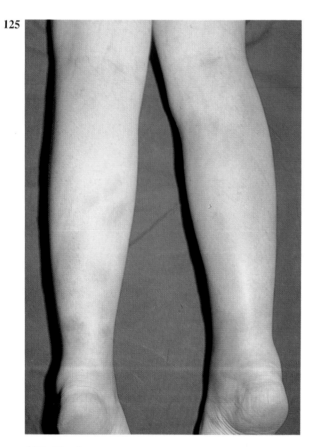

125 Erythema nodosum-like rash is also the result of vasculitis in this patient. The blotchy erythematous areas are slightly raised and painful.

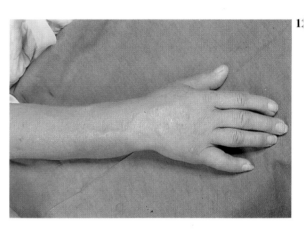

126 Arthritis affecting the larger joints, such as the wrist and elbow, is common. Occasionally an arthritis with all the features of acute rheumatoid arthritis may develop, as in this patient with boggy swelling of the wrist and proximal inter-phalangeal joints.

127 Fibrosing alveolitis. Occasionally, frank fibrosing alveolitis develops. This man's lupoid hepatitis has been inactive for several years as a result of prednisolone therapy. However, he has severe exertional dyspnoea and the chest x-ray shows a honeycomb lung with bullae.

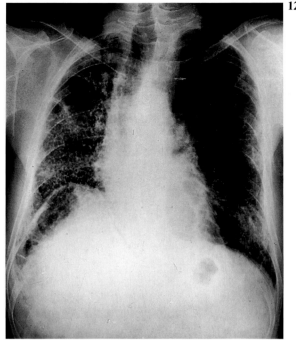

128 Liver biopsy in lupoid chronic active hepatitis usually shows florid changes with infiltration of chronic inflammatory cells expanding the portal tracts and spilling out into the lobule. Liver cell necrosis and rosette formation may be so prominent that they can be seen at low magnification. *(H.&E.×10)*

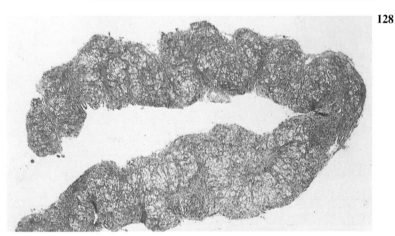

129 Liver biopsy. At a higher magnification the activity of the chronic hepatitis is obvious. Active fibrous septa extend from the enlarged portal tract (1) towards the central vein, enclosing groups of dilated and degenerating liver cells to form rosettes (2). The limiting plate of the portal tract has disappeared as a result of piecemeal necrosis of liver cells and fibrosis. This histological picture is identical to the chronic active hepatitis caused by type B hepatitis. These conditions cannot usually be distinguished on histological grounds using routine stains. *(H.&E.×40)*

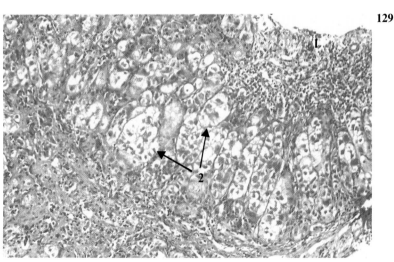

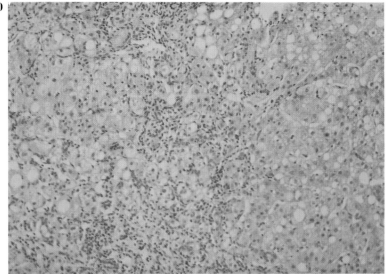

130 Chronic active hepatitis. In a milder case the portal tract (1) is expanded by infiltration with chronic inflammatory cells. Active fibrous septa extend into the lobule. There is piecemeal necrosis of the limiting plate of liver cells around the portal tract and some fatty infiltration. *(H.&E.×40)*

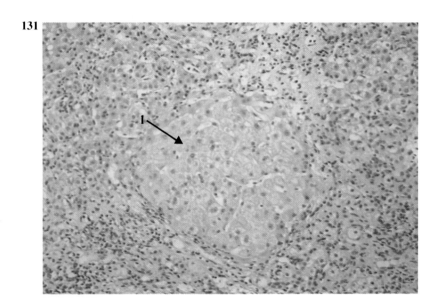

131 Chronic active hepatitis. As the liver cell necrosis and fibrosis progress, regenerative nodules of liver cells develop. This biopsy has included a small regenerative nodule (1) in the midst of an area of active liver cell destruction. *(H.&E.×40)*

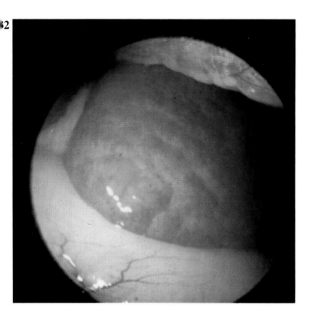

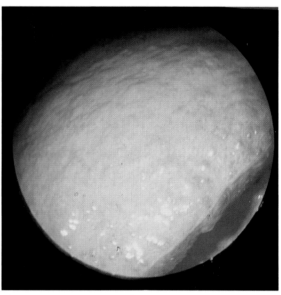

132 Laparoscopy is employed to determine whether lupoid hepatitis has progressed to cirrhosis. The liver biopsy may be insufficient due to the sampling error with a small specimen. The lobulated appearance of the liver in this patient with lupoid hepatitis indicates a non-cirrhotic liver.

133 Laparoscopy in this patient with lupoid hepatitis shows a uniformly nodular liver surface indicating cirrhosis.

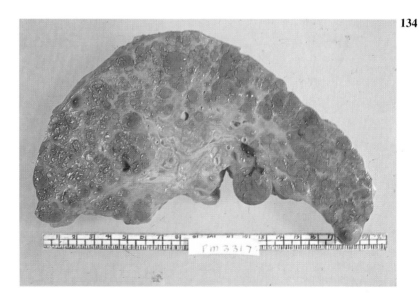

134 Macronodular cirrhosis may be the end result of lupoid hepatitis. As the disease progresses, inflammatory infiltration of the liver decreases and wide fibrous bands, separating nodules of varying sizes, are seen. At autopsy an inactive cirrhosis may be found.

Drug-induced hepatitis

Drugs may cause both acute and chronic hepatitis. Drug-induced hepatitis is often more severe in patients who are also receiving drugs which induce hepatic microsomal enzymes, such as phenobarbitone or alcohol. Liver histology in drug-induced hepatitis is usually indistinguishable from viral hepatitis, except that liver cell necrosis may be more extensive.

Acute drug-induced hepatitis

135 Paracetamol (acetominophen) hepatitis usually results from intentional overdosage. Following ingestion, nausea and vomiting occur. The symptoms then subside for one or two days when mild jaundice and liver tenderness appear. As little as 7.5g (15 tablets) may cause hepatitis and 25g (50 tablets) have been fatal. In severe cases, such as this patient, who had consumed over 100 tablets, drowsiness and coma rapidly develop. Death occurs between the fourth and eighteenth day. The prothrombin time is prolonged.

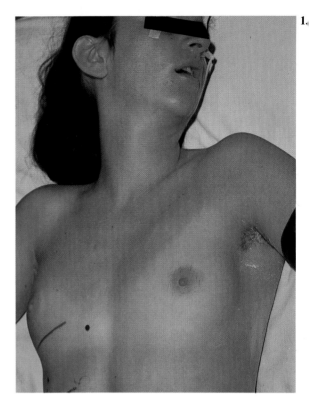

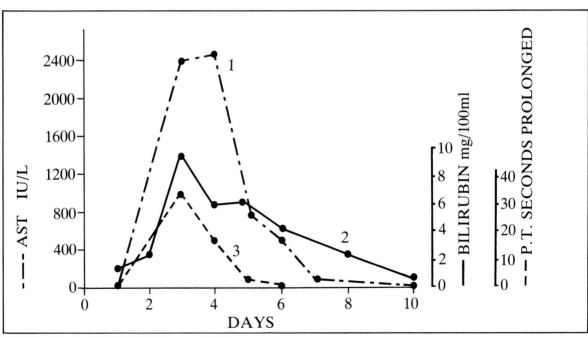

136 Paracetamol hepatitis. This 27-year-old man took an overdose of 130 tablets (65g) of paracetamol and recovered. Three days after the overdose the serum aspartate transaminase (SGOT) concentration (1) had risen to 2400 iu/l and the bilirubin level (2) was 5mg/100ml (85 μmol/l). The prothrombin time (3) was prolonged 40 seconds over the control time. Despite this massive hepatitis, all the tests had returned to normal 10 days after the overdose.

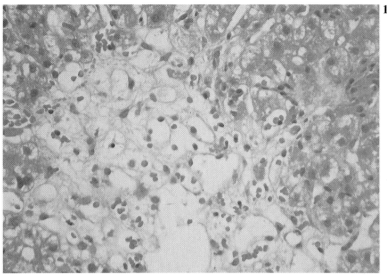

137 Paracetamol hepatitis. The liver biopsy shows well-demarcated centrizonal (zone 3) necrosis of liver cells and collapse of the reticulin framework. In surviving patients the liver lesion heals completely apart from some residual central fibrosis. *(H.&E. ×100)*

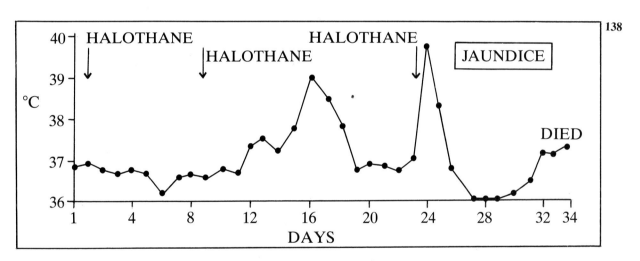

138 Halothane hepatitis is uncommon. It usually follows repeated anaesthetics, often for minor surgical procedures. A history of unexplained fevers five to seven days after a previous halothane exposure is often obtained. Following a subsequent halothane anaesthetic, a moderate to high fever develops early (one to three days) occasionally with a rash and arthralgia. Jaundice appears three to four days later and rapidly deepens. Anorexia, nausea and vomiting may be prominent. The onset of drowsiness and coma indicate a poor prognosis. This patient had three halothane anaesthetics. There was no fever after the first anaesthetic. Six days after the second halothane exposure a pyrexia developed and reached a peak of 39°C. One day after the third anaesthetic he had a fever of 39.5°C and three days later he was jaundiced. The patient died eleven days after the third halothane anaesthetic.

139

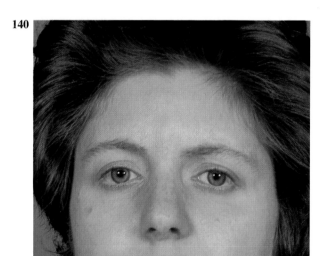

139 Halothane hepatitis. The liver biopsy shows similar changes to viral hepatitis although they are usually more severe. Extensive necrosis and haemorrhage are present around the hepatic vein (1) (zone 3), but the portal tracts (2) are spared. *(H.&E.×40)*

140

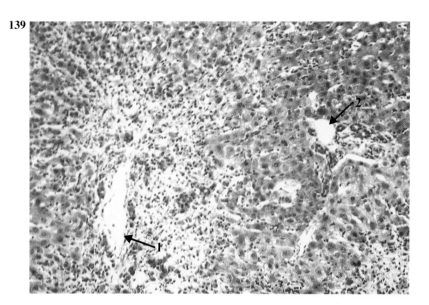

140 Isoniazid hepatitis. Clinical isoniazid hepatitis is uncommon but severe. The patients are usually over 35 years old and have taken isoniazid for three to four months when malaise, lassitude, anorexia and fevers herald the onset of hepatitis. Jaundice with hepatomegaly follows in two to four weeks. The jaundice may be prolonged, even after stopping the drug. This patient had taken isoniazid and rifampicin for six months when jaundice appeared. She was jaundiced with a severe hepatitis for five weeks. Death from acute hepatic failure can occur. This patient recovered.

141

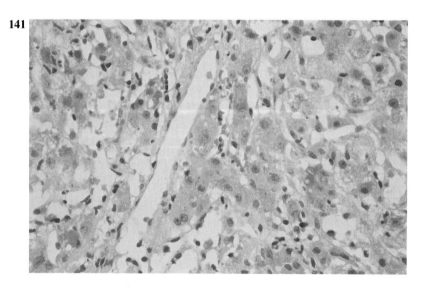

141 Isoniazid hepatitis. The liver biopsy of this patient shows extensive centrizonal (zone 3) necrosis, acute inflammatory infiltration and haemorrhage. In most patients who survive, the liver recovers completely. Rarely, isoniazid may cause chronic active hepatitis which develops insidiously without preceding acute hepatitis. *(H.&E.×100)*

142 Amanita phalloides is the only mushroom known to be hepatotoxic to man. Ingestion causes fulminant hepatic failure, usually in the autumn among holiday-makers who are unfamiliar with the recognition of edible fungi. Amanita phalloides is distinguished by a pale-yellow to olive-green cap and crowded white gills. The stipe (stem) has a bulbous base and is white, but may have a greenish tinge. Symptoms are delayed for six to fifteen hours after poisoning with Amanita phalloides. Nausea, vomiting, abdominal cramps and diarrhoea are followed by signs of dehydration and vasomotor collapse. Jaundice and hepatic coma appear after three days. Signs of renal and central nervous system damage are also prominent.

142

143 Amanita phalloides. The liver biopsy shows massive centrilobular liver cell necrosis, infiltration with acute inflammatory cells and haemorrhage. Many liver cells contain fat droplets. *(H.&E. × 40)*

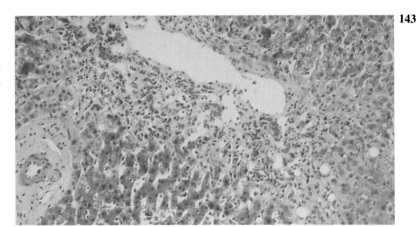

143

Chronic drug-induced hepatitis

144 Oxyphenisatin is one of several drugs which can result in chronic active hepatitis indistinguishable from lupoid hepatitis. Liver damage usually appears after at least a year of regular use of this laxative. The liver biopsy changes are similar to those of lupoid hepatitis. The portal zones (1) are infiltrated with mononuclear cells and there is piecemeal necrosis and active fibrosis. The fibrous septa extend to the centres of the lobules. In some patients the changes reverse on stopping the drug, but in others the hepatitis progresses to cirrhosis. Other drugs that may cause chronic active hepatitis are *methyldopa, isoniazid, ketoconazole* and *flucloxacillin. (H.&E.×40)*

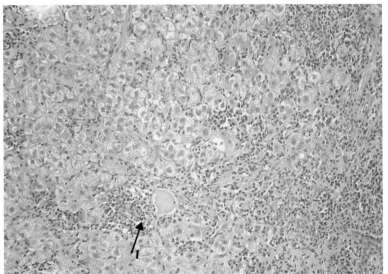

144

Hepatitis in childhood

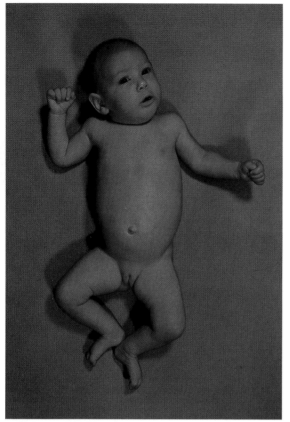

145 Giant cell hepatitis is the common reaction of the liver in infancy to a variety of insults. These include: infections by type B hepatitis, cytomegalovirus, *Herpes simplex*, congenital rubella, coxsackie B and syphilis, metabolic disorders such as galactosaemia and α_1 antitrypsin deficiency and cholestatic syndromes such as biliary atresia. In about 50% of the patients no cause can be found and these are termed *neonatal hepatitis*. Some of the infants are stillborn or die soon after birth, but more commonly a fluctuant cholestatic jaundice appears in the first two weeks. Jaundice has always appeared by two months. The liver and spleen are enlarged and the urine dark and faeces pale. This four-month-old infant had been jaundiced since two weeks old. No cause for her giant cell hepatitis was found. The prognosis is usually poor.

146 Giant cell hepatitis. The liver biopsy is characterized by many multinucleated giant cells (arrow), up to 400μ in diameter, scattered throughout the lobule. The portal tracts are infiltrated with inflammatory cells and there is liver cell swelling and necrosis. Centrilobular cholestasis is often prominent. *(H.&E. ×64)*

3. Fatty infiltration

Infiltration of the liver with fat occurs in a variety of common conditions including obesity, alcoholism and diabetes mellitus. Rare causes of massive fatty change are acute fatty liver of pregnancy and, in children, Reye's syndrome (fatty change with encephalopathy).

147 Focal fat. Fatty infiltration of the liver reduces the density of liver parenchyma in CT scans so that the fatty liver appears darker. This CT scan is from a patient with mild hepatomegaly. Two low attenuation, rather angular, filling defects (arrowed) are present anteriorly and posteriorly in the right lobe of the liver. They had disappeared six months later. Focal fat is a benign condition which may be associated with diabetes, alcoholic liver damage, obesity, hyperalimentation and Cushing's syndrome. The appearances may be confused with malignant infiltration of the liver.

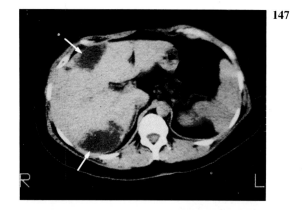

147

148 Diabetic liver. Many liver cells are distended with fat droplets and the nuclei are vacuolated. The fatty change is most marked around the portal zones. During the processing of the section the fat droplets were dissolved, leaving empty spaces. (*H.&E.×100*)

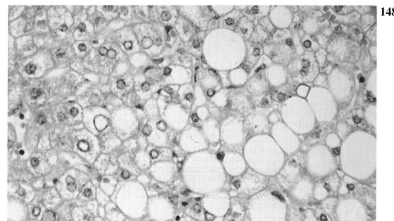

148

149 Diabetic steatonecrosis. Some diabetics develop a liver lesion resembling acute alcoholic hepatitis which may progress to cirrhosis. Hepatomegaly and raised serum transaminases are present. It is related to poor control of the diabetes. This 65-year-old woman had a 10-year history of type 11 diabetes (non-insulin dependent diabetes mellitus). Liver biopsy showed steatonecrosis resembling alcoholic hepatitis but without polymorph infiltration. Note the fatty infiltration and Mallory's hyaline (arrowed). (*H.&E.×100*)

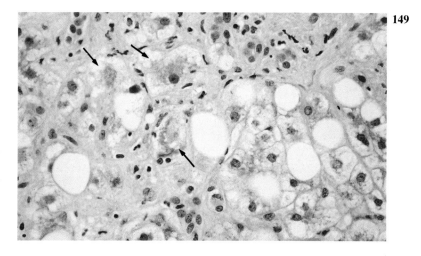

149

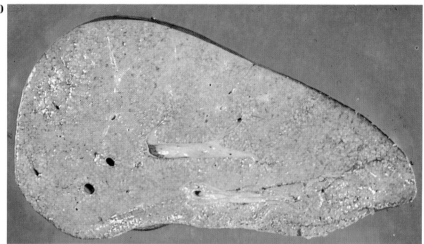

150 Fatty liver. The liver is enlarged and light coloured. The cut surface is greasy and reveals yellow areas of periportal fat. This is the liver of an alcoholic.

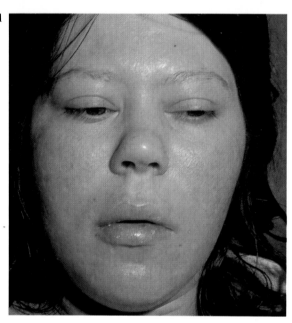

151 Acute fatty liver of pregnancy is a rare cause of jaundice and liver failure in pregnancy. This 23-year-old primiparous patient developed vomiting and epigastric pain followed by jaundice, hepatic encephalopathy and anuria when 37 weeks pregnant.

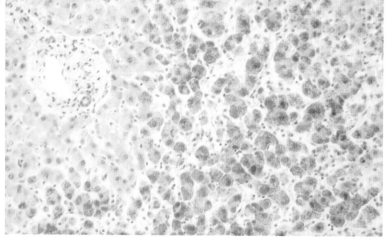

152 Acute fatty liver of pregnancy. A liver biopsy is diagnostic. The liver is massively infiltrated with fat droplets, especially in the centrizonal areas. Liver cell necrosis and inflammation are insignificant. This biopsy has been processed to preserve the fat droplets which are stained red. (*Oil red 0×40*)

153 Jejuno-ileal bypass may cause liver lesions indistinguishable from alcoholic hepatitis. This biopsy shows fat droplets and alcoholic hyaline (arrowed) surrounded by a cuff of polymorphonuclear leucocytes. The patient was a 30-year-old American woman from the 'Bible belt' who had never tasted alcohol. (*Mallory×100*)

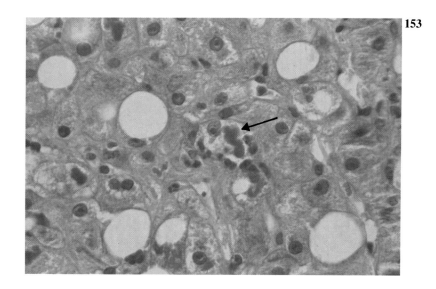

153

154 Amiodarone hepatotoxicity usually develops about one year after starting treatment. The drug has a very long half-life. Hepatomegaly and raised serum transaminases are present, but patients are rarely jaundiced. Amiodarone can cause an acute alcoholic hepatitis-like picture with fibrosis. Fatal cirrhosis can develop. Electron microscopy shows phospholipid-laden lysosomal lamellar bodies containing myelin figures (arrowed).

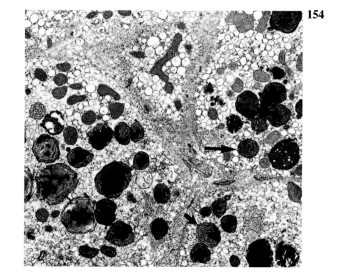

154

155 Reye's syndrome (fatty infiltration with encephalopathy) affects children under ten years of age. Following an upper respiratory infection, this four-year-old boy developed seizures and coma. The prothrombin time was prolonged four seconds over the control value and the arterial ammonia concentration was raised. Hypoglycaemia and intracranial hypertension are frequent complications. The liver biopsy shows massive infiltration with fine droplet (microvesicular) fat (stained red). (*Oil Red 0×200*)

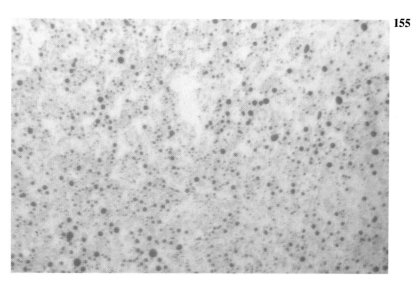

155

4. Cirrhosis

Cirrhosis is defined as widespread fibrosis with nodule formation. Cirrhosis is the result of prolonged liver cell necrosis followed by fibrosis throughout the liver. Liver fibrosis alone is not sufficient for the diagnosis of cirrhosis, as in congenital hepatic fibrosis there is extensive periportal fibrosis but nodules are not present. Conversely, the presence of liver nodules without fibrosis is not cirrhosis. This is seen in the rare condition partial nodular transformation. Cirrhosis may be the end result of many liver diseases, including chronic viral hepatitis, lupoid (autoimmune) chronic active hepatitis, alcoholism, chronic biliary obstruction haemochromatosis, Wilson's disease, heart failure and hepatic venous obstruction, α_1 antitrypsin deficiency and drug toxicity (such as oxyphenisatin and methotrexate). During the development of cirrhosis different patterns of fibrosis may help to distinguish between the different causes. In haemochromatosis the fibrous septa radiate from the portal tracts to give a pointed pattern resembling a holly leaf. In biliary obstruction the fibrosis is mainly in and around the portal tracts and then spreads out to the centres of the lobules. In heart failure fibrosis is most marked in the centrizonal areas. Late in the course of cirrhosis, liver cell necrosis and inflammation disappear and the fibrous septa become inactive and dense, separating regenerating nodules of various sizes. It is then often impossible to identify the cause of the cirrhosis. In a proportion of cirrhotic patients no cause for the cirrhosis can be found and thus it is termed *cryptogenic cirrhosis*. The regenerating nodules disrupt the flow of blood through the liver. Obstruction to portal venous blood flow results in portal hypertension. Shunting of blood through sinusoids at the periphery of the nodules impairs perfusion of the nodules.

Pathological classification

Three types of cirrhosis are recognized, classified according to the size of the regenerating liver cell nodules.

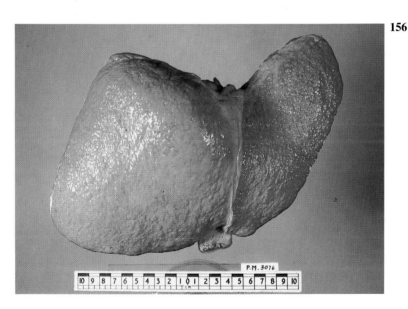

156

156 Micronodular cirrhosis consists of small regenerating nodules of approximately equal size separated by regular bands of fibrous tissue. Every lobule is involved. This type of cirrhosis is usually associated with a continuing liver insult such as alcohol.

157

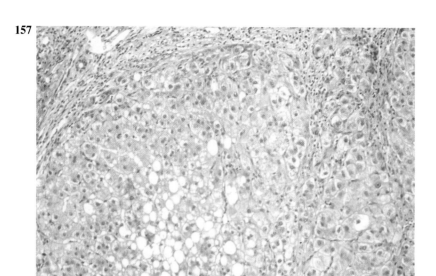

157 Micronodular cirrhosis. The liver biopsy shows fibrous septa enclosing small nodules of liver cells. Many of the hepatocytes are necrotic and there is marked fatty infiltration. This biopsy comes from a patient with alcoholic cirrhosis. (*H.&E.×40*)

158

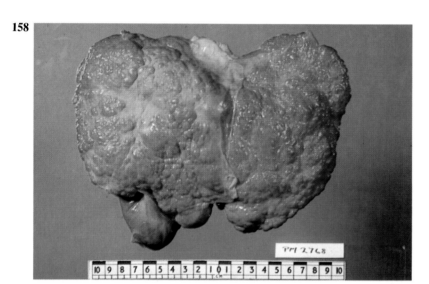

158 Macronodular cirrhosis. The liver is very misshapen and contains nodules of varying sizes. Some of the nodules are large. They are separated by irregular bands of fibrous tissue. In some of the larger nodules, areas with a normal lobular architecture may be found. If a small liver biopsy sample only contains these normal lobules, the presence of a macronodular cirrhosis may be missed. This cirrhosis resulted from chronic type B hepatitis.

159

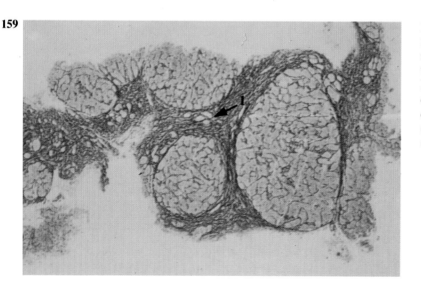

159 Macronodular cirrhosis. The reticulin stain of a liver biopsy shows clearly the variable sizes of the nodules and fibrous septa Previous necrosis and lobular collapse have resulted in the concentration of several portal tracts (1) in the broad fibrous scars. (*×13*)

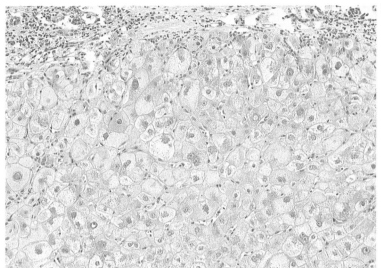

160 Macronodular cirrhosis. Regeneration in cirrhotic nodules often results in liver cell dysplasia. The hepatocytes are of different sizes and many contain large nuclei. Some liver cells are binucleate. The liver cell plates are of varying thickness. A fibrous septum enclosing this nodule is visible at the top of the picture. The liver cell dysplasia in cirrhosis may predispose to the development of primary liver cancer. (*H.&E.×100*)

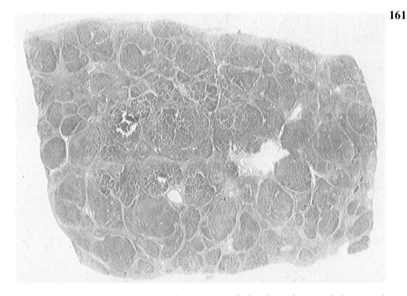

161 Mixed cirrhosis has features of both micronodular and macronodular cirrhosis. Micronodular cirrhosis may develop into a macronodular cirrhosis when the cause of the liver injury is removed. This is seen in alcoholic cirrhotics who stop drinking. A mixed cirrhosis is an intermediate stage.

Clinical signs of cirrhosis

The signs of cirrhosis stem principally from two main causes, portal hypertension and liver cell failure. These signs include spider naevi, paper money skin, palmar erythema, white nails, finger clubbing, endocrine changes, such as gynaecomastia and reduced body hair in males, and fluid retention with ascites and ankle oedema (see Chapter 1). Occasionally signs of the cause of the cirrhosis may be found, such as Kayser–Fleischer rings in the eyes of patients with Wilson's disease. Patients with cirrhosis are classified according to whether the condition is *compensated,* when the patient is relatively well, or *decompensated,* when fluid retention and liver failure are present. Finally, other conditions are associated with cirrhosis, irrespective of the cause.

162

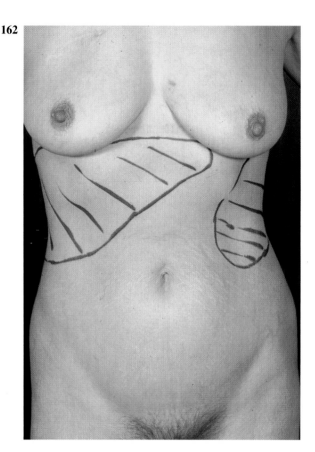

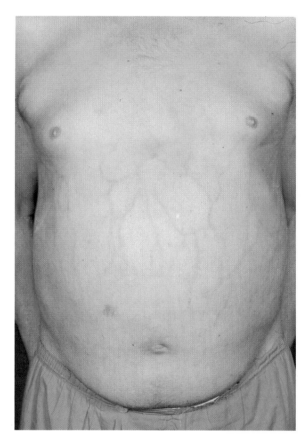

162 Splenomegaly is common in cirrhosis and usually indicates portal hypertension. In this patient with alcoholic cirrhosis the liver is also enlarged due to fatty infiltration. However there are no complications and she feels well. This is an example of a well compensated cirrhosis.

163 Abdominal wall veins in this patient with alcoholic cirrhosis are portal systemic venous collaterals and indicate portal hypertension. The direction of blood flow in these veins is away from the umbilicus. Note the presence of ascites, gynaecomastia and the scanty body hair.

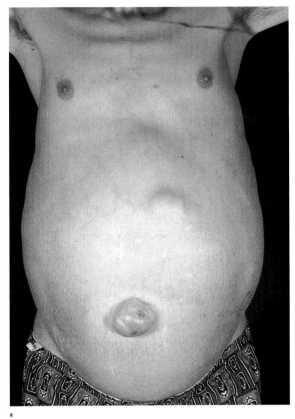

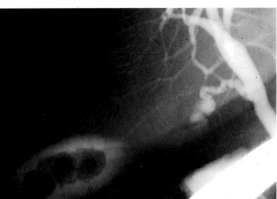

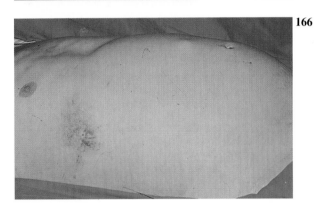
166

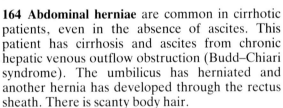

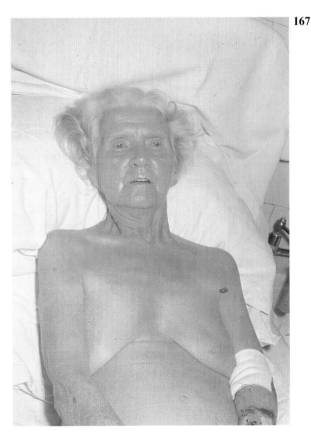
167

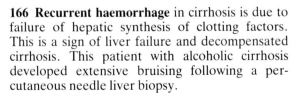

164 Abdominal herniae are common in cirrhotic patients, even in the absence of ascites. This patient has cirrhosis and ascites from chronic hepatic venous outflow obstruction (Budd–Chiari syndrome). The umbilicus has herniated and another hernia has developed through the rectus sheath. There is scanty body hair.

165 Gallstones are present in about 30% of cirrhotic patients compared to about 13% in a matched population. They are usually pigment stones. This endoscopic retrograde cholangiogram from a patient with chronic active hepatitis and cirrhosis has demonstrated three stones in the gall bladder.

166 Recurrent haemorrhage in cirrhosis is due to failure of hepatic synthesis of clotting factors. This is a sign of liver failure and decompensated cirrhosis. This patient with alcoholic cirrhosis developed extensive bruising following a percutaneous needle liver biopsy.

167 Decompensated cirrhosis. Deepening jaundice indicates progressive liver failure. This is usually a late sign in cirrhosis, and purpura and bruising are often associated. This patient had decompensated cryptogenic cirrhosis.

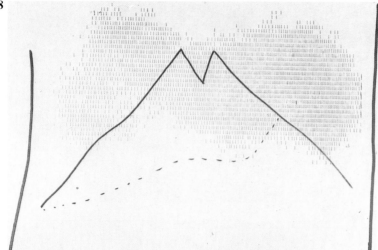

168 Isotope scan in cirrhosis shows reduced liver uptake and increased splenic uptake of ^{99}technetium. In many patients the nodularity of the cirrhotic liver results in a patchy uptake of the isotope, which may be mistaken for space-occupying lesions. In advanced cirrhosis very little isotope is taken up by the liver and most is seen in the spleen, as in this patient with cryptogenic cirrhosis.

169

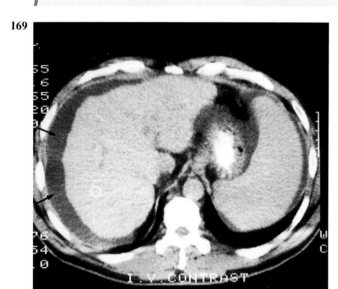

169 CT scan in this patient with hepatic cirrhosis shows a liver with a very irregular nodular margin. Ascites (the opaque area arrowed) is seen between the liver and the abdominal wall and the spleen is enlarged.

170

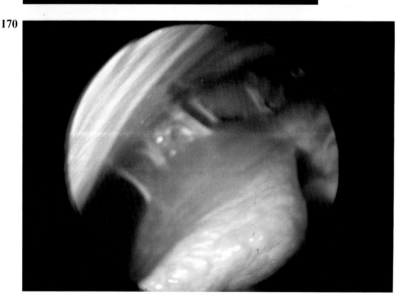

170 Laparoscopy. This patient developed cirrhosis following viral hepatitis. The liver is small and nodular. The adhesions between the liver capsule and the abdominal wall result from inflammation of the liver during acute viral hepatitis. Laparoscopy also permits biopsy of suspicious areas, such as nodules of primary liver cancer which may develop in cirrhosis.

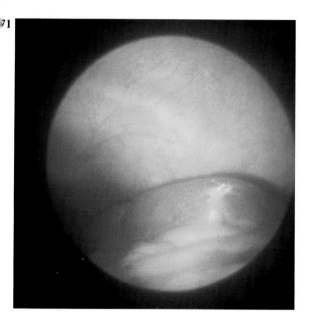

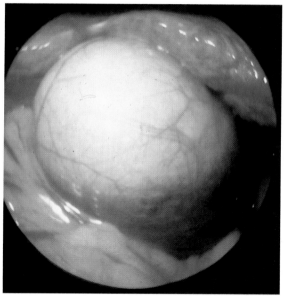

171 Laparoscopy. A normal spleen is not usually visible. In this patient with cryptogenic cirrhosis the spleen is clearly seen and therefore enlarged, indicating the presence of portal hypertension.

172 Laparoscopy. This enlarged gall bladder is a normal appearance in cirrhosis and does not indicate biliary obstruction. Note the normal reddish-pink colour of the cirrhotic liver in this patient with cryptogenic cirrhosis.

Alcoholic liver disease – clinical signs

173 Fatty liver. Hepatomegaly due to a fatty liver is an early sign of alcoholic liver disease. The liver is usually tender. On withdrawal of alcohol, fatty infiltration disappears and the liver returns to a normal size.

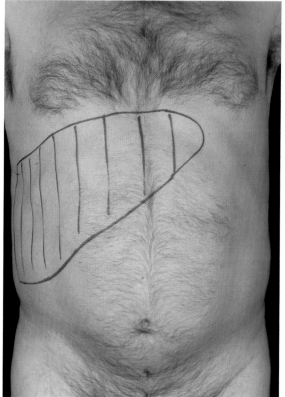

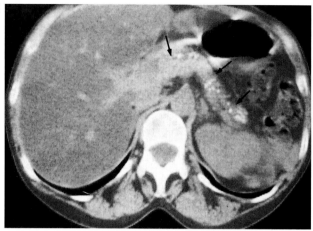

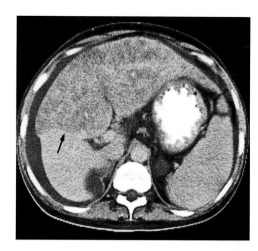

174 Alcoholic fatty liver and chronic pancreatitis. Abdominal CT (unenhanced) shows an enlarged fatty liver evidenced by its low attenuation. The intrahepatic blood vessels are prominent even though no intravenous contrast medium has been given. The pancreas is enlarged and calcified (arrowed).

175 Alcoholic pseudo-tumour. This 45-year-old businessman with fever, jaundice and leucocytosis was suffering from acute alcoholic hepatitis. He felt a mass in his upper abdomen. A liver tumour was suspected and an abdominal CT scan (with oral contrast) showed an extensive low attenuation area suggestive of hepatocellular carcinoma (arrowed). Directed needle liver biopsy sampling showed only acute alcoholic hepatitis. This is a rare type of alcoholic hepatitis affecting particularly one part of the liver.

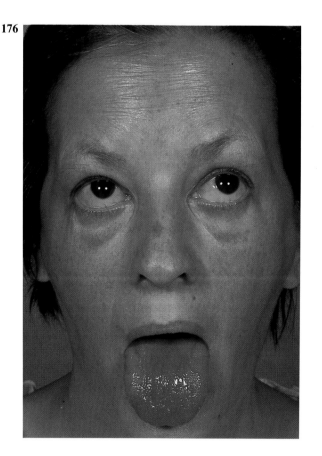

176 Acute alcoholic hepatitis is the next stage of alcoholic liver disease. It usually follows a particularly heavy drinking bout. Deep jaundice, as in this patient, is a bad sign. Note the prominent spider naevus on this patient's nose and her raw red tongue. The liver is usually enlarged, due to fatty infiltration in addition to the hepatitis.

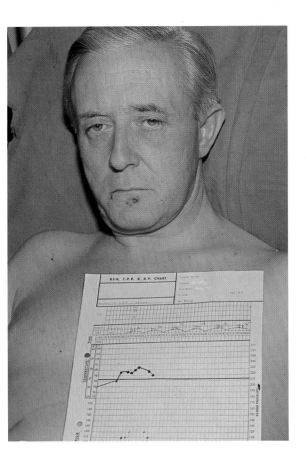

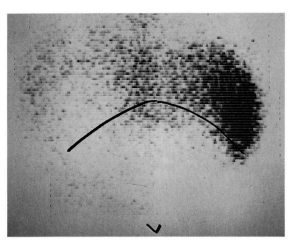

177 Acute alcoholic hepatitis. These patients often have a persistent fever and a polymorph leucocytosis. Alcoholic hepatitis may be confused with acute viral hepatitis. However, the florid spider naevi of the alcoholic, seen on the chest of this patient, a large liver and a leucocytosis are not found in viral hepatitis.

178 Isotope scan. In severe alcoholic hepatitis, uptake of ^{99}technetium by the liver may be negligible. Only splenic uptake is seen. Hepatic blood flow is increased and an arterial murmur may be heard over the liver.

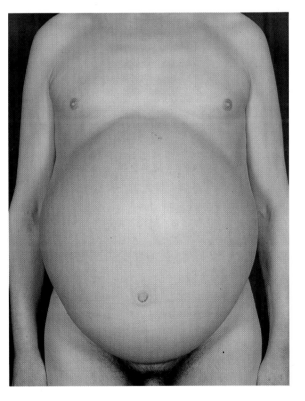

179 Decompensated alcoholic cirrhosis is the final stage of alcoholic liver disease. Note the tense ascites and scanty body hair. In contrast to acute alcoholic hepatitis, jaundice is usually absent.

180 Spider naevi are usual and often florid. The shoulder of this alcoholic patient is covered with spider naevi.

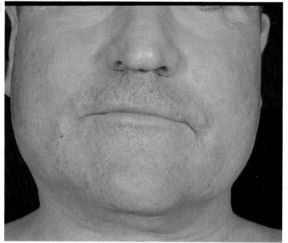

181 Parotid enlargement occasionally occurs in alcoholic liver disease. The swelling is bilateral and painless.

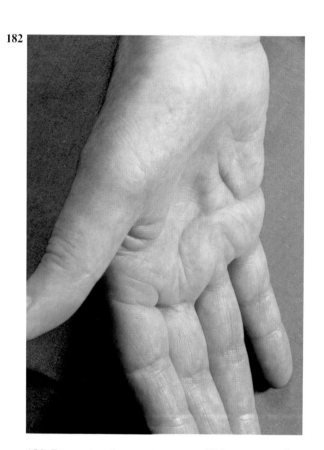

182 Dupuytren's contracture. This progressive fibrosis of the palmar fascia may cause fixed flexion deformities of the fingers. Dupuytren's contracture is more common in alcoholics than in a control population. It is especially frequent among alcoholic cirrhotics, but is related to the alcoholism and not to the cirrhosis. Dupuytren's contracture may also be familial.

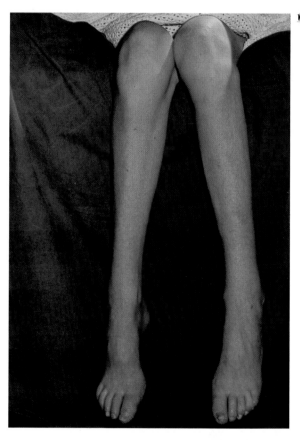

183 Alcoholic neuropathy occasionally develops in poorly nourished alcoholics. Paraesthesiae, impaired pin-prick and light touch sensation and absent ankle jerks are early signs of this peripheral neuropathy. In severe cases, such as this woman, gross muscle wasting results. The calf muscles are especially wasted.

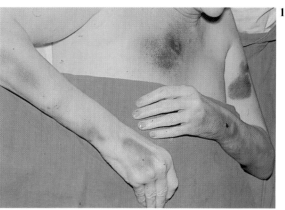

185 Bruising, which may be extensive, is common in alcoholics and usually due to repeated falls while drunk. This patient had alcoholic cirrhosis.

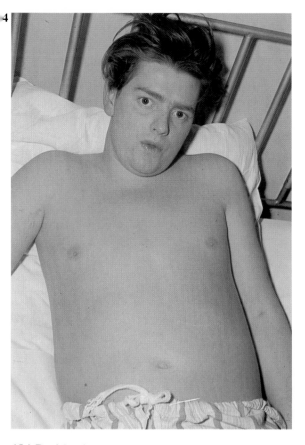

184 Beri-beri, a rare complication of alcoholism, develops when malnutrition has resulted in gross thiamine deficiency. The 'wet' beri-beri syndrome presents as severe congestive cardiac failure which responds dramatically to thiamine. This patient has pitting oedema up to his chest.

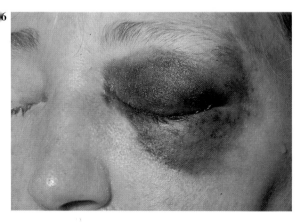

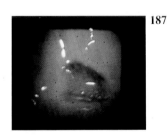

187 Duodenal ulcer. The incidence of duodenal ulcer is higher in alcoholic cirrhosis than in other forms of cirrhosis. This endoscopic picture from an alcoholic shows a large duodenal ulcer covered by a pale slough.

186 Bruising around the eye of this woman with alcoholic cirrhosis followed a fight.

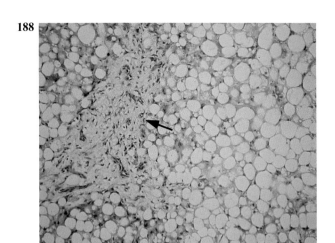

188 Chronic pancreatitis with biliary stricture.
This patient who abused alcohol presented with mild alcoholic hepatitis, but with an unexpectedly high serum bilirubin and alkaline phosphatase level. Liver biopsy showed marked fatty change, but also portal (zone 1) fibrosis (arrowed) with some ductular proliferation. The zone 1 features suggested biliary obstruction. (*H.&E.×120*)

189 Chronic calcific pancreatitis is associated with alcoholism and is a cause of recurrent abdominal pain. An abdominal x-ray in this patient shows pancreatic calcification lying behind the duodenal bulb which is filled with air.

190 Chronic pancreatitis with biliary stricture.
Endoscopic cholangiogram in the patient whose liver biopsy is shown in **188** showed that the biliary obstruction was caused by a stricture (bent knee deformity) (arrowed) of the distal common bile duct due to compression from chronic alcoholic pancreatitis. The pancreatogram showing a dilated pancreatic duct with dilated side branches confirms the chronic pancreatitis. Biliary stricture due to chronic pancreatitis is an important cause of cholestatic (obstructive type) jaundice in alcoholics.

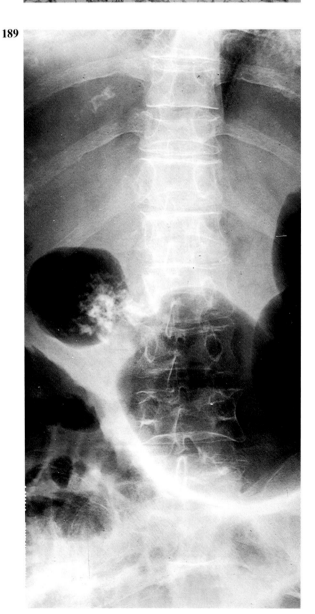

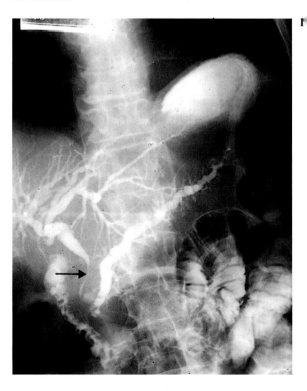

191 Fatty liver develops early in alcoholic liver disease. A biopsy shows most of the liver cells contain large fat droplets. During the processing of this section the fat droplets have dissolved out leaving empty holes. (*H.&E. ×40*)

191

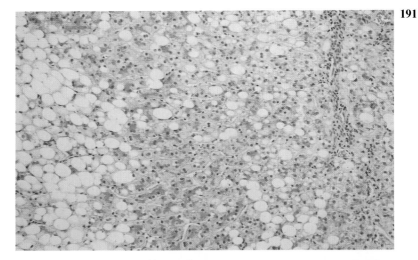

192 Fatty liver. Laparoscopy shows an enlarged swollen liver, which is pale due to heavy fatty infiltration.

192

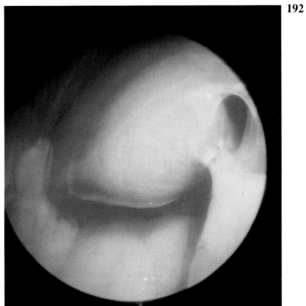

193 Fatty liver. The yellow colour of this liver from an alcoholic is due to massive fatty infiltration.

193

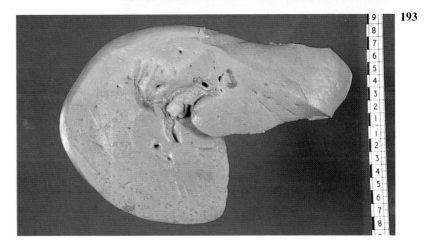

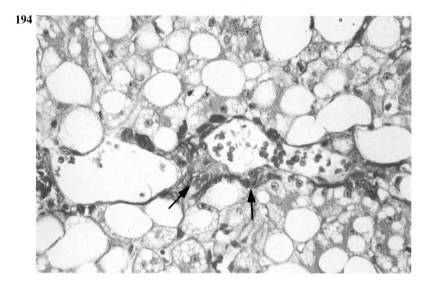

194 Alcoholic liver injury. Early in the course of alcoholic liver disease fine fibrous septa develop around central veins (zone 3) following liver cell necrosis. These septa of new collagen extend into the lobule dividing the liver into regular small nodules. The process can eventually lead to a micronodular cirrhosis. This picture shows spreading perivenular fibrosis (arrow) in zone 3 (central) with fat in the hepatocytes (*chromophobe aniline blue ×80*). This appearance is also known as sclerosing central hyaline necrosis and is an important factor in the development of portal hypertension in alcoholic liver disease.

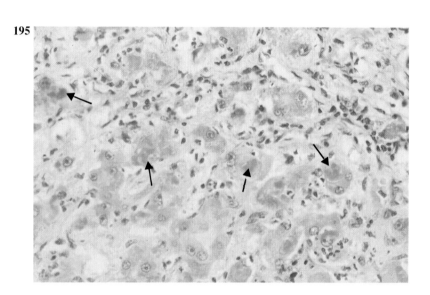

195 Mallory's alcoholic hyaline. In acute alcoholic hepatitis centrizonal (zone 3) liver cell necrosis and acute inflammatory cell infiltration develop, as in any hepatitis. Additionally, the cytoplasm of degenerating liver cells contains irregular clumps of refractile eosinophilic material. This is Mallory's alcoholic hyaline (arrowed). This pink staining material may rarely be found in other chronic liver diseases, such as diabetic steatonecrosis and amiodarone toxicity (see Chapter 3). (*H.&E. ×100*)

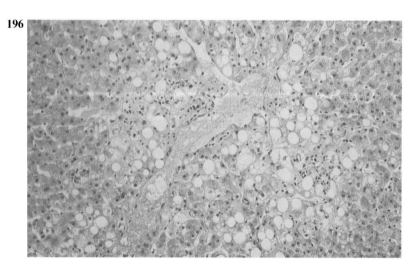

196 Acute alcoholic hepatitis. An acute hepatitis, with liver cell necrosis, inflammatory cell infiltrates, fatty change and alcoholic hyaline, is evident around the central vein (zone 3). There are no signs of cirrhosis. This patient continued to drink. (*H.&E. ×40*)

197 Acute alcoholic hepatitis and cirrhosis. Three years later a second biopsy from the patient shown in **196** demonstrated progression of the liver disease. Now, in addition to alcoholic hepatitis, active fibrous septa are dividing the liver into nodules. An active cirrhosis has developed. The patient then stopped drinking. (*H.&E.×40*)

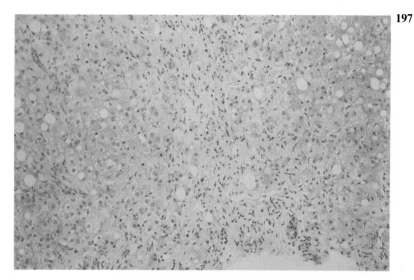

197

198 Inactive micronodular cirrhosis. Five years after the first biopsy (**196**) a third biopsy in this patient shows an inactive cirrhosis. The inflammation and liver cell necrosis have disappeared and fibrous septa separate small nodules. (*H.&E.×40*)

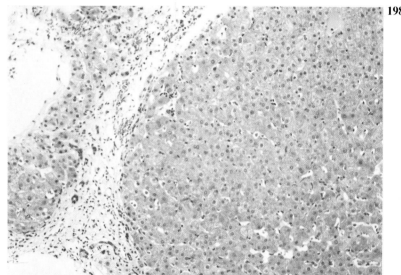

198

199 Laparoscopy in a patient with late alcoholic cirrhosis shows a small liver. The surface is finely nodular indicating a micronodular cirrhosis.

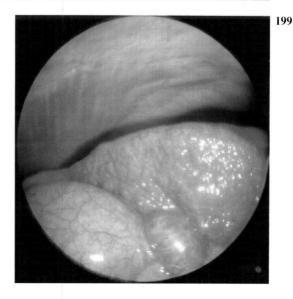

199

Rare causes of cirrhosis

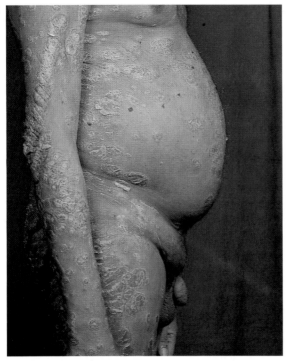

200 Methotrexate therapy causes portal zone (zone 1) fibrosis in the liver. During prolonged treatment with methotrexate the portal fibrosis may progress to cirrhosis. This is seen in patients with psoriasis who receive the drug for long periods. The development of cirrhosis is related to both the dose and duration of methotrexate treatment. This psoriatic patient had been on the drug for four years when ascites appeared.

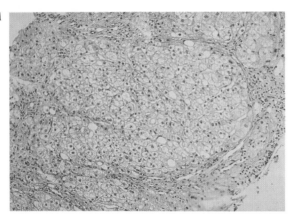

201 Methotrexate. The liver biopsy shows fibrous septa surrounding nodules of liver tissue. Fatty change is present in some hepatocytes, but inflammatory cells are conspicuously absent. This is a late stage of methotrexate toxicity; fibrosis alone is more common.

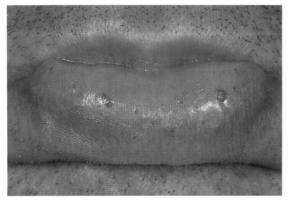

202 Hereditary haemorrhagic telangiectasia. Hepatomegaly is common in this rare disease. Cirrhosis may be due to viral hepatitis contracted from the blood transfusions these patients require. In some cases cirrhosis appears to be associated with the telangiectases. In this cirrhotic patient thin-walled telangiectases are present on the lips.

203 Hereditary haemorrhagic telangiectasia. The venous phase of a selective coeliac axis arteriogram shows a marked and prolonged venous 'blush' in an enlarged liver. The numerous dense pools of contrast are caused by the telangiectases in the liver.

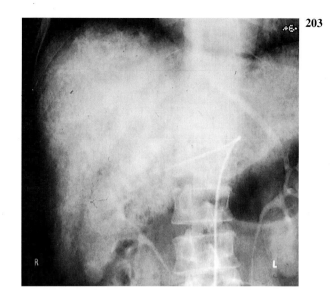
203

204 Hereditary haemorrhagic telangiectasia. The wedge liver biopsy from the patient in **202** shows an inactive cirrhosis. The fibrous septa surrounding the regenerative nodules contain numerous telangiectases.

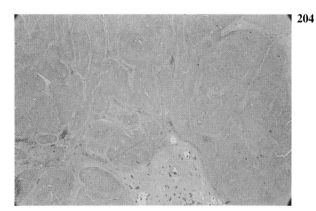
204

5. *Familial non-haemolytic jaundice*

Unconjugated hyperbilirubinaemia

In these patients the serum total bilirubin concentration is above the upper limit of the normal range (greater than 1mg/100ml; 17μmol/l) and most of the bilirubin is unconjugated (non-esterified). However, all other liver function tests are normal. Fasting causes the serum bilirubin level to rise. Gilbert's syndrome is both the commonest and the mildest unconjugated hyperbilirubinaemia. The serum bilirubin level in Gilbert's syndrome rarely exceeds 3mg/100ml (51μmol/l). The prognosis is excellent. Very rarely a severe unconjugated hyperbilirubinaemia is encountered when jaundice is present from birth. This is the Crigler–Najjar syndrome. Most infants affected die in the first year of life from kernicterus. Occasionally these patients develop normally to adult life.

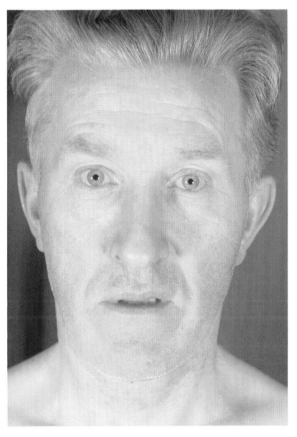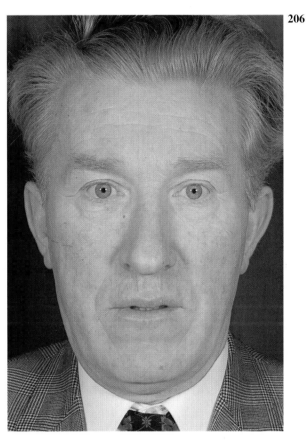

206

205,206 Crigler–Najjar syndrome. This man had been deeply jaundiced since birth. The serum total bilirubin concentration varied between 19mg/100ml (323μmol/l) and 21mg/100ml (357 μmol/l) and was totally unconjugated. Apart from the jaundice, this patient remained in good health. Phenobarbitone therapy may lower the bilirubin level dramatically in some of these cases. The patient was treated with phenobarbitone and his serum bilirubin concentration fell to 5mg/100ml (85μmol/l).

Conjugated hyperbilirubinaemia

Chronic intermittent jaundice due to conjugated hyperbilirubinaemia is seen in the Dubin–Johnson and Rotor syndrome. Since the bilirubin is conjugated it appears in the urine. Other liver function tests are normal. The principal distinction between these two syndromes is a darkly pigmented liver in the Dubin–Johnson type. These conditions are benign.

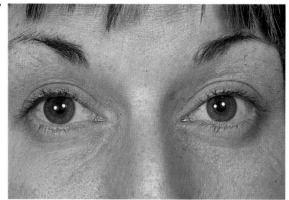

207 Dubin–Johnson syndrome. Clinical jaundice is usually intermittent. It may present during pregnancy or in patients starting the oral contraceptive pill.

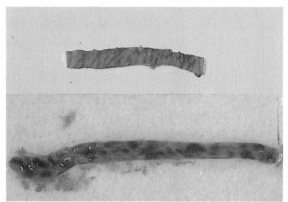

208 Dubin–Johnson syndrome. The liver is a greenish-black colour and this striking feature is easily recognized in a liver biopsy. The lower liver biopsy comes from a Dubin–Johnson patient. The upper biopsy is normal.

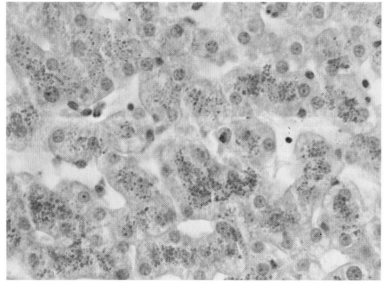

209 Dubin–Johnson syndrome. The dark colour of the liver is due to granules of a brown pigment in the liver cells and Kupffer cells. The pigment is most dense in the centrizonal areas and stains like a lipofuscin. (*H.&E.×160*)

6. Cholestasis

Cholestasis is defined as the failure of bile flow from the hepatocyte to the duodenum. Previously the term 'obstructive jaundice' was used, but this was inaccurate because in many cholestatic patients no bile duct obstruction can be found. Cholestasis is classified as either *extrahepatic*, where there is a mechanical block in the bile ducts, or *intrahepatic*, where no biliary obstruction is present. Many of the signs of cholestasis are the same irrespective of the cause (see Chapter 1 for the clinical signs of cholestasis). Occasionally, associated signs indicate the diagnosis. Examples are a palpable enlarged gall bladder where a cancer of the head of the pancreas obstructs the bile duct, and Sjögrens syndrome in primary biliary cirrhosis. Prolonged cholestasis lasting months or years leads to progressive liver damage and eventually to a biliary cirrhosis with formation of regenerative nodules and fibrosis. The development of a biliary cirrhosis is usually heralded by ascites and signs of hepatocellular failure including portal-systemic encephalopathy.

210 Anatomy of the intrahepatic biliary tree. Bile canaliculi empty into ductules which are found largely in the portal tracts of the liver. The ductules pass into interlobular bile ducts, which are the first bile channels to be accompanied by branches of the hepatic artery and portal vein. Interlobular bile ducts are also found in the portal tracts. These channels unite with one another to form septal bile ducts and so on until the two main hepatic ducts emerge from the left and right lobes of the liver at the porta hepatis.

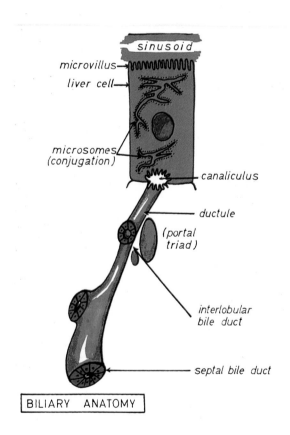

BILIARY ANATOMY

Investigation of cholestasis

The first objective in the investigation of cholestasis is to determine whether the cause is intrahepatic or extrahepatic. Most cases are due to gallstones (see Chapter 14), cancer of the pancreas and biliary tree or secondary cancer, causing extrahepatic cholestasis (see Chapter 11), and viral, drug or alcoholic hepatitis, causing intrahepatic cholestasis (see Chapters 2 and 4).

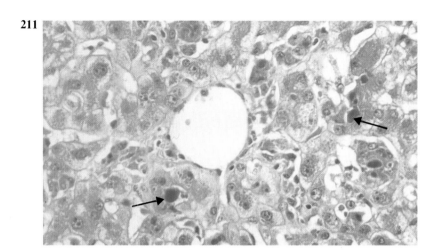

211 Liver biopsy. Bile pigment (arrow) accumulates in the liver cells, Kupffer cells and the bile canaliculi. The pigment is mainly conjugated bilirubin and is most dense in the centrizonal areas (zone 3). (*H.&E.×100*)

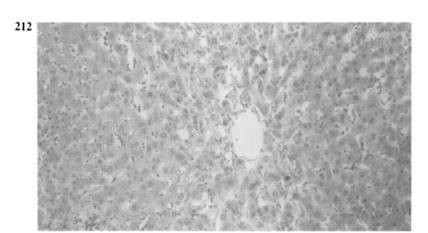

212 Liver biopsy. The centrizonal distribution of bile pigment in cholestasis is clearly seen in this biopsy from a patient with carcinoma of the bile duct. Large amounts of yellow material are deposited around a central vein. (*H.&E.×40*)

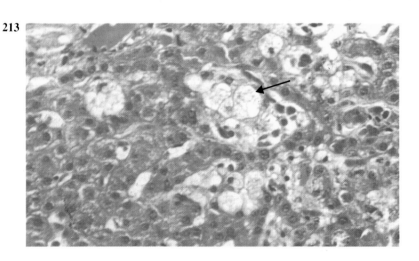

213 Liver biopsy. Some centrizonal liver cells undergo 'feathery' degeneration (arrow) and are surrounded by mononuclear cells. Centrizonal accumulations of bile pigment and 'feathery' degeneration develop in all forms of cholestasis, whether intrahepatic or extrahepatic. (*H.&E. ×100*)

214 Liver biopsy. An extrahepatic cholestasis is usually characterized by marked changes in the portal tracts (1). The bile ducts proliferate and are tortuous, with a wide lumen. The portal tracts are enlarged by infiltration with acute inflammatory cells. These are mainly polymorphonuclear and indicate infection above the obstruction. Oedema and portal zone fibrosis also develop. In this patient gallstones were obstructing the common bile duct. Occasionally, areas of focal liver cell necrosis become bile stained, forming 'bile lakes'. (*H.&E.* ×*40*)

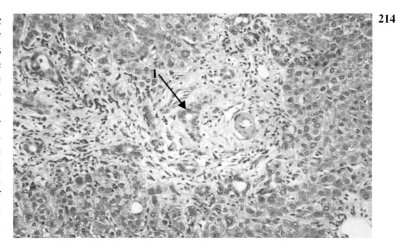

214

215 Ultrasonography of the liver in a patient with extrahepatic cholestasis shows a star-shaped filling defect (1) in the liver (2). This is due to dilated intrahepatic bile ducts. A cancer of the pancreas was obstructing the common bile duct.

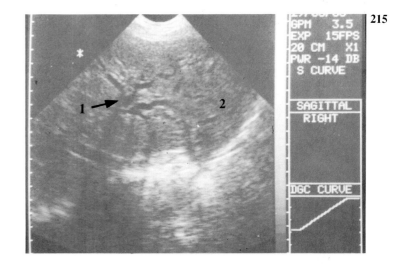

215

216 Laparoscopy in cholestasis shows the liver to be enlarged and green. This patient had a cancer of the head of the pancreas obstructing the bile duct.

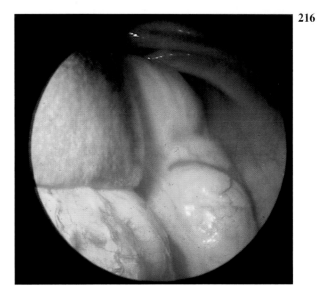

216

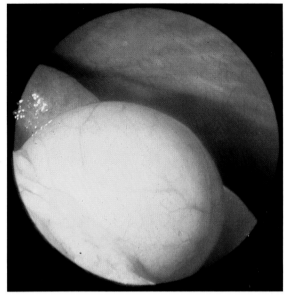

217 Laparoscopy. Another view in the patient shown in **216** reveals a tense enlarged gall bladder. This indicates that the bile duct obstruction is below the level of the cystic duct.

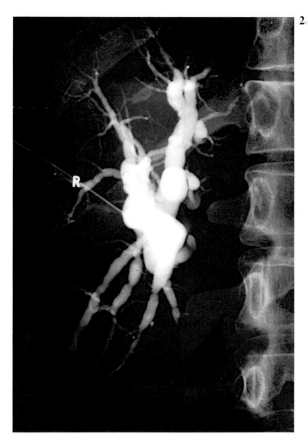

218 Percutaneous cholangiography. In this jaundiced patient the needle has entered a grossly dilated intrahepatic biliary system. No contrast flowed down the common bile duct. This obstruction was due to a carcinoma of the bile duct at the porta hepatis.

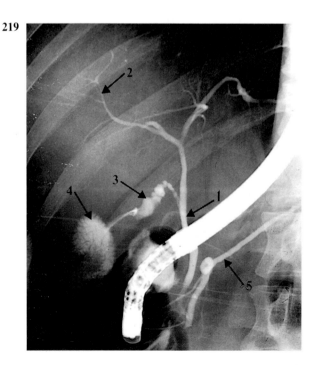

219 Endoscopic retrograde cholangiography is also employed to determine the cause of a cholestasis. In this patient the study revealed a normal common bile duct (1), intrahepatic ducts (2), cystic duct (3) and gall bladder (4). The pancreatic duct (5) was also normal. The cause of the cholestasis was chlorpromazine.

Uncommon causes of cholestasis

1 Sclerosing cholangitis

This syndrome has many causes. The end result is progressive fibrosis and ultimately disappearance of intrahepatic or extrahepatic ducts or both.

Primary sclerosing cholangitis

This condition is of unknown cause although there is a strong genetic predisposition. The HLA-DRw52a antigen appears to be present in all patients. All parts of the biliary system can be involved in a chronic fibrosing inflammatory process which results in obliteration of the biliary tree and ultimately in biliary cirrhosis. It usually affects patients about 40 years old; 60% are male and 75% also suffer from ulcerative colitis. The patient may be asymptomatic or may have bouts of jaundice and abdominal pain. Patients ultimately develop a constant deep cholestasis with secondary biliary cirrhosis and its complications.

220 Primary sclerosing cholangitis. An ERCP shows an irregular common bile duct. The intrahepatic bile ducts are alternately stenosed and dilated resulting in the typical beaded appearance. Diverticulum-like outpouchings may be seen along the common bile duct (arrowed).

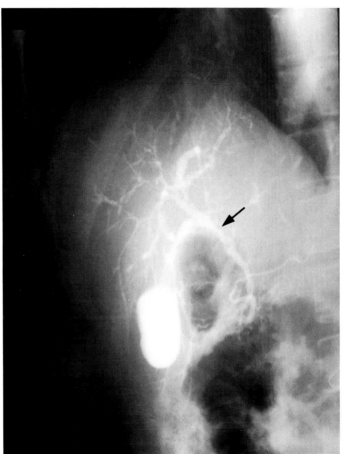

220

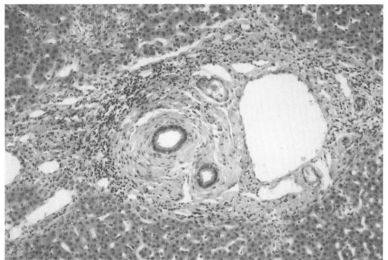

221 Primary sclerosing cholangitis. Liver biopsy from the patient shown in **220** shows fibrosis and inflammation in the portal tracts. Intrahepatic bile ducts show abnormal epithelium and are surrounded by rings of fibrous tissue (onion skin fibrosis). (*H.&E.×40*)

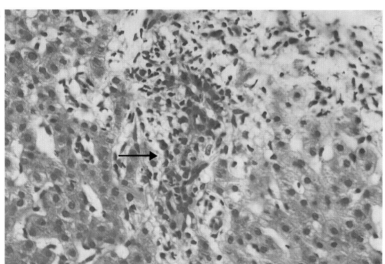

222 Pericholangitis in primary sclerosing cholangitis. The portal tract (zone 1) is oedematous and expanded with proliferated bile ducts and an inflammatory cell infiltrate (arrowed). These changes are not diagnostic of primary sclerosing cholangitis. (*H.&E.×160*)

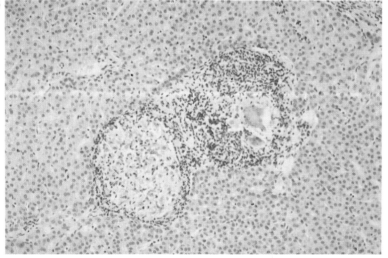

223 Granulomas are found in 10% of liver biopsies from patients with primary sclerosing cholangitis and a third of liver biopsy specimens contain lymphoid aggregates. The granulomas may be well developed with a cuff of lymphocytes enclosing epithelioid cells and giant cells. Caseation does not occur. The presence of granulomas and lymphoid aggregates may lead the liver biopsy in primary sclerosing cholangitis to be confused with primary biliary cirrhosis. (*H.&E.×40*)

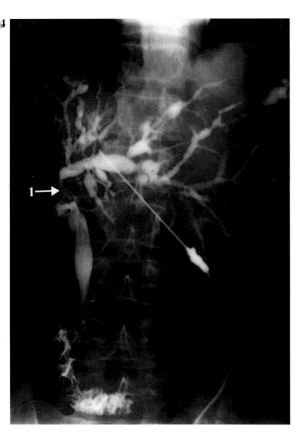

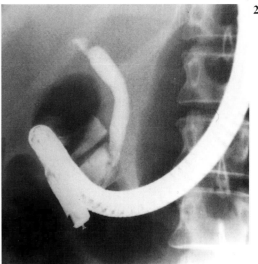

225 Carcinoma of the bile ducts. ERCP in this patient with primary sclerosing cholangitis complicated by bile duct carcinoma shows the common bile duct obstructed and terminating in a nipple-like deformity.

224 Carcinoma of the bile ducts may complicate primary sclerosing cholangitis. It should be suspected if the patient shows progressive jaundice and the intrahepatic bile ducts become dilated. It is difficult to obtain histological (cytological) proof. This percutaneous cholangiogram from a patient with primary sclerosing cholangitis and ulcerative colitis shows the beaded intrahepatic bile ducts of primary sclerosing cholangitis. The intrahepatic ducts are dilated. The stricture at the porta hepatis (arrowed) is due to a bile duct carcinoma.

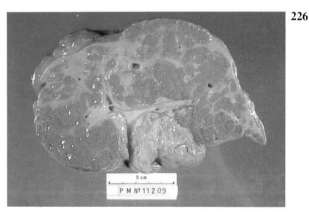

226 Macronodular cirrhosis is an uncommon association with ulcerative colitis. This liver, from a patient with ulcerative colitis, shows the typical large nodules and irregular fibrous septa of a macronodular cirrhosis. Chronic active hepatitis may also be seen.

Similar cholangiographic and liver biopsy appearances to those of primary sclerosing cholangitis can be found in patients with biliary infections. These include children with primary immunodeficiencies and patients with the acquired immunodeficiency syndrome (AIDS) (see Chapter 9). Secondary sclerosing cholangitis is also found in patients treated by hepatic arterial infusion of cytotoxic drugs and after the introduction of caustics into hydatid cysts.

227

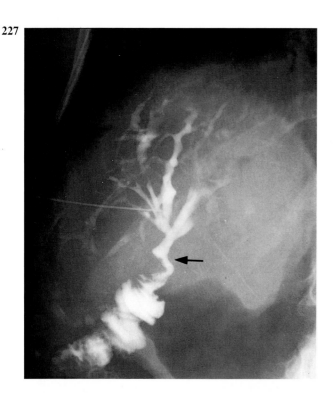

227 Sump syndrome with secondary sclerosing cholangitis. If the common bile duct or hepatic duct is surgically anastomosed to a stagnant loop of duodenum, continued access of gut organisms to the biliary system can result in bacterial cholangitis with biliary obstruction. This patient had a hepaticoduodenostomy (arrow), allowing ascending infection into the biliary tree. Percutaneous cholangiography shows no obstruction to the flow of contrast into the duodenum, but an intrahepatic sclerosing cholangitis, marked by strictures and beading, has developed. This sequence can also complicate choledocholithiasis, biliary strictures and stenosis of biliary-enteric anastomoses.

228

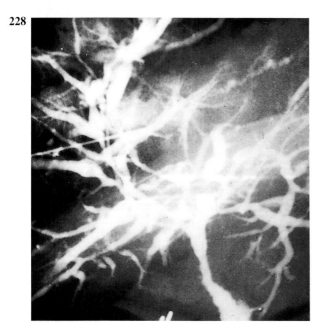

228 Sclerosing cholangitis secondary to hepatic arterial chemotherapy. This patient with hepatic metastases from a colonic cancer had received 5-fluorodeoxyuridine (5-FUDR) by a constant infusion into the hepatic artery every two weeks for one year. Cholangiography shows diffuse sclerosis of the intrahepatic bile ducts. The hepatic metastases have regressed, but they did not disappear.

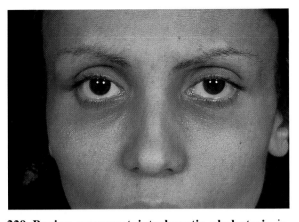

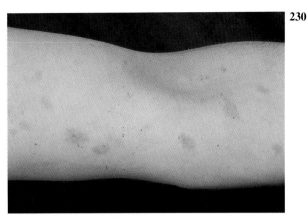

229 Benign recurrent intrahepatic cholestasis is rare. The patient suffers repeated attacks of cholestatic jaundice. This was the patient's seventh attack and her serum bilirubin concentration was 21mg/100ml (357µmol/l). The syndrome may be familial. There is no bile duct obstruction. The cholestasis is self-limiting and usually lasts about two months, but this varies.

230 Macular eruption in this man always preceded attacks of benign recurrent intrahepatic cholestasis. A proportion of patients complain of transient rashes on the shoulders and arms associated with the cholestasis.

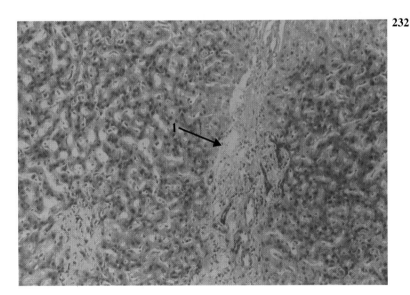

231 Pruritus is usually the first sign of a cholestatic attack and appears before the jaundice. The pruritus is often severe and may dominate the patient's illness. The scratch marks on this girl's legs result from severe pruritus.

232 Liver biopsy during the cholestatic attack shows centrizonal (zone 3) cholestasis and moderate mononuclear infiltration of the portal zones. Between attacks the liver is normal apart from mild portal zone fibrosis (1). (*H.&E.×40*)

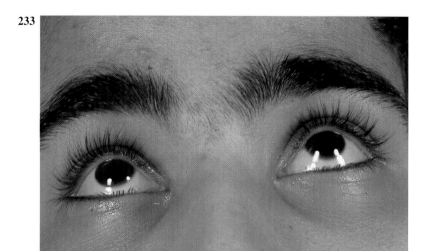

233 Sickle cell crisis may result in a severe intrahepatic cholestasis. Characteristically the serum bilirubin level is enormously increased. In this Arab boy the serum total bilirubin level was 54mg/100ml (918μmol/l); most of the bilirubin was conjugated.

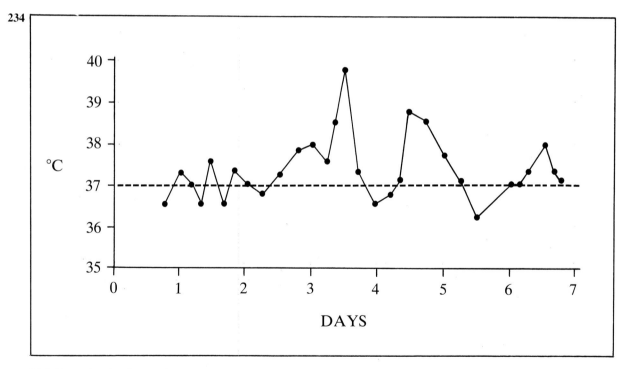

234 Pyrexia. An intermittent pyrexia is commonly present during a sickle cell crisis. Fevers up to 40°C were recorded in the patient shown in **233**. No infective cause could be found for the fever.

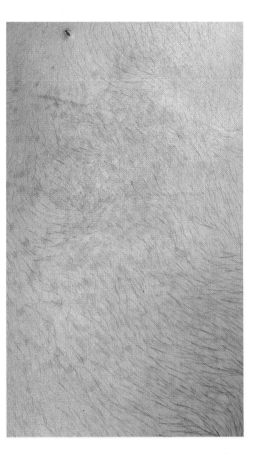

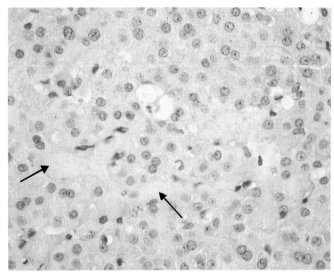

235 Septicaemia. During a sickle cell crisis patients are especially prone to infections. One day before his death this purpuric rash appeared on the abdomen, buttocks and legs of the patient shown in **233**. The purpura was due to gram negative septicaemia. Bone infections also occur.

236 Liver biopsy in a sickle cell crisis. The hepatic sinusoids are dilated and full of clumps of sickled red blood cells (arrowed). (*H.&E.×100*)

4 Drug-induced cholestasis

237 Oral contraceptive drugs may rarely cause an intrahepatic cholestasis. The jaundice usually develops by the second cycle. The liver biopsy changes are confined to centrizonal (zone 3) cholestasis. The portal tracts are normal. Recovery follows when the drug is stopped. These patients may also develop cholestasis of late pregnancy. A dose-dependent pure cholestasis may also follow ingestion of C17-α substituted testosterones, such as methyl testosterone. (*H.&E.×100*)

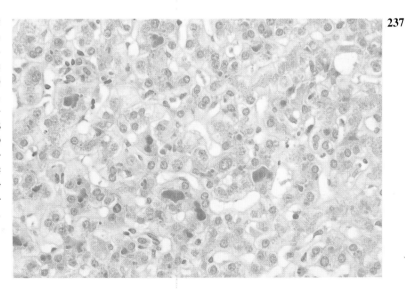

237

238

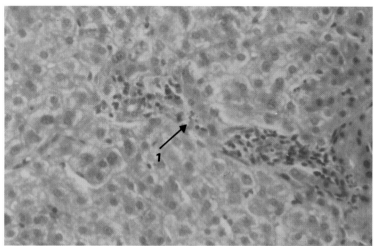

238 Chlorpromazine may cause an intrahepatic cholestasis. The jaundice usually appears by the third week together with signs of a hypersensitivity reaction. The liver biopsy shows centrizonal cholestasis and some 'feathery degeneration' of liver cells. Chlorpromazine causes a portal zone reaction (1) with mononuclear cell and eosinophil infiltration. Complete recovery is usual. A similar hypersensitivity-type cholestasis is associated with other phenothiazine derivatives, tolbutamide, anti-thyroid drugs and gold. (*H.&E.×100*)

239

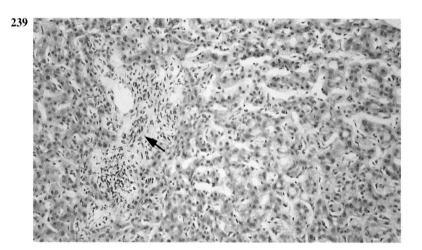

239 Chronic drug cholestasis. Occasionally a hepatic drug reaction causes chronic cholestasis lasting many months or even years. Recovery is usually complete, but sometimes small intrahepatic bile ducts are destroyed and liver transplantation can be required. Drugs at fault include chlorpromazine, procarbazine, flucloxacillin and thiabendazole. This liver biopsy comes from a middle-aged woman who developed cholestatic jaundice four weeks after starting procarbazine. Icterus persisted for six months and then cleared with complete recovery. Liver biopsy shows a portal area (zone 1) markedly expanded with mononuclear cells and some fibrous tissue, and containing a damaged bile duct (arrowed). (*H.&E.×40*)

5 *Primary biliary cirrhosis*
(also called chronic non-suppurative destructive cholangitis and 'Hanot's cirrhosis')

Primary biliary cirrhosis mainly affects women, usually between the ages of 40 and 59 years. The onset is insidious and typically pruritus is the first symptom. Months or years later cholestatic jaundice appears. Pigmentation of the skin and xanthomas are common. A serum mitochondrial antibody is found in 83–98% of patients. Some collagen diseases are associated with primary biliary cirrhosis including Sjögren's syndrome, Raynaud's phenomenon, rheumatoid arthritis, dermatomyositis and scleroderma. Autoimmune thyroiditis and renal tubular acidosis also occur.

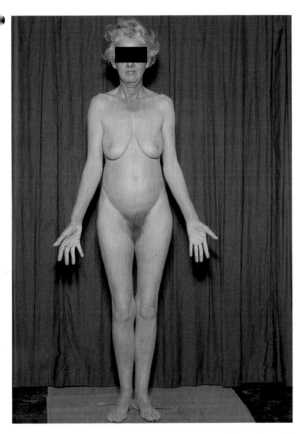

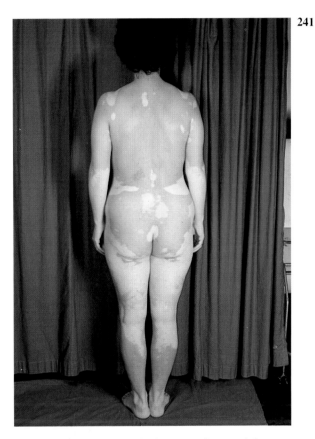

240 Primary biliary cirrhosis. The patient is well nourished, mildly jaundiced and pigmented. Hepato-splenomegaly is usual.

241 Vitiligo. Patchy depigmentation and hyper-pigmentation occasionally develop in primary biliary cirrhosis.

242 Arthritis. The late changes of rheumatoid arthritis have developed in this patient with primary biliary cirrhosis. There is ulnar deviation of the hand, subluxation of the metacarpo-phalangeal joints and wasting of the small muscles of the hand.

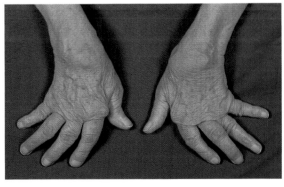

242

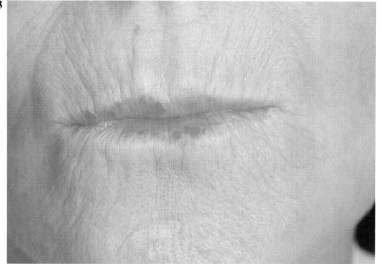

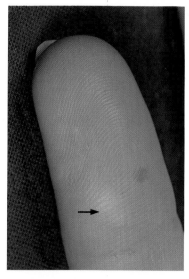

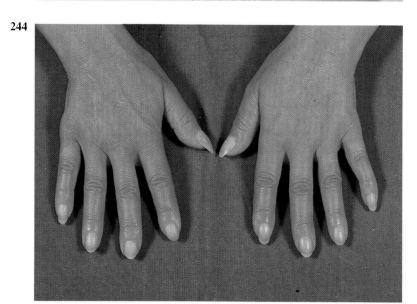

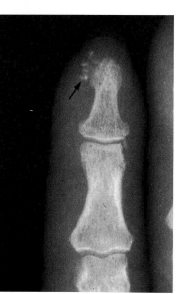

243–246 CRST syndrome. The syndrome comprises calcinosis, Raynaud's phenomenon, sclerodactyly and telangiectasia. Telangiectases are present on the lips (**243**) and tongue of this patient with primary biliary cirrhosis. Other sites include the palate, forehead and hands.

Sclerodactyly is the cause of the thickened shiny skin on the patient's fingers. In the later stages the skin atrophies and the fingers become spindle-shaped.

Calcinosis, which are small white patches of subcutaneous calcification (**245**), are present on the patient's finger (arrowed). A telangiectasis can also be seen. An x-ray (**246**) of the finger shows the calcinosis as spotty subcutaneous calcification adjacent to the distal phalanx.

247 Dermatomyositis may be associated with primary biliary cirrhosis. The patient developed the typical lilac-coloured (heliotrope) rash on her cheeks and over the bridge of her nose. Periorbital oedema is usually marked. Her main complaint was profound muscle weakness due to a proximal myopathy.

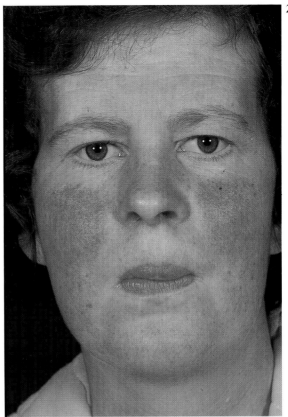

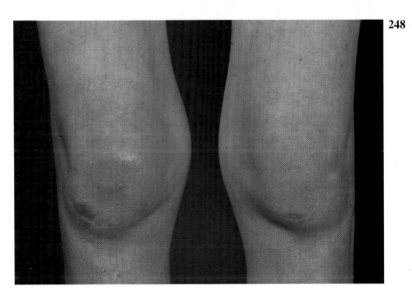

248 Dermatomyositis. The itchy dermatitis was also present on the knees of the patient shown in **247**. Note the wasting of quadriceps femoris due to a proximal myopathy.

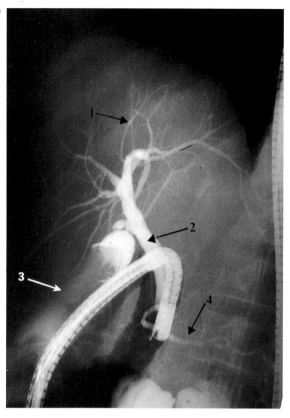 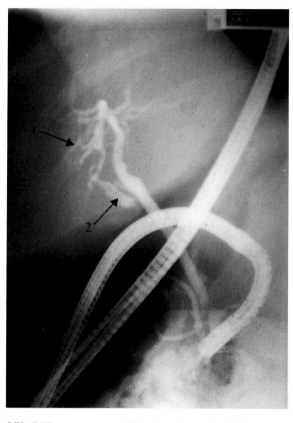

249 Biliary system. Primary biliary cirrhosis only affects the very small bile ducts in the liver. The larger elements of the biliary system are normal, unless cirrhosis has developed when their course is distorted by nodule formation. This endoscopic retrograde cholangiogram from a patient with primary biliary cirrhosis shows normal smoothly tapering intrahepatic bile ducts (1). The common bile duct (2), gall bladder (3) and pancreatic duct (4) are all normal. In this patient cirrhosis had not developed.

250 Biliary system. The intrahepatic bile ducts (1) are pruned and their course is tortuous in this patient with primary biliary cirrhosis. The intrahepatic bile ducts have been distorted by cirrhotic nodules. Note the shrunken gall bladder (2) which contains small stones. Patients with primary biliary cirrhosis often develop gallstones.

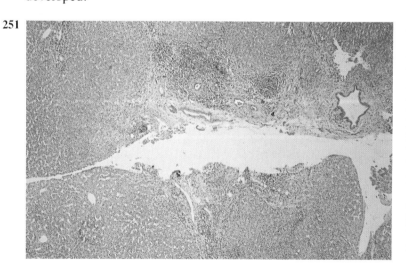

251 Primary biliary cirrhosis. The liver biopsy shows heavy infiltration of the portal tracts (zone 1) with lymphocytes, histiocytes and epithelioid cells. Lymphoid follicles with germinal centres and granulomas may form in the portal tracts in relation to damaged bile ducts. Fibrosis begins in the portal tracts and fibrous septa later spread into and around the lobules. Primary biliary cirrhosis involves the septal and larger interlobular bile ducts, so that if these are not included in the biopsy, the characteristic changes may be missed. (*H.&E.×10*)

252 Primary biliary cirrhosis. At higher magnification the patho-gnomonic sign of primary biliary cirrhosis is seen. An enlarged portal tract is infiltrated with chronic inflammatory cells and contains a granuloma adjacent to a damaged bile duct (arrowed). (*H.&E. ×64*)

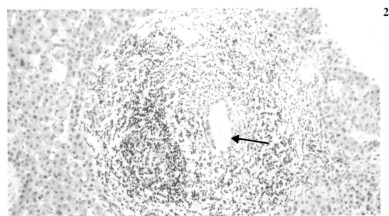

253 Primary biliary cirrhosis. Copper accumulates in the liver cells in any prolonged cholestasis. This is due to impaired biliary excretion of copper. The rhodamine stain shows a heavy load of copper-binding protein as red granular deposits in the liver cells of a patient with primary biliary cirrhosis. (*×100*)

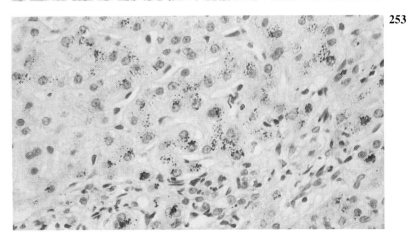

254 Primary biliary cirrhosis. At autopsy the liver is enlarged, green and coarsely nodular.

6 Secondary biliary cirrhosis

Prolonged extrahepatic biliary obstruction may result in secondary biliary cirrhosis. This is most commonly due to a benign bile duct stricture or to gallstones. Malignant strictures of the bile duct, such as cancer of the head of the pancreas, rarely lead to secondary biliary cirrhosis. The patient usually dies from the cancer before biliary cirrhosis has had time to develop.

255,256 Benign biliary stricture usually follows a cholecystectomy. The jaundice is cholestatic and of variable intensity and is often accompanied by fevers and pain due to cholangitis. This patient has a biliary stricture following a cholecystectomy. The serum bilirubin level was 18mg/100ml (306μmol/l).

Recurrent cholangitis caused temperatures up to 39.5°C in this patient (Charcot's intermittent biliary fever). During the fevers the white blood cell count rose to 24,000mm³ and consisted predominantly of polymorphonuclear leucocytes. *E. coli* were cultured from the blood.

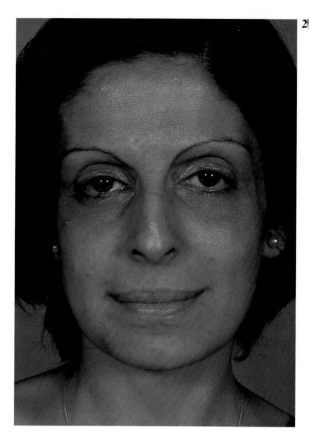

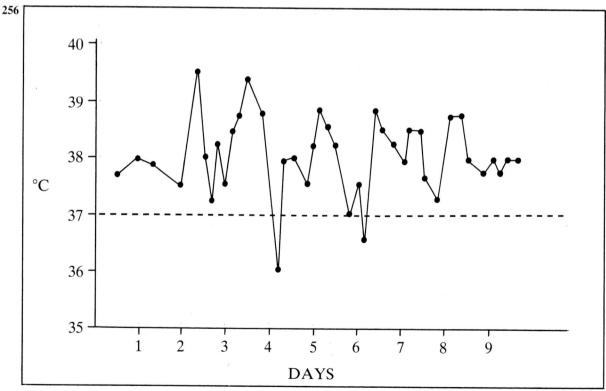

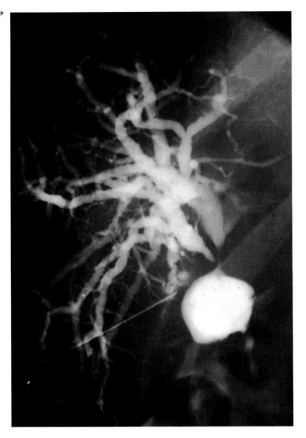

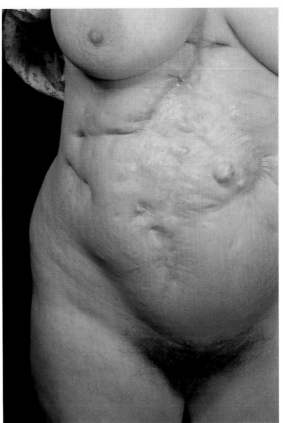

257 Benign biliary stricture. A percutaneous cholangiogram from the patient in **255** shows a dilated intrahepatic biliary tree above a tight stricture of the common bile duct. A collection of contrast has accumulated in the gall bladder bed.

258 Benign biliary stricture. The abdominal walls of these patients are typically marked by many scars which have followed repeated surgical attempts to repair the stricture. This patient had had a biliary stricture for 11 years.

259 Benign biliary stricture in the patient shown in **258** has led to secondary biliary fibrosis. The reticulin stain shows portal fibrosis (1) and septa extending to link portal tracts and central veins. (×*10*)

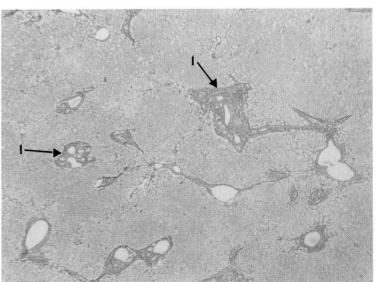

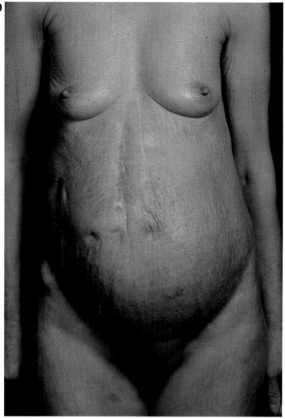

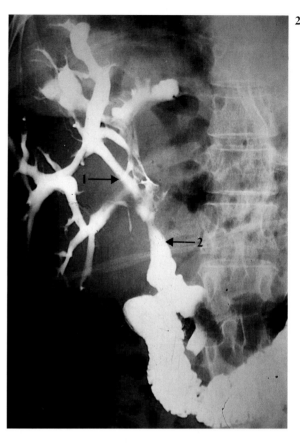

260 Decompensated biliary cirrhosis may be the end result of a benign bile duct stricture. Chronic cholestasis has led to pigmentation in this patient and the ascites indicates a decompensated cirrhosis. Hepato-splenomegaly was present. She suffered repeated attacks of cholangitis

261 Secondary sclerosing cholangitis has developed in the patient shown in **260** as a result of repeated ascending biliary tract infections. The percutaneous cholangiogram shows saccular dilatations and stenoses of the intrahepatic bile ducts, indicating secondary sclerosing cholangitis. The anastomosis between the bile duct (1) and jejenum (2) is patent.

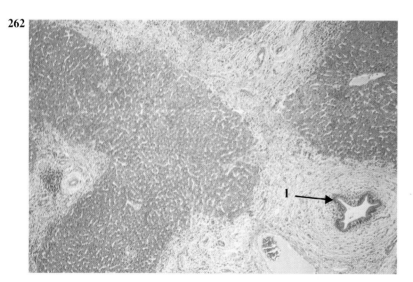

262 Secondary biliary cirrhosis was fully developed in the patient shown in **260**. Extensive portal fibrosis (zone 1) was present. This is especially obvious around a large bile duct (1). Fibrous septa have spread out to link portal tracts, isolating nodules of liver cells. Note the clear margins of the nodules; there is no piecemeal necrosis. (*H.&E.×24*)

7 Cholestatic syndromes in infancy and childhood

Jaundice is common in early infancy. In the early neonatal period jaundice is usually due to haemolysis and impaired bilirubin conjugation. After two weeks jaundice is usually cholestatic with conjugated hyperbilirubinaemia. There are many causes of cholestasis in infancy and childhood. The most common are biliary atresia, neonatal hepatitis and cytomegalovirus infection (see Chapter 2), and intrahepatic biliary atresia (paucity of intrahepatic bile ducts). Biliary atresia is agenesis or malformation of the *extrahepatic* biliary tract and causes a steadily deepening jaundice and biliary cirrhosis. Intrahepatic biliary atresia is reduction or loss of *intrahepatic* bile ducts which causes cholestatic jaundice, itching and xanthomas. In intrahepatic biliary atresia the extrahepatic biliary tree is normal. Untreated patients with intrahepatic biliary atresia survive longer than those with extrahepatic biliary atresia. The initial step in cholestatic infants is differentiating intrahepatic from extrahepatic biliary atresia. This may be difficult in the first months of life since the clinical and laboratory findings are similar. Scintiscanning and percutaneous or endoscopic cholangiography are required.

Intrahepatic biliary atresia (paucity of intrahepatic bile ducts) can be classified further into those with a non-syndromatic type and those with a syndromatic type (Alagille's syndrome). Children with non-syndromatic intrahepatic biliary atresia develop cirrhosis in later childhood. In contrast, those with syndromatic intrahepatic biliary atresia (Alagille's syndrome) tend to recover normal liver function as they become adolescent.

263 Biliary atresia. This child is deeply jaundiced and pigmented. Bile is not secreted into the intestine so the stools (1) are pale and the urine (2) dark. Note the grossly enlarged liver which is indenting the abdominal wall. Ascites and portal hypertension are late features. Untreated, these children usually die by six months.

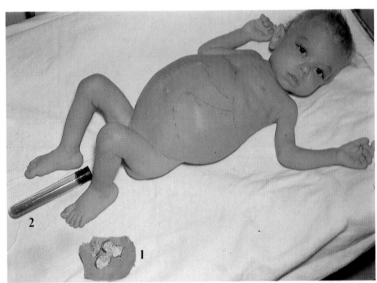

263

264 Biliary atresia. The liver biopsy shows a severe cholestasis, which is mainly centrizonal (zone 3). Bile plugs are present in the biliary canaliculi. In the portal tracts (1) there is bile ductular proliferation. Giant cells are common, making the distinction from neonatal hepatitis difficult. At laparotomy the bile ducts may be absent or replaced by fibrous strands. (*H.&E.×70*)

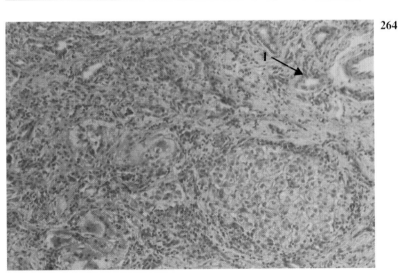

264

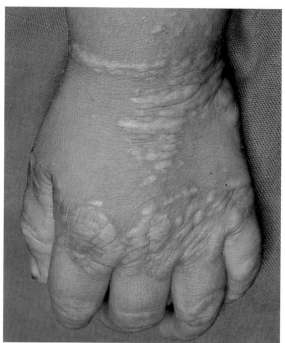

265 Intrahepatic biliary atresia. The infants are usually jaundiced in the neonatal period, but presentation may be delayed until later in childhood. This infant was jaundiced as a neonate. When one year old he presented with xanthomas and pruritus. Xanthomas are present on the hands.

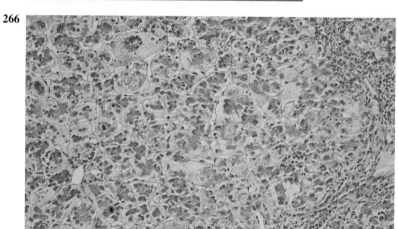

266 Intrahepatic biliary atresia. The liver biopsy shows a prominent giant cell reaction. In the portal tracts bile ductules are reduced or absent. (*H.&E.×40*)

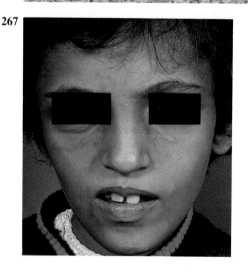

267 Alagille's syndrome or syndromatic chronic intrahepatic biliary atresia is due to loss of intrahepatic bile ducts. The prognosis is better than for non-syndromatic intrahepatic biliary atresia. This 10-year-old boy shows pigmentation and jaundice and has a rather flattened and triangular shaped face. Pulmonary stenosis, vertebral abnormalities and changes in the eye (embryotoxon) are also associated with this syndrome.

268 Pigmentation of the teeth may develop in children with intrahepatic biliary atresia. This is due to staining of the growing teeth with bile pigments.

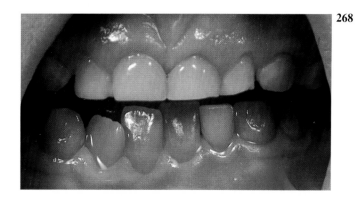

269 Secondary biliary cirrhosis may develop in patients with intrahepatic biliary atresia. However progression to cirrhosis is not inevitable in these patients. Thick fibrous septa separate well-demarcated nodules in this biopsy. No bile ducts can be seen. The cirrhosis resulted in portal hypertension and bleeding from oesophageal varices. (*H.&E.×40*)

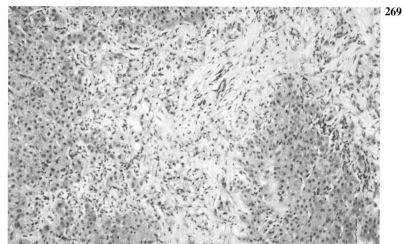

270 Pruritus may be intense in children with intrahepatic biliary atresia. This 6-year-old girl was not clinically jaundiced but pruritus led to these extensive scratch marks.

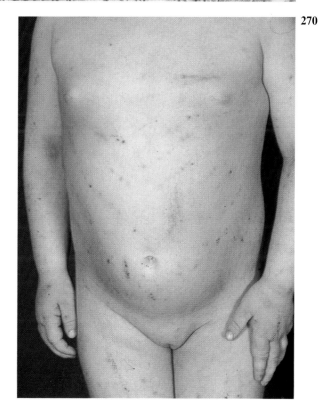

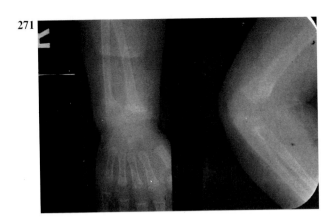

271 Biliary rickets may complicate intrahepatic biliary atresia. The general density of the bones is reduced. The metaphyses are widened and 'cupped', and the depth of the epiphyseal cartilage is increased.

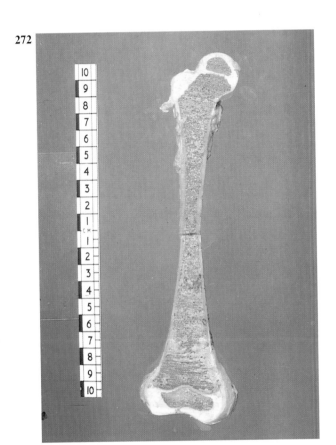

272 Biliary rickets. The widening of the epiphyses and cupping of the metaphyses due to biliary rickets are seen in the femur from a case of intrahepatic biliary atresia. Note the green staining of the bone.

7. Vascular diseases

Portal hypertension

Venous blood from the gastrointestinal tract flows back to the liver through the portal venous system. The inferior mesenteric vein usually enters the splenic vein. The union of the splenic vein and the superior mesenteric vein forms the portal vein. On entering the liver, at the porta hepatis, the portal vein divides into right and left branches to the major lobes of the liver. The umbilical vein joins the left branch of the portal vein.

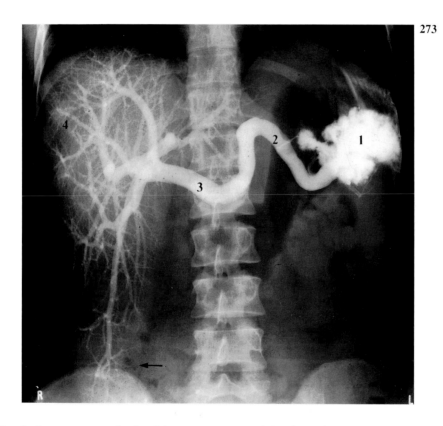

273

273 Normal splenic venogram obtained by percutaneous injection of contrast material into the spleen. All the contrast in the spleen (1) rapidly flows through the splenic vein (2) and portal vein (3) into the liver. Note the smoothly tapering intrahepatic portal veins (4) extending to the periphery of the liver. This normal liver has a large Riedel's lobe (arrowed).

Obstruction to the portal venous system results in portal hypertension. The obstruction may be *intrahepatic* (most commonly due to cirrhosis) or *extrahepatic* due to blockage of the portal vein. In response to portal hypertension an extensive collateral circulation develops, draining portal venous blood into the systemic veins. The collateral circulation at the cardia of the stomach leads to oesophageal and gastric varices, and at the anus haemorrhoids may develop . Other sites include the umbilical veins in the falciform ligament, veins from the liver to the diaphragm, veins in the lieno-renal ligament and collaterals to the left renal vein. Patients with portal hypertension usually present with gastrointestinal haemorrhage from oesophageal varices. In cirrhotic patients bleeding may cause decompensation of the liver disease, and ascites, jaundice and portal-systemic encephalopathy then develop. With a very large collateral circulation the portal pressure may fall and the liver shrink.

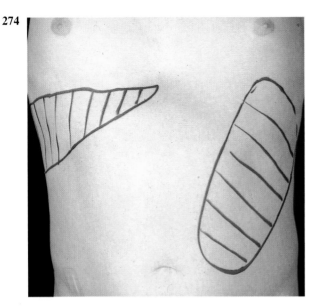

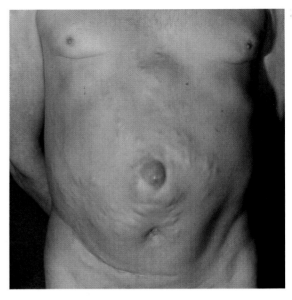

274 Splenomegaly is an important sign of portal hypertension. The spleen progressively enlarges as the portal pressure rises. This patient had cirrhosis following chronic active hepatitis and presented with a haematemesis from ruptured oesophageal varices. Regenerating nodules in the liver obstruct the portal venous blood flow. Note the scanty body hair.

275 Abdominal wall veins in this alcoholic cirrhotic were due to a collateral circulation between the left branch of the portal vein via the umbilical vein and the systemic veins on the anterior abdominal wall. The direction of blood flow is away from the umbilicus. The blue colour of the umbilicus is due to a large vein. Stigmata of chronic liver disease, gynaecomastia and reduced body hair are also present.

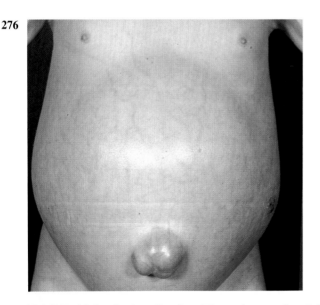

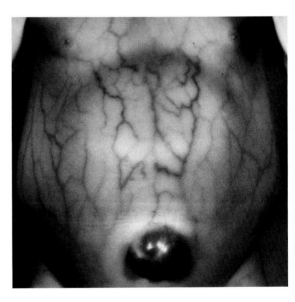

276,277 Abdominal wall veins. The veins on the abdomen of this alcoholic cirrhotic are portal systemic shunts. Ascites is present and the umbilicus has herniated. Vascular spiders are seen in the necklace area.

An infra-red photograph (**277**) of the patient shows much more clearly the extent of the portal-systemic collaterals on the abdominal wall.

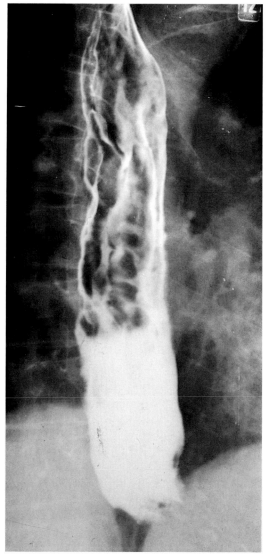

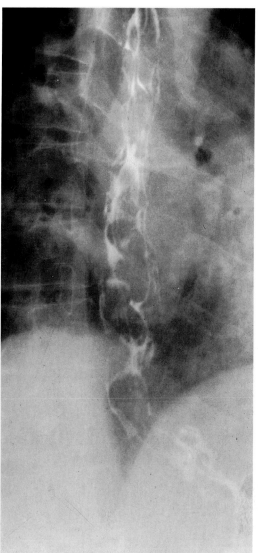

278 Oesophageal varices. Submucosal varices in the oesophagus can be demonstrated radiologically by a barium swallow examination. The x-ray shows a dilated oesophagus which contains thick worm-like filling defects, representing the varices.

279 Oesophageal varices are best demonstrated with very little barium in the oesophagus. This x-ray comes from the barium swallow shown in **278**. The worm-like filling defects caused by oesophageal varices are now seen extending the whole length of the oesophagus.

280 Portal hypertension. Endoscopic appearances in the oesophagus show white and blue varices. White varices and small blue varices have a low risk of rupture.

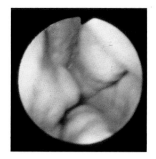

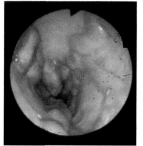

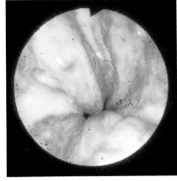
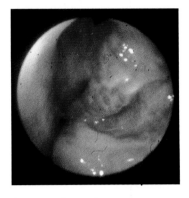

281 Portal hypertension. Endoscopic oesophageal appearances show oesophageal varices with cherry-red spots on them. These are due to venous channels uncovered by epithelium. Cherry-red spots indicate that rupture of the oesophageal varices is likely.

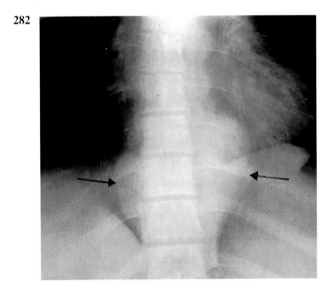

282 Oesophageal varices. Rarely very large varices can be seen in a well-penetrated x-ray of the chest. The mass in the lower part of the mediastinum (arrowed) in this patient is due to oesophageal varices.

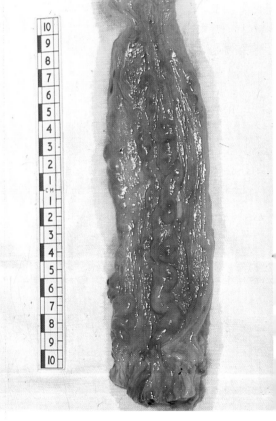

283 Oesophageal varices usually collapse at autopsy so that grossly distended varices are rarely seen. This oesophagus has been laid open and the sinuous dark purple varices can be seen lying under the oesophageal mucosa.

284 Haemorrhoidal varices have developed in this cirrhotic patient. They represent the collateral circulation between the superior haemorrhoidal vein of the portal system and the middle and inferior haemorrhoidal veins of the systemic venous system.

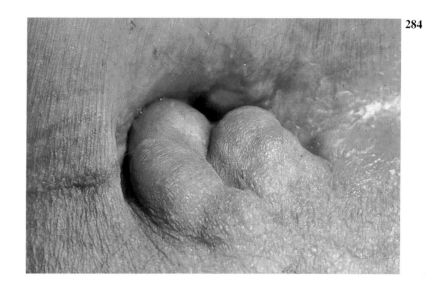

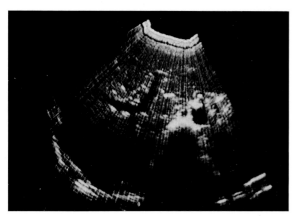 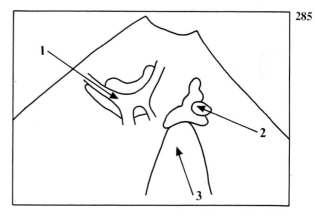

285 Grey-scale ultrasonography. Intrahepatic portal hypertension causes dilation of the portal vein (1) which can be shown by ultrasonography. The aorta (2) and a vertebral body (3) are also shown. The portal vein cannot be identified in cases of portal vein thrombosis. Ultrasonography is a useful non-invasive technique to distinguish between intrahepatic and extrahepatic portal hypertension.

286 Cirrhosis with portal hypertension. Intravenous contrast-enhanced CT scans will show the portal systemic collaterals that develop in portal hypertension. This enhanced CT scan shows contrast-filled portal-systemic collateral veins (1) around the oesophagus (2). The liver is very small (3).

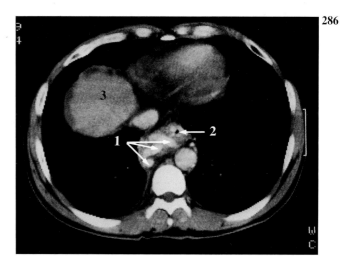

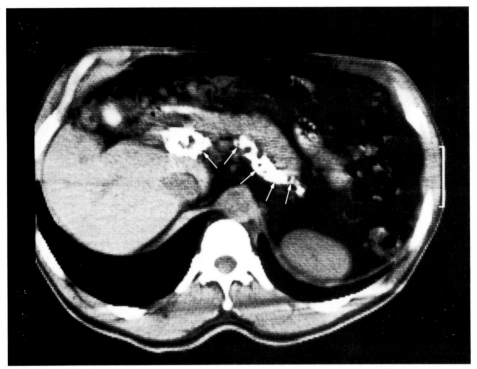

287 Calcified portal vein. Portal hypertension may lead to calcification of the portal vein. This follows damage to the portal vein which includes endothelial haemorrhages, mural thrombi and intimal plaques. These calcified veins are unsuitable for anastomosis in porta-caval shunts or liver transplantation. CT scans are particularly sensitive to the detection of portal vein calcification. This patient developed splenic and portal vein obstruction secondary to chronic pancreatitis. Abdominal CT scan (enhanced with contrast) shows heavy calcification in the portal and splenic veins (arrowed).

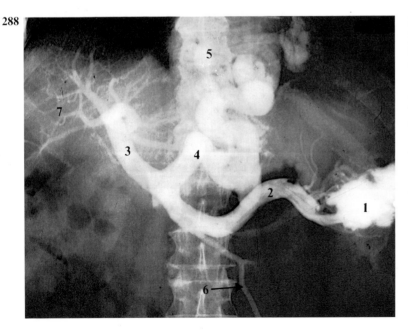

288 Splenic venogram from a patient with portal hypertension due to alcoholic cirrhosis. Injection of contrast into the enlarged spleen (1) has filled the splenic vein (2) and portal vein (3). A large proportion of the contrast is diverted via a dilated and tortuous left gastric vein (4) into a leash of gastric and oesophageal varices (5). There is retrograde flow of contrast down the inferior mesenteric vein (6). The intrahepatic portal veins (7) are pruned, indicating cirrhosis ('tree in winter' appearance).

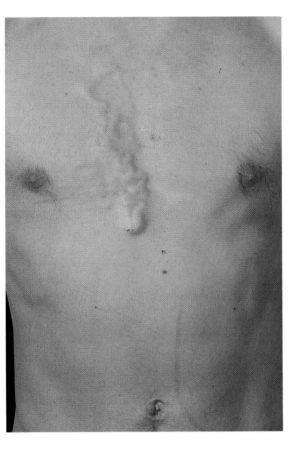

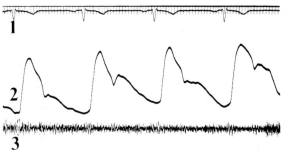

289,290 **Venous hum** was heard over these portal-systemic collaterals at the lower end of the sternum. The patient had cirrhosis following chronic active hepatitis. The spleen was enlarged. The hum was due to blood flow through a large umbilical vein in the falciform ligament supplied by the left branch of the portal vein.

A phonocardiogram (**290**) recorded over the site of the venous hum shows a continuous low pitched noise (3) unrelated to the electrocardiogram (1) or the carotid pulse (2).

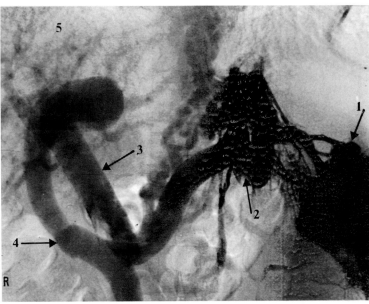

291 Splenic venogram from the patient shown in **289**. Splenic injection (1) has filled the splenic vein (2) and portal vein (3). Most of the contrast flowed down the left branch of the portal vein into a very large umbilical vein (4) and little entered the liver (5). The clarity of this x-ray has been achieved by the use of a 'subtraction' technique.

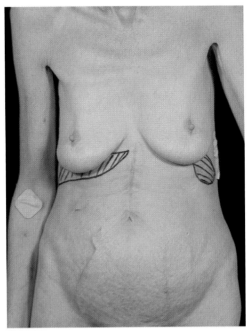 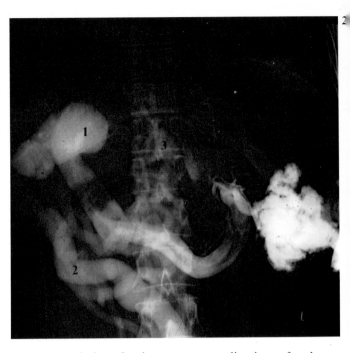

292,293 Chronic dementia due to portal-systemic encephalopathy is a rare complication of a large collateral circulation in cirrhotic patients. This patient presented with dementia. She had a small inactive cirrhotic liver. The portal vein pressure was normal due to the large portal systemic shunt, hence the spleen was not enlarged. Note the veins on the abdominal wall which are portal-systemic collaterals.

The splenic venogram (**293**) shows a very large shunt from the left branch of the portal vein (1) down the umbilical vein (2). Later films showed the umbilical vein draining via the iliac veins into the inferior vena cava. Only a few oesophageal varices (3) have filled, reflecting the decompression of the portal venous system down the umbilical vein.

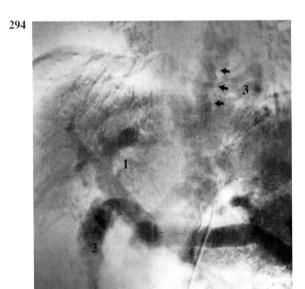

294 Coeliac axis arteriography. The portal venous system may be seen in the venous phase of a coeliac axis arteriogram. However, this technique does not usually opacify the portal venous system as well as splenic venography. The catheter has been placed in the splenic artery. The venous phase of this study shows the portal vein (1), umbilical vein (2) and oesophageal varices (3).

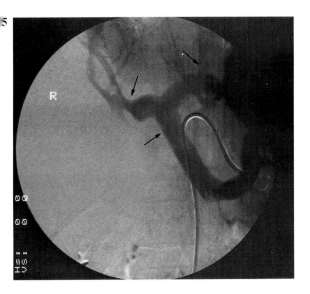

295 Digital subtraction angiography (DSA) is replacing splenic venography for visualizing the portal vein because of its lower morbidity and higher quality. This DSA of the venous phase of a coeliac axis arteriogram clearly shows the portal vein and its branches (arrowed).

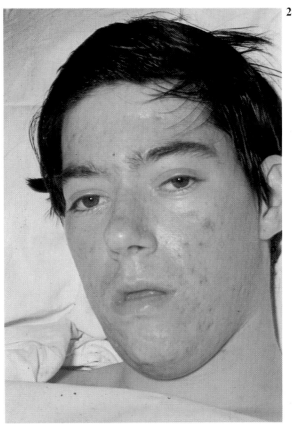

296 Portal-systemic encephalopathy is an important complication of porta-caval shunts. This cirrhotic patient underwent a porta-caval shunt for recurrent variceal haemorrhage. Subsequently he became drowsy with a fetor and a coarse flapping tremor.

297 Steal syndrome. In some patients with portal hypertension due to cirrhosis, blood does not enter the liver via the portal vein, but escapes by the collateral circulation. Portal venography may be misinterpreted as showing portal vein block. In this cirrhotic patient all the contrast escapes via collateral channels (1) and the portal vein appears to taper to an obstruction (2). However the portal vein is patent, but there is no blood flow through it into the liver.

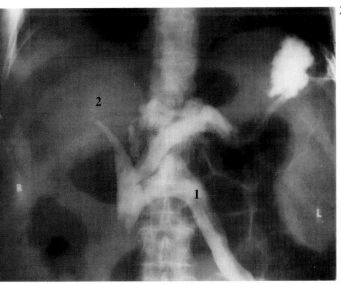

Rare causes of intrahepatic portal hypertension

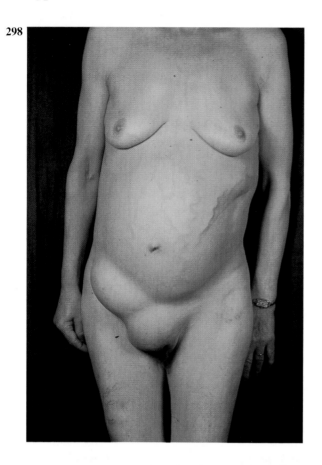

298 Partial nodular transformation is a rare cause of portal hypertension. The hilum of the liver is replaced by nodules. The remainder of the liver is normal. The hilar nodules compress the portal vein resulting in portal hypertension. This patient had partial nodular transformation of the liver. Note the portal systemic shunts on the abdominal wall and the hernias.

299 Partial nodular transformation. A large nodule (arrowed) at the porta hepatis obstructed the portal vein and caused portal hypertension in this patient. The remainder of the liver was normal.

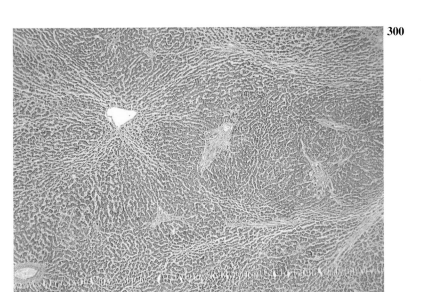

300 Partial nodular transformation. A biopsy of the nodule in **299** showed the liver dissected by slender fibrous septa. The hepatic architecture in the nodule is not grossly disorganized, as in cirrhosis. (*H.&E.×10*)

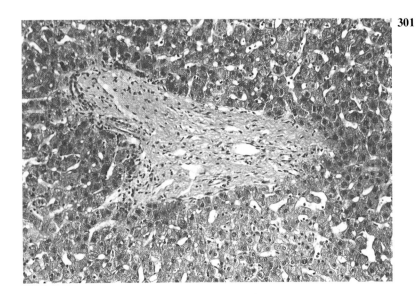

301 Hepatoportal sclerosis or sclerosis of the portal veins in the portal tracts may result in portal hypertension. The extensive portal fibrosis and obliteration of the portal veins in this patient was due to chronic inorganic *arsenic* ingestion. For many years he had received sodium arsenite (Fowler's solution) for the relief of psoriasis. A similar picture may be seen in workers exposed to *vinyl chloride monomers*, which are used in the synthesis of the plastic PVC.

Extrahepatic portal hypertension

Thrombosis of the portal vein is the commonest cause of extrahepatic portal hypertension. This usually follows neonatal infection of the umbilicus. The infection spreads up the umbilical vein to the left branch of the portal vein and thence to the main portal vein causing thrombosis. Other causes include: intra-abdominal sepsis, such as appendicitis or a perforated duodenal ulcer, tumours of the pancreas and blood diseases with increased blood coagulation such as polycythaemia rubra vera.

302 Portal vein thrombosis following neonatal infection of the umbilicus. These children develop normally. Examination reveals an enlarged spleen, as in this child. Splenomegaly often causes a pancytopenia. The liver is normal.

303 Portal vein thrombosis. Signs of previous umbilical infection may be present. This Arab child had extrahepatic portal vein thrombosis. The circular scar around the umbilicus results from native treatment at birth.

304 Enlarged spleen (arrowed) was visible in an x-ray of the abdomen in this patient with portal vein thrombosis. The liver was of normal size.

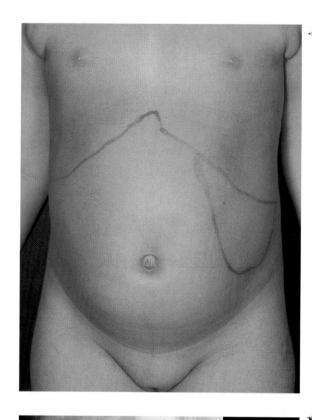

303

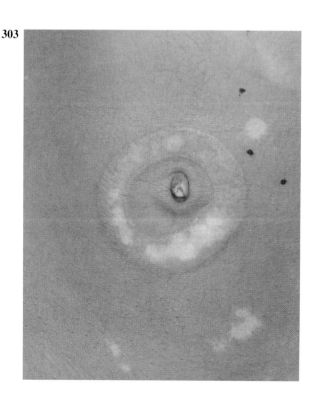

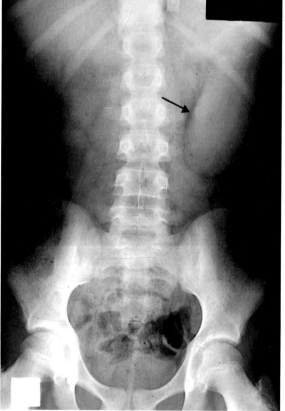

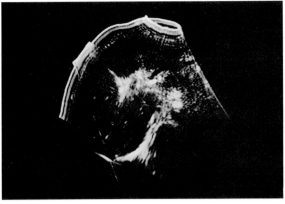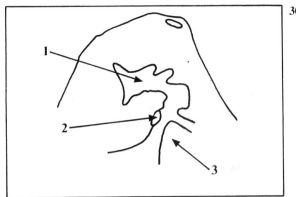

305 Grey-scale ultrasonography will normally identify the portal vein in the porta hepatis (1). In portal vein thrombosis the portal vein is absent. In this scan the inferior vena cava (2) and a vertebral body (3) can also be seen.

306 Splenic venogram in portal vein thrombosis. The splenic injection (1) filled the splenic vein (2) and collaterals to a mesh of oesophageal and gastric varices (3). There is retrograde flow down the inferior mesenteric vein (4). The portal vein had been replaced by many small collaterals (5). In this patient no cause was found for the portal vein thrombosis.

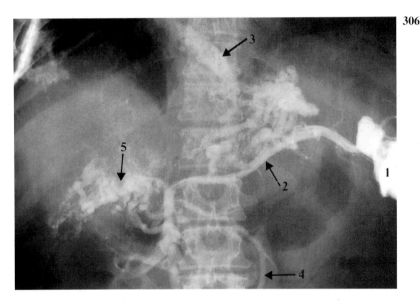

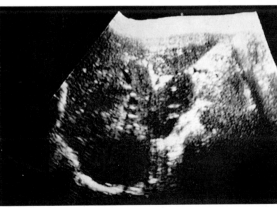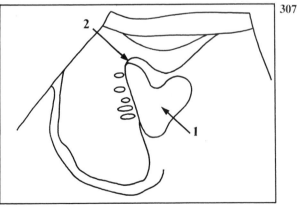

307 Cancer of the pancreas occasionally results in portal vein thrombosis. This 55-year-old man presented with bleeding oesophageal varices due to portal hypertension. An ultrasound scan showed a pancreatic mass (1) extending into the porta hepatis (2). The portal vein was not identified, suggesting portal vein obstruction.

308 Cirrhosis is a rare cause of portal vein thrombosis. A thrombosed portal vein (arrow) is visible at the porta hepatis in this section of a cirrhotic liver. Thrombosis of the portal vein is probably due to the sluggish portal circulation in cirrhosis. More commonly in cirrhotic patients, non-filling of the portal vein, during splenic venography, is due to diversion of blood through a large collateral circulation while the portal vein is in fact patent.

Hepatic artery

309

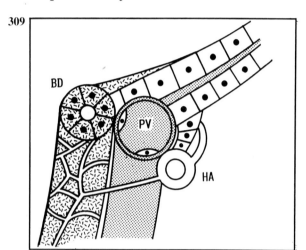

309 Hepatic artery. This diagram shows the hepatic artery (HA), portal vein radicle (PV) and bile duct (BD) in zone 1 of the liver (portal tract). Note that the hepatic artery provides a peri-biliary arterial plexus (arrow) supplying the bile duct. Interference with this blood supply leads to bile duct injury and often disappearance of the bile ducts.

310

310 Hepatic artery occlusion leads to infarction of the liver. The pale infarcted areas are surrounded by red haemorrhagic zones. This rare condition may follow polyarteritis nodosa, emboli from bacterial endocarditis, biliary tract surgery and liver transplantation (see Chapter 12). Hepatic artery occlusion is rarely diagnosed during life.

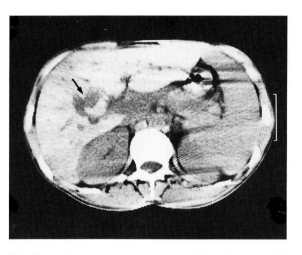

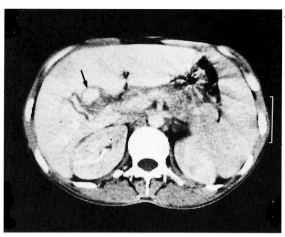

311 Hepatic artery aneurysm. This 45-year-old man suffered from sub-acute bacterial endocarditis. He complained of pain over the liver. Upper abdominal CT (without contrast enhancement) showed a filling defect (arrowed).

312 Hepatic artery aneurysm. Abdominal CT after intravenous contrast in the patient shown in **311** showed that the filling defect was highlighted (arrowed) indicating that it was due to a hepatic artery aneurysm.

Hepatic veins

The hepatic veins drain into the inferior vena cava where it passes through the liver. The number of hepatic veins is variable. In general, one vein drains the left lobe and two veins drain the right lobe. The caudate lobe of the liver is drained separately into the inferior vena cava by a variable number of small veins.

313 Hepatic venous obstruction (Budd–Chiari syndrome). In the acute type the patient usually dies in liver failure. More commonly, a chronic form is encountered, as in this patient. The liver was enlarged and tender. Obstruction of the inferior vena cava caused the dilated veins on her abdominal wall (arrowed) and oedema of the legs. The flow of blood in these veins was upwards. In this patient the hepatic vein obstruction was associated with the oral contraceptive pill. Other causes include congenital webs, clotting diseases such as polycythaemia rubra vera, protein C deficiency, antithrombin 3 deficiency, lupus anticoagulant and paroxysmal nocturnal haemoglobinuria.

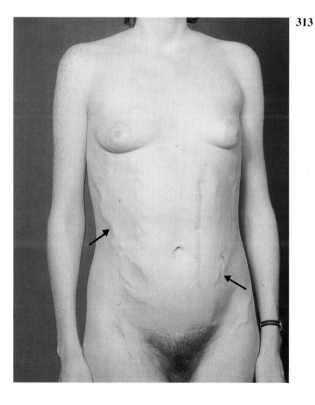

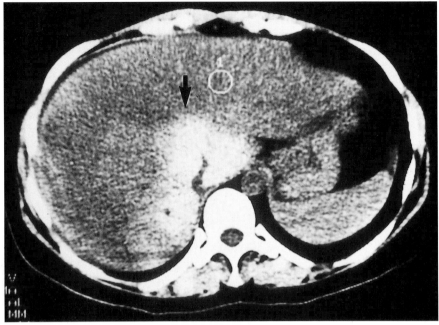

314 Budd–Chiari syndrome. This young woman had thrombosis of the hepatic veins secondary to polycythaemia rubra vera. Abdominal CT (enhanced) shows a large liver. The caudate lobe is well perfused (arrowed), while the rest of the liver is underperfused. The spleen is not enlarged.

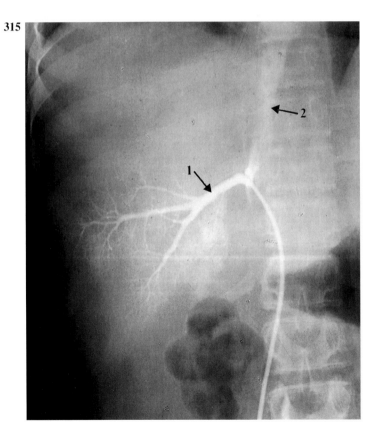

315 Hepatic venography. Cannulation of the hepatic veins through the superior or inferior vena cava is essential to determine the site of the hepatic vein block. This x-ray shows the normal branching pattern in one of the right hepatic veins (1). Some contrast can be seen flowing up the vena cava (2).

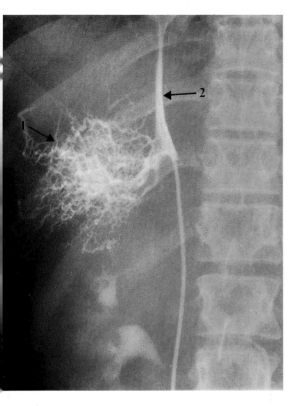

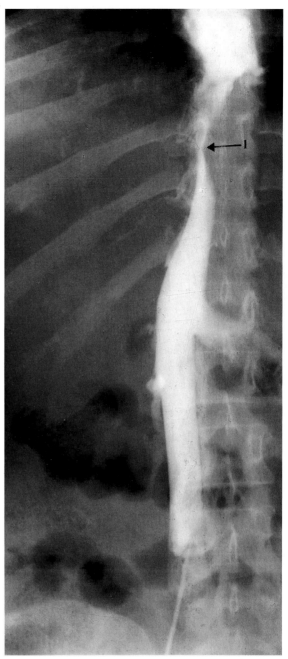

316 Hepatic venography in hepatic venous obstruction. The right hepatic vein has been cannulated via the inferior vena cava. The normal 'tree-like' pattern of the hepatic veins in the liver has been replaced by a characteristic 'lace-like' pattern (1). Contrast is escaping up the vena cava (2). In some patients extensive thrombosis in the hepatic veins will prevent cannulation. In this patient the Budd–Chiari syndrome followed trauma to the liver.

317 Inferior vena-cavography should also be performed in the Budd–Chiari syndrome. This usually reveals a narrowed segment (1) where the inferior vena cava passes through the liver due to compression by the hypertrophied caudate lobe. A supra-hepatic web obstructing the inferior vena cava may also be shown. Pressure measurements along the course of the inferior vena cava will establish the degree and site of obstruction due to a caudate lobe or vena-caval web.

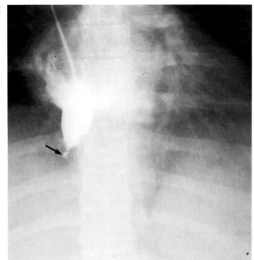

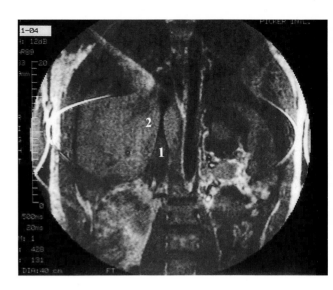

318 Budd–Chiari syndrome secondary to systemic lupus erythematosus. Inferior vena-cavography by catheter via the right atrium shows a nipple-like obstruction to the right hepatic vein (arrowed).

319 Budd–Chiari syndrome. Magnetic resonance imaging (MRI) is particularly useful in showing blood vessels. In this abdominal MRI scan, taken in the sagittal plane, the hepatic veins are not visualized, but the inferior vena cava (1) is shown to be compressed by an enlarged caudate lobe (2).

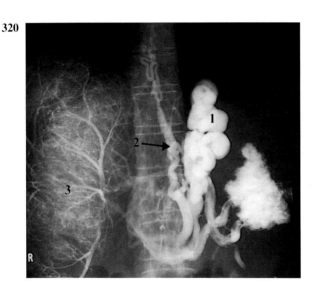

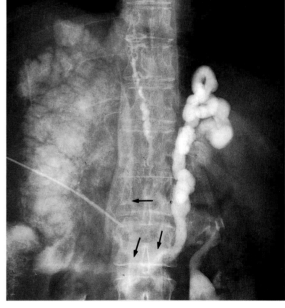

320 Portal hypertension develops in chronic hepatic venous obstruction. This splenic venogram shows an extensive collateral circulation arising from the splenic and portal veins. A large retroperitoneal collateral (1) and shunts to oesophageal varices (2) have filled. The liver is grossly enlarged (3) and there is 'pooling' of the contrast in the liver. The Budd–Chiari syndrome in this patient followed the oral contraceptive pill.

321 Transhepatic portal venogram in the patient shown in **320**. A later x-ray in this study shows circular collections of contrast in the enlarged liver. This appearance may be mistaken for malignant deposits in the liver. A splenorenal–inferior vena caval shunt is shown (arrowed).

322 Hepatic venous obstruction.
A thrombosed hepatic vein (1) is visible on laying open the intra-hepatic portion of the inferior vena cava in this patient with the Budd−Chiari syndrome. However the obstruction may be at any point along the length of the hepatic veins.

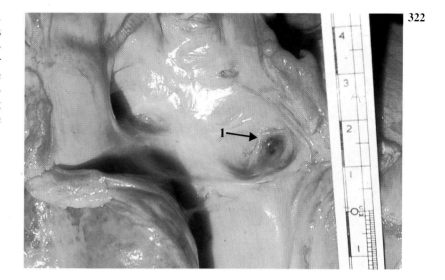

323 Hepatic venous obstruction.
In this section of the liver at autopsy the dark areas are congested due to venous obstruction. The pale areas are regenerating liver tissue. Note the marked hypertrophy of the caudate lobe (arrowed).

324 Hepatic venous obstruction.
Liver biopsy shows congestion and haemorrhage around the central veins (zone 3). *(H.&E. ×10)*

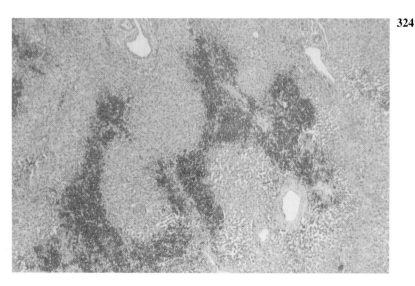

Circulatory failure

A rise in right atrial pressure is readily transmitted to the hepatic veins. This results in impaired hepatic blood flow and oxygen supply especially to the centrizonal liver cells. Impaired tissue perfusion due to arterial hypotension further aggravates the oxygen supply to the hepatocytes in circulatory failure.

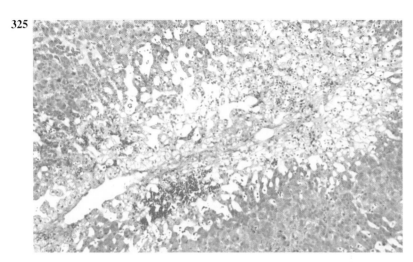

325 Acute heart failure. This biopsy came from a man who suffered a coronary thrombosis and prolonged hypotension. Around the central vein (which is stained blue) some liver cells have disappeared and others are necrotic. The sinusoids are dilated and there are areas of haemorrhage. The reticulin framework is preserved. These are the hepatic changes which develop in shock. *(Picro-Mallory×25)*

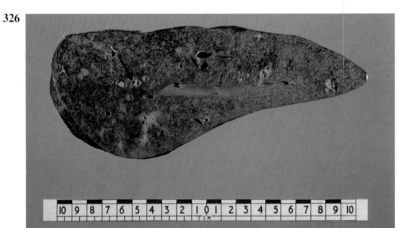

326 Congestive cardiac failure when prolonged gives a 'nutmeg' liver. The cut surface shows yellow areas caused by fatty peripheral zones alternating with red areas due to centrizonal congestion and haemorrhage. The hepatic veins (1) are prominent and their walls are thickened. Prolonged heart failure results in condensation of the centrizonal reticulin and later fibrous bands link the central veins. Finally, a cardiac cirrhosis may develop.

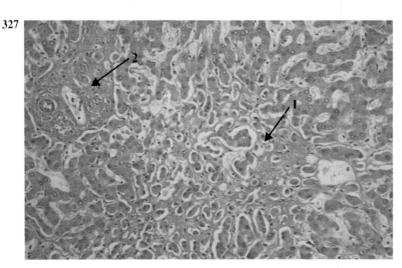

327 Congestive cardiac failure. Extensive fibrous tissue, stained pale blue, has developed around the central vein (1) in this patient with long-standing heart failure. Fibrous septa extend from the centrizonal areas to link the central veins. In chronic cases the portal tracts (2) are surrounded by a cuff of fibrous tissue. *(Martius-Scarlet-Blue×40)*

328 Cardiac cirrhosis. In prolonged heart failure centrizonal fibrosis increases and fibrous septa extend to link the central veins, isolating nodules of liver cells. In this severe case a cardiac cirrhosis has developed. *(H.&E.×40)*

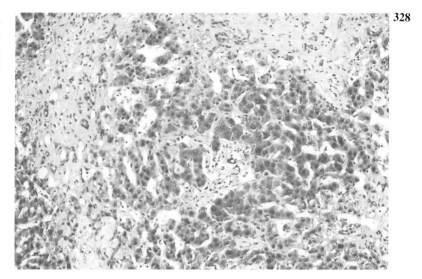

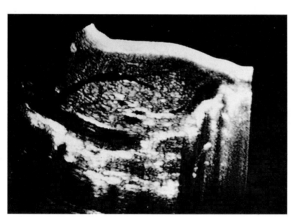

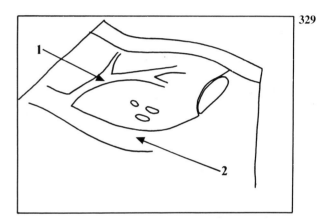

329

329 Congestive cardiac failure. Grey-scale ultrasonography shows dilatation of the hepatic veins (1) and inferior vena cava (2) in this patient with congestive cardiac failure. This is caused by transmission of the high right atrial pressure.

330 Constrictive pericarditis has a similar effect on the liver as does congestive cardiac failure. Patients usually present with marked ascites and a hard, enlarged, non-pulsatile liver. Other features of constrictive pericarditis must be sought, including a paradoxical arterial pulse, the characteristic jugular venous pulse and a calcified pericardium. This patient was treated by stripping the tough fibrous pericardium (1) from the heart (2).

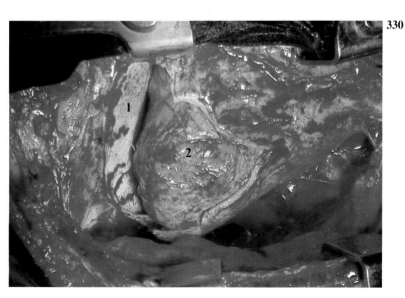

330

331 Peliosis hepatis is a very rare condition in which the liver has a bluish colour and contains numerous blue-black blood-filled sacs. Rupture of the cysts may result in severe haemorrhage. The aetiology of peliosis hepatis is unknown, but it is associated with fatal tuberculosis, anabolic steroids and oral contraceptives (see also Adenomas of the liver, in Chapter 11).

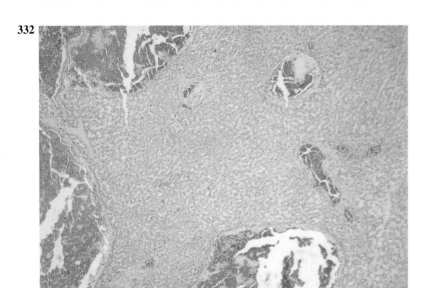

332 Peliosis hepatis. A liver biopsy shows normal liver tissue studded with large blood-filled spaces. Some have no endothelial lining, while others are dilated sinusoids, portal or central veins. *(H.&E.×10)*

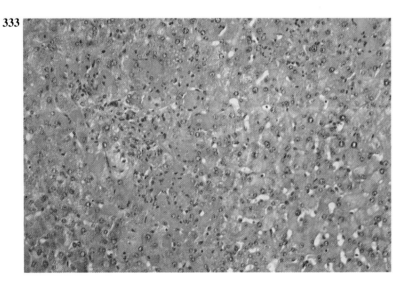

333 Eclampsia of pregnancy. Jaundice is terminal and usually follows the grand mal seizures. The liver shows extensive periportal pink-staining fibrin deposition in the sinusoids. Centrizonal changes of necrosis and haemorrhage indicate shock. Characteristically there is no inflammatory reaction. This biopsy came from a 34-year-old woman. She was 36 weeks pregnant with twins when eclampsia suddenly developed. *(H.&E.×40)*

8. *Storage diseases of the liver*

Iron storage diseases

These are classified as *haemochromatosis*, where iron deposition has resulted in liver injury (usually cirrhosis), and *haemosiderosis*, where there is excessive iron deposition in the liver but no tissue damage. Primary (hereditary) haemochromatosis is due to increased intestinal absorption of iron. The primary haemochromatosis gene is closely associated with the HLA-A3 gene on the short arm of chromosome 6. It is not known how the primary haemochromatosis gene causes increased intestinal absorption of iron. Rarely, secondary haemochromatosis develops after repeated transfusions, chronic haemolytic anaemia or excessive iron ingestion (Bantu siderosis).

334 Primary haemochromatosis typically presents in middle-aged men. The patient is pigmented and body hair is scanty or absent. The liver is enlarged and the spleen may be palpable, as in this patient. Diabetes mellitus is common.

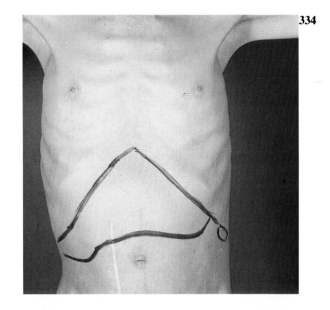

334

335 Primary haemochromatosis. The skin pigmentation is a slate-grey colour and is due to increased melanin in the skin. It is maximal in the axillae, groins and exposed areas. The pigmented hands on the left come from a patient with haemochromatosis, the hand on the right is from an unaffected relative. Note the arthropathy affecting the first and second metacarpophalangeal joints.

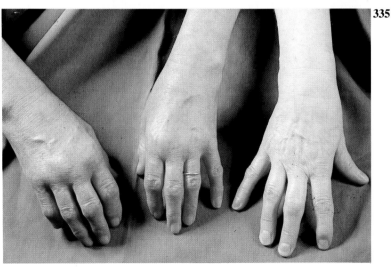

335

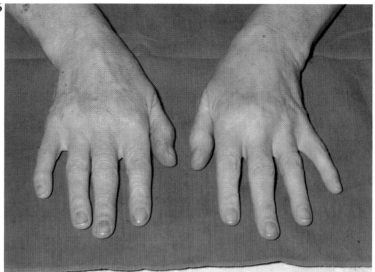

336 Primary haemochromatosis. Many patients develop an arthropathy causing swelling of the first and second metacarpophalangeal joints. The arthritis is related to pyrophosphate crystal deposition. An x-ray of the hands may show chondrocalcinosis in the articular cartilage.

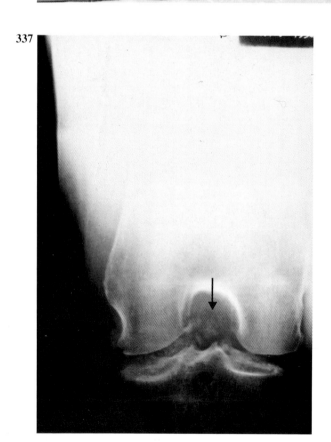

337 Primary haemochromatosis. The pyrophosphate arthropathy also affects the knees. This x-ray of the knee in flexion shows chondrocalcinosis (arrowed) of the menisci and articular cartilage.

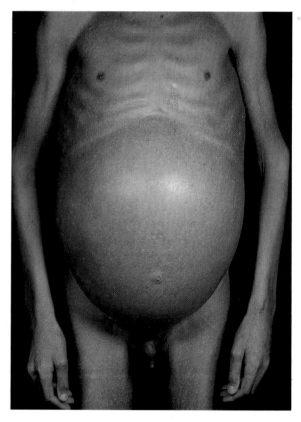

338 Primary haemochromatosis. Primary liver cancer develops in some patients. Sudden clinical deterioration, with the development of ascites, often heralds a primary liver cancer, as in this patient. Note the pronounced skin pigmentation and muscle wasting.

339 Primary haemochromatosis.
The liver is nodular and the iron deposition gives it a bronze-like colour. Ultimately a macronodular cirrhosis develops.

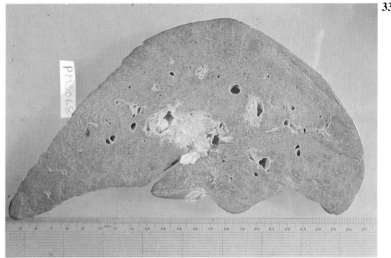

340 Primary haemochromatosis.
Iron deposited in the pancreas gives it a bronzed colour. This picture shows the pancreas laid open; the pancreatic duct is arrowed. The iron causes destruction of the pancreatic parenchyma and fibrosis. Diabetes mellitus is a common sequel. Bronze diabetes was an early name for primary haemochromatosis.

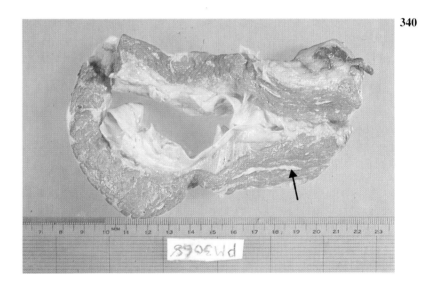

341 Primary haemochromatosis.
A liver biopsy shows iron (stained blue) deposited mainly in the liver cells but also in the Kupffer cells. Most of the iron is concentrated around the portal tracts (arrowed). Fibrous septa extend from the portal tracts giving a 'holly leaf' appearance. *(Perls×16)*

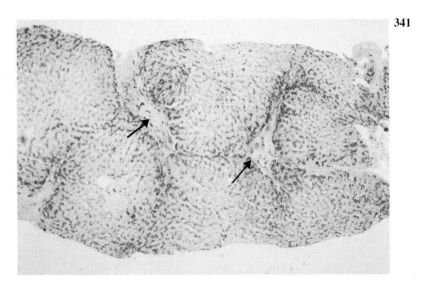

342

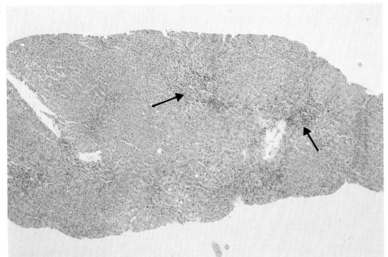

342 Primary haemochromatosis. Stained with haematoxylin and eosin, the biopsy in **341** shows focal areas of inflammation (arrowed) and active fibrous septa around portal tracts. The brown material is iron. *(×16)*

343

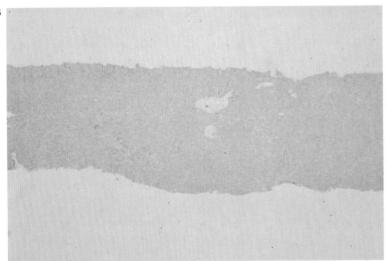

343 Primary haemochromatosis. Four years later, after repeated venesections, a further biopsy from the patient in **341** shows complete removal of iron from the liver. *(Perls×16)*

344

344 Primary haemochromatosis. A haematoxylin and eosin stain of the biopsy in **343** shows that, following the removal of iron, the liver histology had returned to normal.

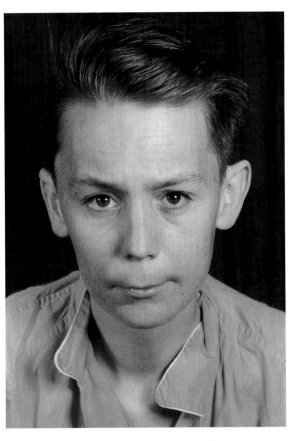

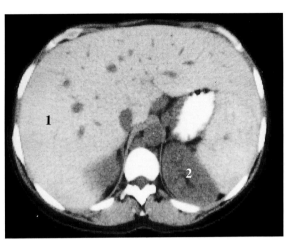

346 Thalassaemia major. Secondary haemosiderosis followed multiple blood transfusions. This unenhanced CT scan shows that the liver density (1) is greater than that of the kidney (2). Portal vein radicles are very prominent. The appearances are due to increased iron in the liver.

345 Secondary haemochromatosis. The slate-grey skin pigmentation can be seen on the face. A congenital haemolytic anaemia was the cause of iron overload in this young man.

347 Secondary haemochromatosis. This patient had idiopathic sideroblastic anaemia. Iron absorption is increased because of the excessive erythropoietic activity. Iron overload caused the skin pigmentation on her buttocks and the hepatomegaly. Secondary iron overload is also seen in thalassaemia and sickle cell anaemia.

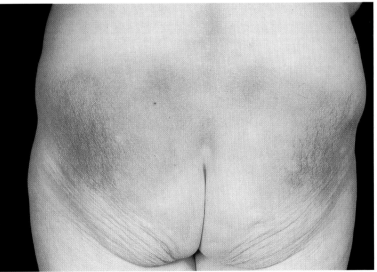

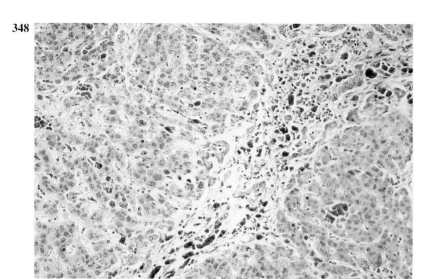

348 Secondary haemochromatosis. Cirrhosis had developed in the patient in **347**. Fibrous septa separate nodules of liver cells. The brown pigment represents iron deposits. *(H.&E. ×40)*

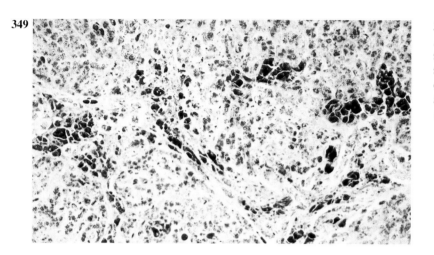

349 Secondary haemochromatosis. A Perls stain of the biopsy in **348** shows the widespread iron as blue staining material. Iron is first deposited in the Kupffer cells and later in the hepatocytes. *(×40).*

Wilson's disease (hepatolenticular degeneration)

This is a rare cause of inherited cirrhosis principally affecting children and young adults. It is characterized by cirrhosis, degeneration of the basal ganglia, renal tubular damage and brown rings in the cornea (Kayser−Fleischer rings). Copper accumulates in many organs.

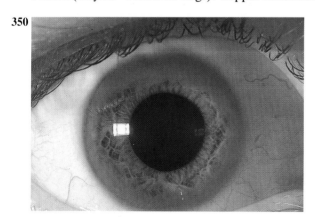

350 Kayser−Fleischer rings are greenish-brown rings at the periphery of the cornea. They are caused by the deposition of copper on the posterior surface of the cornea and appear first at the upper pole. Kayser−Fleischer rings are present in practically every symptomatic case of Wilson's disease, but a slit lamp examination may be required to detect them.

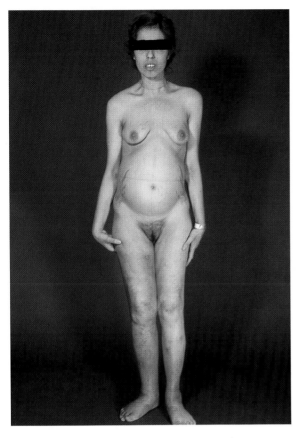

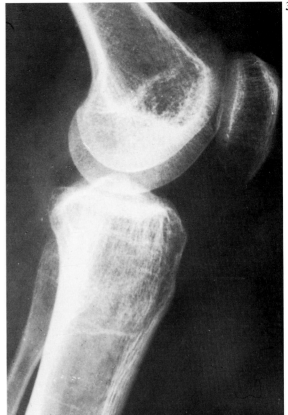

351 Wilson's disease may present with an episode of jaundice due to haemolysis, as a well-compensated cirrhosis or as fulminant liver failure. Alternatively Wilson's disease can mimic chronic active hepatitis, as in this young woman. Note the abdominal striae and leg oedema. The posture and fatuous expression in this patient are due to the basal ganglia changes of Wilson's disease, which usually develop some years after the liver disease.

352 Wilson's disease. The bones may be demineralized. Sub-articular cysts and fragmentation of bone also develop. Note the demineralized femur and tibia in this patient.

353 Wilson's disease. A liver biopsy shows fatty infiltration and vacuolated nuclei (glycogenic vacuolation). Some of the liver cells are ballooned and the inflammatory reaction is usually slight. A fibrous septum is present (arrowed). *(H.&E.×100)*

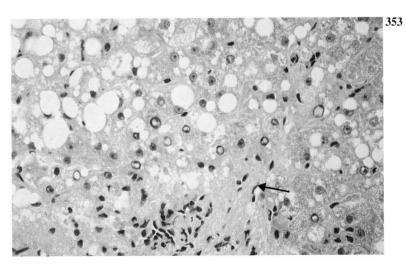

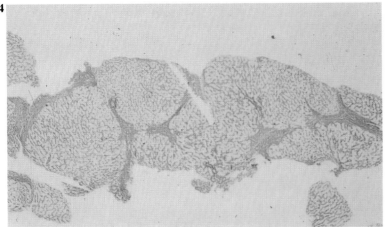

354 Wilson's disease. A reticulin stain of the biopsy showed cirrhosis with fibrous septa separating nodules of varying sizes. Cirrhosis is usual in symptomatic patients. *(×10)*

355 Wilson's disease. The large accumulation of copper in the liver cells has been stained reddish-pink in this biopsy. Histological stains for copper are unreliable for the diagnosis of Wilson's disease as the copper deposition may be irregular, causing sampling errors. *(Rhodamine×40)*

Alpha₁ anti-trypsin deficiency

This inherited metabolic defect is associated with neonatal hepatitis and cirrhosis in children and pulmonary emphysema in adults. In most patients the cholestatic neonatal hepatitis subsides by about seven months, but later hepato-splenomegaly develops due to a cirrhosis. However, the presentation of alpha₁ anti-trypsin deficiency is variable and rarely patients present with cirrhosis in later life. The serum alpha₁ anti-trypsin concentration is low.

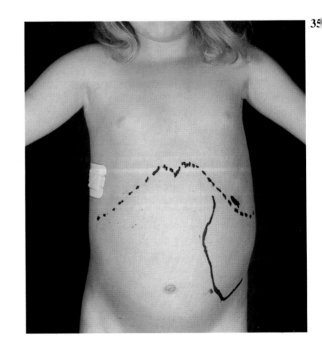

356 Alpha₁ anti-trypsin deficiency. This girl had neonatal hepatitis. Aged 5, cirrhosis was present with splenomegaly due to portal hypertension. At age 9 (shown here), she suffered repeated haematemeses from oesophageal varices. Her brother also had alpha₁ anti-trypsin deficiency.

357 Alpha₁ anti-trypsin deficiency.
A liver biopsy showed a cirrhotic liver with brightly staining diastase-resistant inclusions concentrated around the portal tracts. *(Diastase periodic acid Schiff×10)*

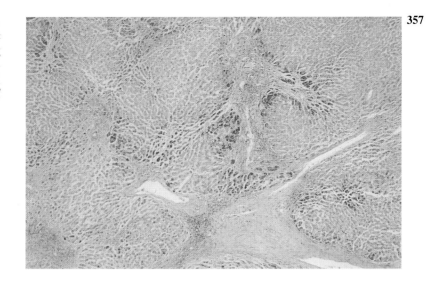

358 Alpha₁ anti-trypsin deficiency.
At a higher magnification the bright red granular inclusions are seen to be in the liver cells around the portal tracts. *(Diastase periodic acid Schiff×100)*

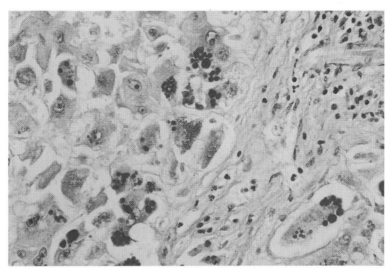

359 Alpha₁ anti-trypsin deficiency.
This biopsy has been stained specifically with a fluorescent bound antibody to alpha₁ anti-trypsin. The blue granules represent accumulation of alpha₁ anti-trypsin in the liver cells. *(×400)*

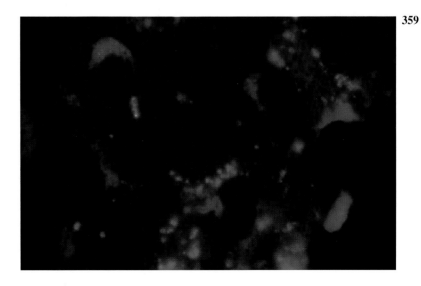

Glycogen storage diseases

There are many varieties of these inherited defects of glycogen metabolism. The severity and prognosis of the disease depends on the type. Typically, patients present in childhood with hepatomegaly and episodes of hypoglycaemia and ketosis.

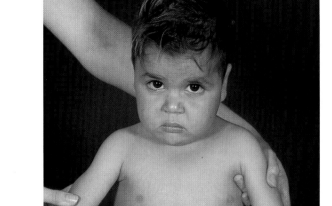

360 Glycogen storage disease. This two-year-old child presented with massive hepatomegaly, but characteristically the spleen was not enlarged. Although reduced in height, his weight was normal for his age.

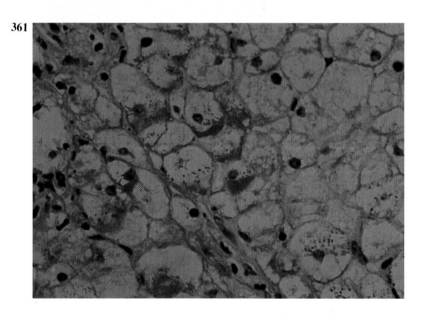

361 Glycogen storage disease. A liver biopsy shows swollen liver cells and vacuolated nuclei full of glycogen. Enzyme analysis of the liver biopsy will determine the type of glycogen storage disease. *(Periodic acid Schiff×100)*

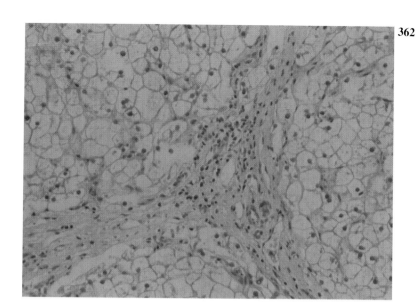

362 Glycogen storage disease. In a liver biopsy processed in formol saline, the glycogen is washed out of the cells. The liver cells then appear clear like plant cells. *(H.&E.×40)*

363 Galactosaemia is an inborn disorder of carbohydrate metabolism. Galactose-1-phosphate accumulates, derived mainly from dietary milk. Infants present with diarrhoea, vomiting and frequently jaundice. A macronodular cirrhosis and cataracts develop. This biopsy shows an enlarged fibrotic portal tract containing inflammatory cells surrounded by regenerative nodules. Giant cells and pseudo-acini may be prominent. *(Periodic acid Schiff ×40)*

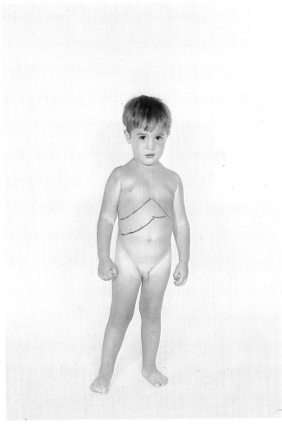

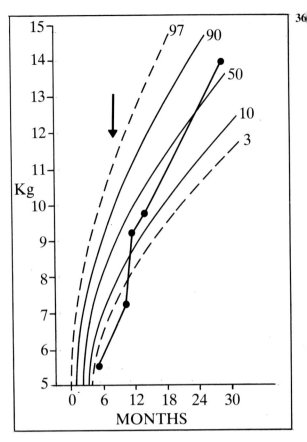

364 Hereditary fructose intolerance. This 2½-year-old boy presented with nausea, vomiting and hepatomegaly. Hypoglycaemia, jaundice and aminoaciduria may also develop. Fructose intolerance resembles galactosaemia, but the presentation is usually delayed until fruit and sucrose are introduced to the diet.

365 Hereditary fructose intolerance. Development is retarded. At presentation this child's weight was below the third percentile. After removal of fructose and sucrose from his diet, his weight rapidly returned to normal.

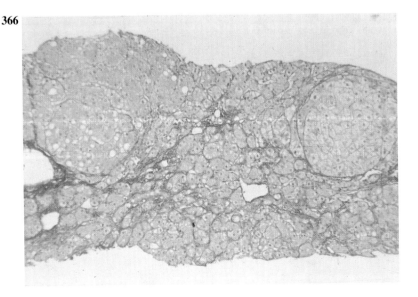

366 Hereditary fructose intolerance. In the liver fatty infiltration, liver cell necrosis, fibrosis and bile ductular proliferation develop. In this patient prolonged fructose ingestion had led to cirrhosis. (*×16*)

367 Hereditary fructose intolerance. A higher magnification of the biopsy in **366** shows chronic inflammatory cell infiltration, fatty change and fibrosis. Groups of liver cells forming pseudo-acini (arrowed) are prominent. *(×100)*

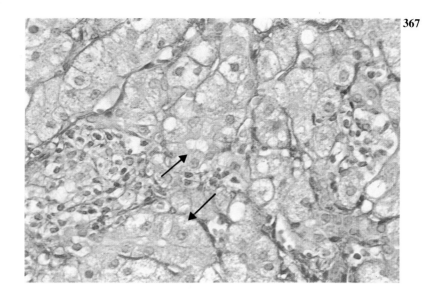

Lipid storage diseases

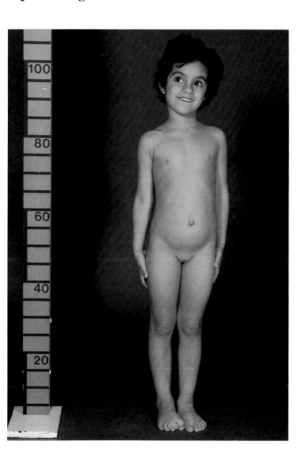

368 Familial hypercholesterolaemia. The heterozygote develops skin xanthomas and ischaemic heart disease in middle age. The homozygous state is rare and presents in childhood. The development of this five-year-old homozygote girl was normal when she presented with skin xanthomas. Her serum cholesterol level was 420mg/100ml.

369 Familial hypercholesterolaemia. Tuberous xanthomas had developed on the hands of the patient shown in **368.** Tendon xanthomas were also present.

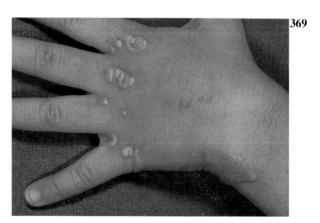

369

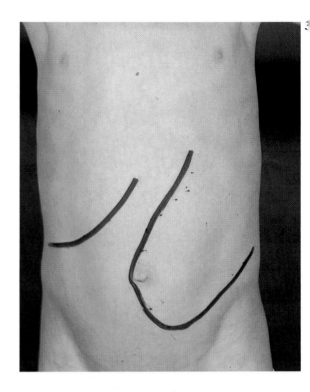

370 Familial hypercholesterolaemia. The white band at the upper pole of the cornea in the child shown in **368** is an arcus senilis, reflecting the high serum cholesterol concentration.

371 Gaucher's disease. In this rare inherited metabolic defect, a cerebroside accumulates in the reticulo-endothelial cells. The affected children present with hepato-splenomegaly. A chronic adult form of Gaucher's disease is more commonly encountered.

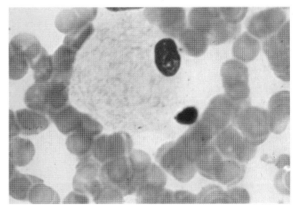

372 Gaucher's disease. A bone marrow aspirate may reveal the characteristic Gaucher cells. These are large, pale staining oval or polygonal cells 70–80μm in diameter. The cytoplasm is fibrillary and contains one or more hyperchromatic nuclei. *(May−Grünwald−Giemsa×600)*

373 Gaucher's disease. A liver biopsy reveals heavy infiltration of pink staining Gaucher cells among the pale staining liver cells. *(Diastase periodic acid Schiff ×63)*

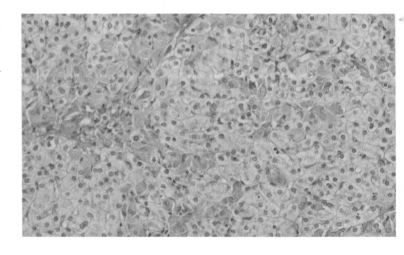

374 Gaucher's disease. At a higher magnification, the whole field is occupied by large pale staining Gaucher cells in this liver biopsy. *(H.&E.×254)*

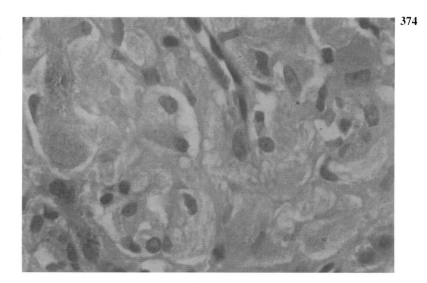

375 Niemann—Pick disease is a rare familial lipid storage disorder. Sphingomyelin accumulates in the reticulo-endothelial cells. The disease affects infants who die before two years of age. Hepato-splenomegaly and lymph node enlargement develop. The skin becomes waxy and yellow-brown. A cherry-red spot may be seen at the macula of the ocular fundus (also seen in Tay Sach's disease). This liver biopsy from a one-year-old child shows the characteristic pale, swollen reticulo-endothelial cells packed with sphingomyelin (1). The liver cells are stained pink due to glycogen, but also contain fine vacuoles of sphingomyelin (2). *(Periodic acid Schiff×100)*

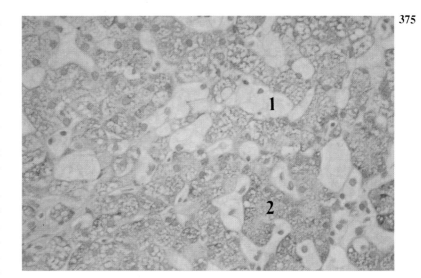

376 Niemann—Pick disease. An electron micrograph of the biopsy in **375** shows a liver cell (1) and two non-parenchymal cells (2). The cells are loaded with vacuoles (cytosomes) containing concentrically laminated material. This is sphingomyelin. *(×1900)*

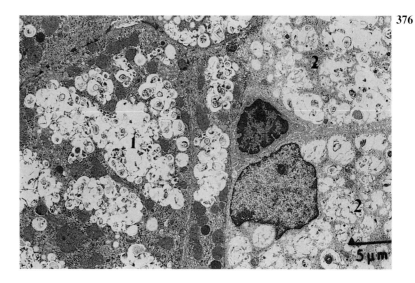

Amyloidosis

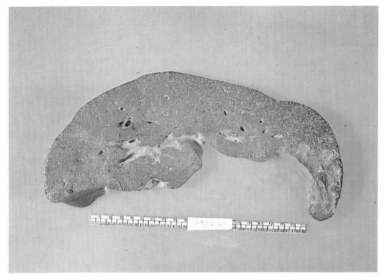

377 Amyloid infiltration of the liver leads to hepatomegaly. The cut surface has a firm, waxy texture. The amyloid deposits have been stained a reddish-brown colour with a dilute iodine solution. Staining with congo red is specific for amyloid. This patient developed amyloidosis following long-standing rheumatoid arthritis. Amyloidosis of the liver may complicate many other chronic diseases including tuberculosis, leprosy, pulmonary suppuration, ulcerative colitis, Crohn's disease, multiple myeloma and Hodgkin's disease. Primary amyloidosis (pericollagen or atypical) is a further rare form.

378

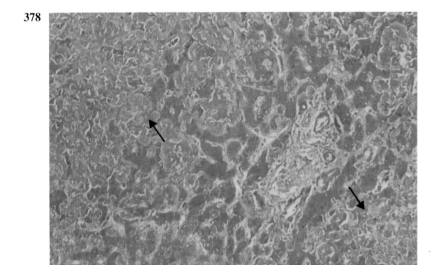

378 Amyloid is widely distributed in the liver and easily detected in a liver biopsy. The amorphous, dark staining amyloid is deposited between the liver cells and the sinusoidal wall in the Space of Disse (arrowed). *(Methyl violet×40)*

Cystic fibrosis (mucoviscidosis)

The commonest effects of this recessively inherited disorder are pancreatic insufficiency and recurrent chest infections. Cystic fibrosis may also involve the liver causing fatty change and a characteristic biliary cirrhosis.

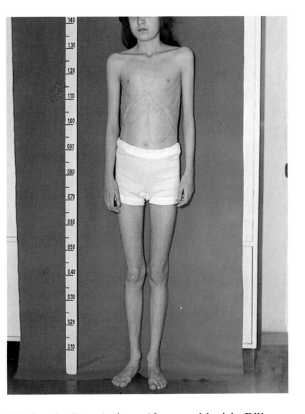

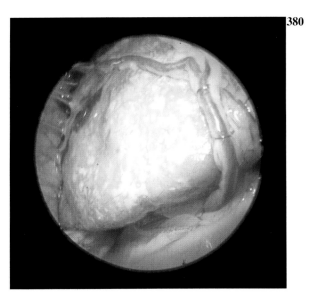

380 Cystic fibrosis. Peritoneoscopy in a seven-year-old boy with biliary cirrhosis and portal hypertension. A portal-systemic collateral vein is coursing over the surface of the nodular liver.

379 Cystic fibrosis in a 13-year-old girl. Biliary cirrhosis and portal venous hypertension have caused hepato-splenomegaly. Note the muscle wasting and barrel-shaped chest.

381 Cystic fibrosis. A liver biopsy from the boy in **380** shows a portal tract expanded by fibrosis and dilated proliferating bile ducts. The cast of eosinophilic material (arrowed), obstructing an intrahepatic bile duct, is the typical finding in cystic fibrosis. Fibrous septa radiate from the portal tracts and result in a coarse biliary cirrhosis. (*H.&E. ×175*)

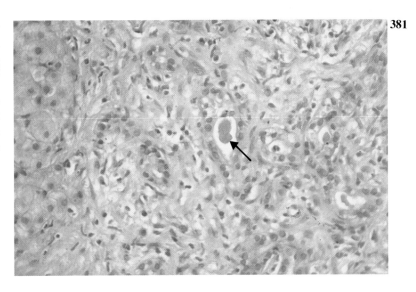

145

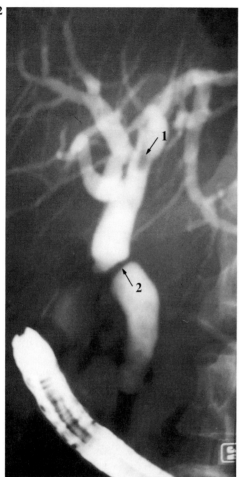

382 Cystic fibrosis. Endoscopic cholangiography shows abnormalities of the biliary tree at all levels. The intrahepatic bile ducts are dilated and contain filling defects (1) due to gallstones forming in the viscid bile. Strictures develop in the common bile duct (2). Subclinical liver disease is present in 24% of patients, but is found in 40% at postmortem.

Porphyria

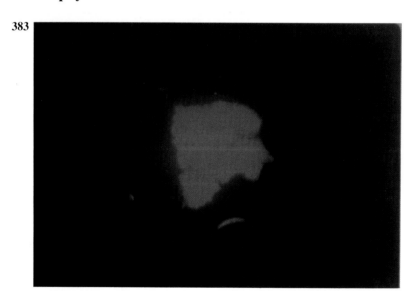

383 Porphyria cutanea tarda (symptomatic cutaneous hepatic porphyria). Uroporphyrin in a fresh fragment of liver biopsy gives a red fluorescence in ultra-violet light. Light microscopy shows a hepatitis or cirrhosis and iron overload. Symptoms include photosensitivity with blistering and scarring of the skin. Alcoholism is a common association. Urinary uroporphyrin excretion is increased.

9 Infections of the liver

Pyogenic infections

Pyogenic infections of the liver usually arise from the biliary tract (*cholangitis*) or the portal venous system (*portal pyaemia*). Stones or strictures in the biliary tract are the commonest causes of cholangitis. Portal pyaemia may follow intra-abdominal sepsis, such as appendicitis, diverticulitis or a perforated duodenal ulcer. Both cholangitis and portal pyaemia may lead to a *pyogenic liver abscess*. Liver abscesses may rarely arise from the hepatic artery in the course of a *septicaemia*. In a proportion of patients no cause for the liver abscess can be found; these are termed *'cryptogenic'*. Organisms of the gut flora are usually cultured in these infections, including the aerobes, such as *E. coli, str. faecalis, pr. vulgaris*, and staphylococci and anaerobes, such as bacteroides, aerobacter and anaerobic streptococci.

384 Recurrent cholangitis. This patient presented with recurrent rigors, sweating and fevers. He was not jaundiced. During the rigors, the white blood count rose to $18,000/mm^3$ and were mainly polymorphonuclear leucocytes. *E. coli* was cultured from his blood. This endoscopic retrograde cholangiogram showed a grossly dilated biliary tree with two large gallstones obstructing the lower end of the bile duct.

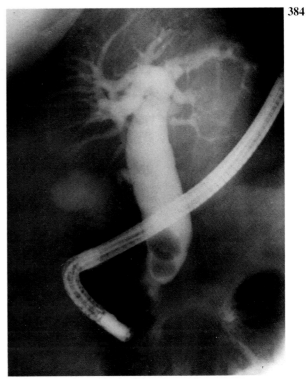

384

385 Recurrent cholangitis. A liver biopsy from the patient in **384** shows a severe cholangitis in the portal tracts. There is proliferation of the bile ductules and a heavy infiltrate of acute inflammatory cells. Culture of this biopsy yielded *E. coli*. (*H.&E.×100*)

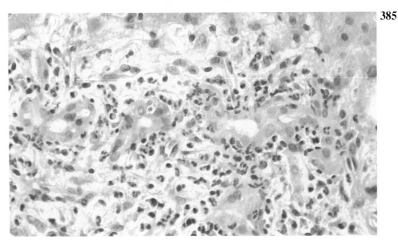

385

386

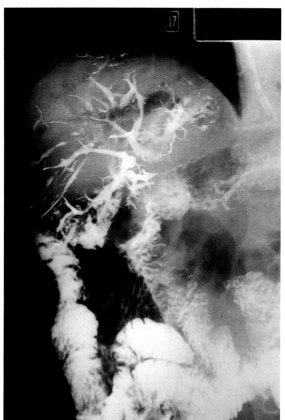

386 Recurrent cholangitis may follow surgical operations which permit reflux of the gut contents up the bile ducts. Following a choledochojejunostomy this patient had many attacks of cholangitis. A barium meal examination showed free reflux of the barium from the jejunum into the biliary tree. The small intrahepatic bile ducts, outlined by barium, showed that the changes of secondary sclerosing cholangitis had followed the recurrent infections.

387

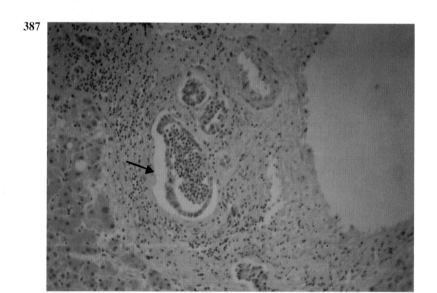

387 Suppurative cholangitis. A liver biopsy shows an enlarged portal zone massively infiltrated with acute inflammatory cells. A bile duct (arrowed) is full of pus. Culture of this biopsy yielded *E. coli. (H.&E.×64)*

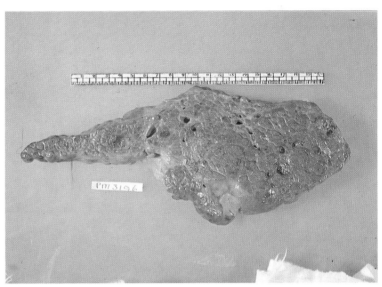

388 Pyogenic liver abscesses following acute suppurative cholangitis. A cut section of the liver shows multiple abscess cavities, about 1cm in diameter.

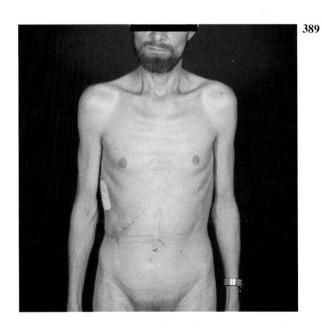

389 Pyogenic liver abscess following portal pyaemia. This patient developed rigors and a tender liver 10 days after a partial gastrectomy. Note the marked muscle wasting.

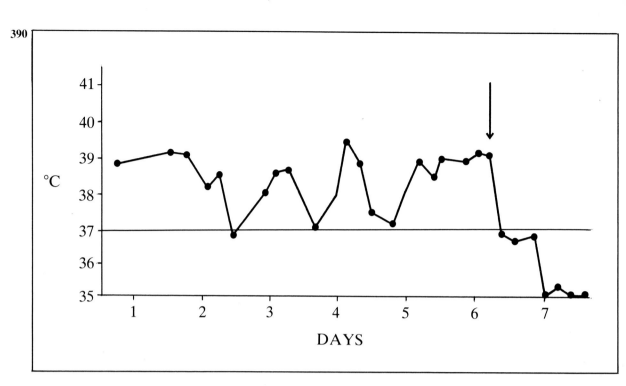

390 Pyogenic liver abscess. The temperature chart of the patient in **389** showed recurrent fevers up to 39.5°C. After surgical drainage of the abscess (arrowed) the temperature rapidly fell to normal.

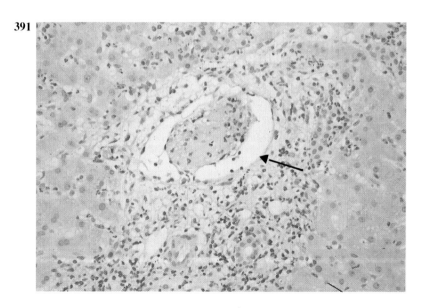

391 Pyogenic liver abscess. A liver biopsy from the patient in **389** showed pylephlebitis (septic phlebitis) of the portal vein. The portal tract is enlarged and contains an acute inflammatory infiltrate around the portal vein (arrowed). There is a thrombus in the portal vein. Portal vein thrombosis is a late complication of pylephlebitis. *(H.&E.×63)*

392 Pyogenic liver abscess. A chest x-ray of the patient in **389** showed a right-sided pleural effusion and a pulmonary reaction. This is a common finding with a liver abscess or sub-phrenic abscess.

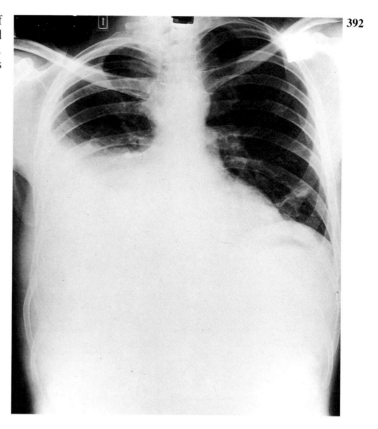

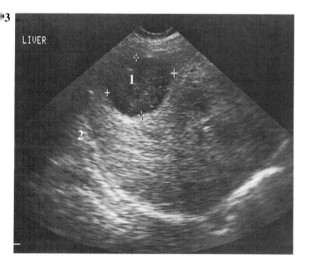

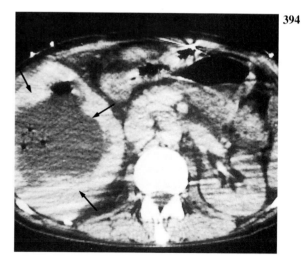

393 Ultrasound of a pyogenic liver abscess shows a low density lesion (1) containing echogenic material which is pus and necrotic liver tissue. The acoustic enhancement (2) beyond the lesion is characteristic of a liver abscess.

394 Pyogenic liver abscess. This previously healthy man of 60 presented with fever and weight loss. A CT enhanced scan showed a large space-occupying lesion in the right lobe of the liver (arrowed) with an irregular thick wall and a fluid-filled centre. Percutaneous aspiration yielded foul-smelling green pus which contained Gram-negative organisms and which, on culture, grew *E. coli*. A primary source for the infection was not found.

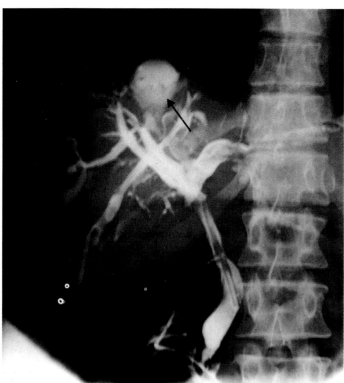

395 Pyogenic liver abscess. The abscess (arrowed) often involves the biliary tree and fills with contrast in a T-tube cholangiogram.

Amoebiasis of the liver

The protozoan parasite *Entamoeba histolytica* normally lives in the wall of the colon where it exists in two forms, a motile trophozoite and a non-motile cyst. The motile trophozoite invades the colonic mucosa where it may cause a colitis or enter the portal venous system and be carried to the liver. In the liver, *E. histolytica* secrete proteolytic enzymes which lyse liver tissue, resulting in abscess formation. These abscesses may burst into the pleural or peritoneal cavities. Amoebiasis is distributed throughout the world, but most infections are seen in the tropics.

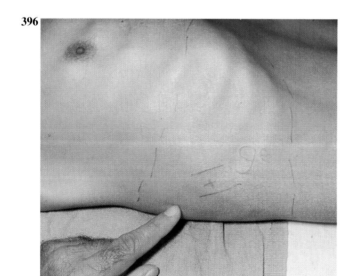

396 Amoebic liver abscess. The patient is typically a young adult male. The liver may be enlarged and tender. An amoebic liver abscess is usually single and commonly found supero-anteriorly in the right lobe. Palpation may reveal an area of exquisite tenderness in the intercostal space overlying the abscess ('punch tenderness'). In this patient the tender point has been marked with a cross. A moderate polymorphonuclear leucocytosis develops. Only a small proportion of patients give a history of amoebic dysentery.

397 Amoebic liver abscess. A chest x-ray may show an elevated right hemidiaphragm, as in this patient. In addition, a pleural effusion and a pulmonary reaction have developed.

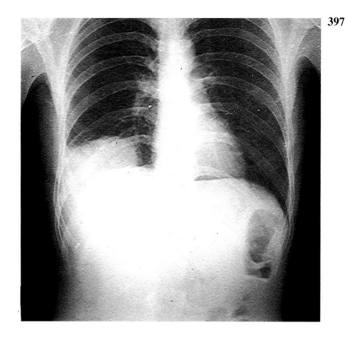

397

398 Amoebic liver abscess. A grey-scale ultrasonogram demonstrated an amoebic abscess (1) in the liver (2) lying posteriorly against the diaphragm (3). The anterior abdominal wall (4) is also shown. (Scanned 10cm right of the umbilicus.)

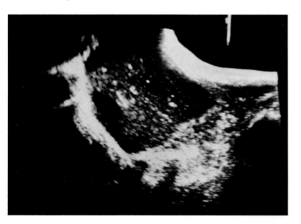

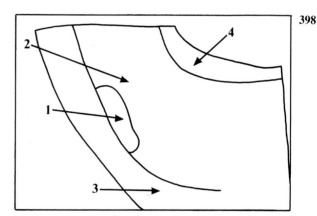

398

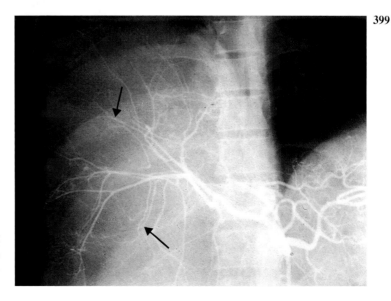

399

399 Amoebic liver abscess in the right lobe of the liver displaced and stretched the intrahepatic vessels (arrowed) in this selective coeliac axis arteriogram.

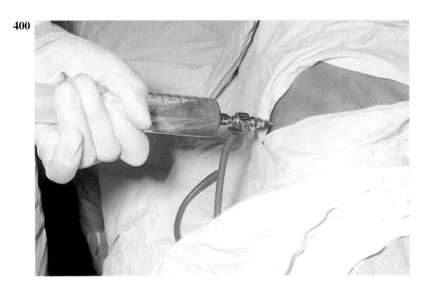

400 Amoebic liver abscess. Percutaneous drainage of an amoebic abscess yields reddish-brown pus ('anchovy sauce' or 'chocolate sauce'). The 'pus' consists of amoebae, degenerate and lysed liver cells and red blood cells. Secondary infection of the abscess occurs in a proportion of patients and the pus turns yellow or green and foul smelling.

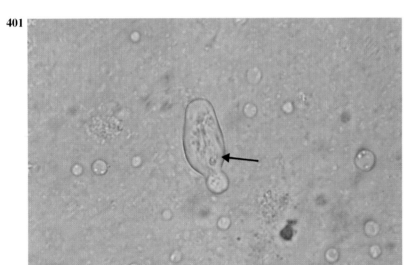

401 Amoebic liver abscess. A motile amoeba (arrowed) was found in the pus aspirated from the patient in **400**, confirming the diagnosis.

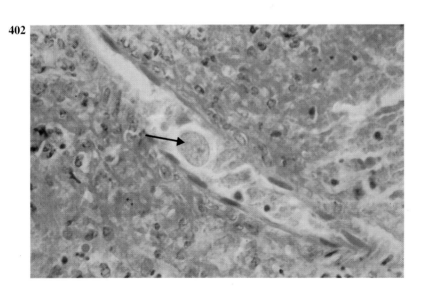

402 Amoebic liver abscess. The liver around the amoebic abscess shows necrotic liver cells. An amoeba (arrowed) is present in a small portal vein radicle. *(H.&E. ×100)*

403 Amoebic colitis. Sigmoidoscopy and examination of fresh warm stools are essential in patients with a suspected amoebic abscess. In this patient an active amoebic colitis was seen and the rectal biopsy showed many motile amoebae (arrowed). The amoebae contain ingested red blood cells, identifying them as *E. histolytica*. This is rare. Usually amoebic abscesses are not found in association with a very active colitis.

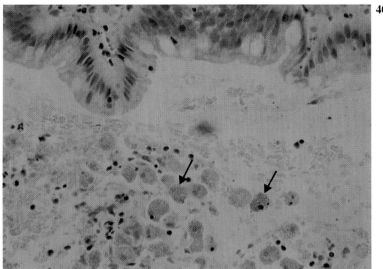

Hydatid disease

The tapeworm *Echinococcus granulosus* lives in the intestines of dogs. The ova shed by the tapeworm develop into cysts in the intermediate hosts: man, sheep and cattle. Dogs become infected by eating infected offal from sheep or cattle. Man is infected by contamination with dog faeces containing the ova. The ingested ova burrow through the intestinal wall and gain access to the liver via the portal venous system. In the liver the ova develop into hydatid cysts. Daughter cysts develop from the germinal layer of the wall of the hydatid cyst. Rarely, ova reach the systemic circulation and hydatid cysts develop in the lungs, spleen, brain and bone.

404 Hydatid cysts usually present with symptomless hepatomegaly, as in this man. Some patients complain of a dull ache or distension in the right upper quadrant. Note the healthy appearance of the patient. Complications include secondary infection of the cyst and rupture of the cyst into the peritoneal or pleural cavities or the biliary system.

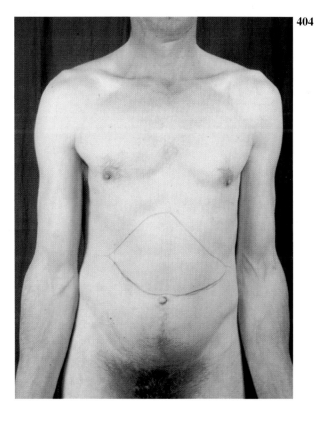

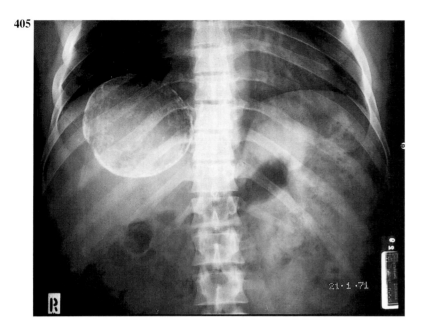

405 Hydatid cyst. This 50-year-old woman left a farm in southern Greece at the age of 16. A routine x-ray of the abdomen showed a space-occupying lesion with a thin calcified wall in the right lobe of the liver under the diaphragm.

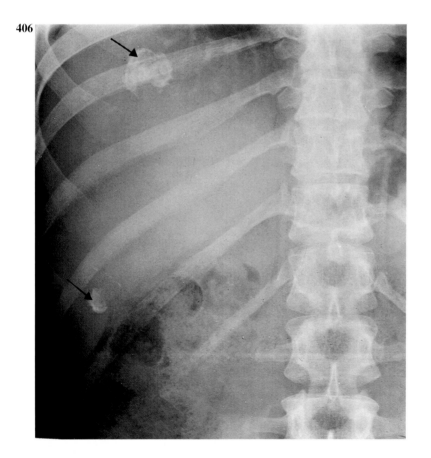

406 Hydatid cyst. In some patients the parasites die and the cysts degenerate and shrink. The calcium deposits in the cyst wall then appear like crumpled eggshells. Two dead hydatid cysts are present in this x-ray (arrowed).

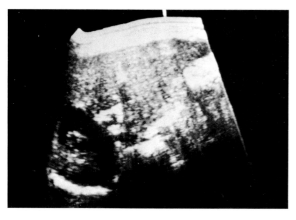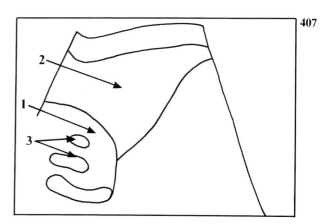

407 Hydatid cysts. To detect uncalcified cysts other techniques are used. This grey-scale ultrasonogram shows a hydatid cyst (1) in the right lobe of the liver (2). Daughter cysts (3) can be identified inside the large cyst. (Scanned 13cm above the umbilicus.)

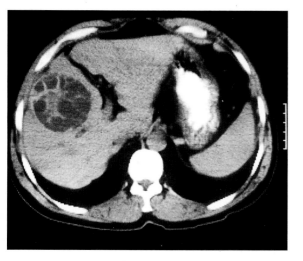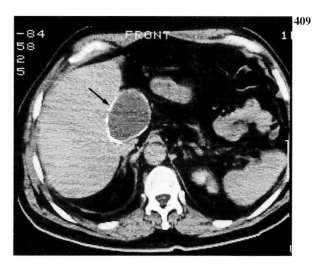

408 Hydatid cyst. Abdominal CT (contrast enhanced) shows a hydatid cyst in the right lobe of the liver with patchy calcification of the wall and containing multiple septae produced by daughter cysts.

409 Hydatid cyst. Abdominal CT (contrast enhanced) shows a calcified hydatid cyst (arrow) in the quadrate lobe of the liver.

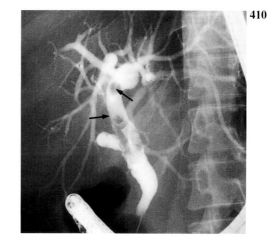

410 Hydatid disease. This patient with hydatid disease presented with upper abdominal pain and obstructive jaundice. The endoscopic cholangiogram shows a dilated biliary tree obstructed by several daughter cysts (arrowed) from the rupture of a hydatid cyst into the biliary system.

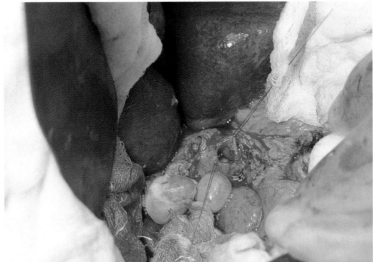

411 **411 Hydatid cyst.** At operation in the patient shown in **410** pale, glistening hydatid cysts can be seen emerging from the common bile duct.

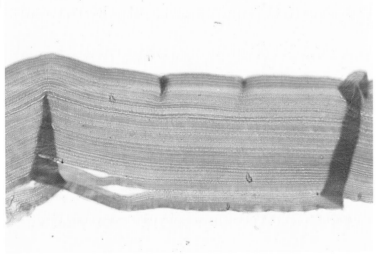

412 **412 Hydatid cyst.** Four hydatid cysts (one bile stained) were removed surgically from the common bile duct of the patient shown in **411**.

413 **413 Hydatid cysts.** Histological examination of a daughter cyst shown in **412** reveals the characteristic chitinous wall of a hydatid cyst. *(H.&E.×63)*

414 Hydatid cysts. A selective coeliac axis arteriogram may show stretching of vessels around the hydatid cysts. In this patient, the margins of three large cysts can be identified (arrowed).

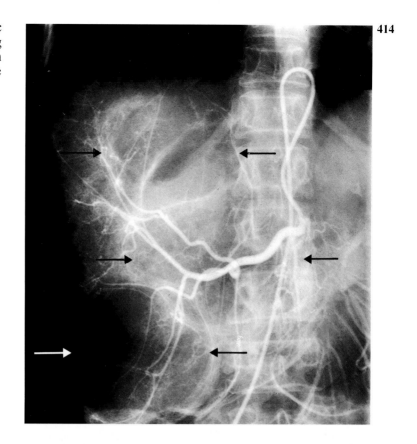

414

415 Hydatid cysts. In the venous phase of the coeliac axis arteriogram shown in **414** the cysts appear as avascular areas (arrowed).

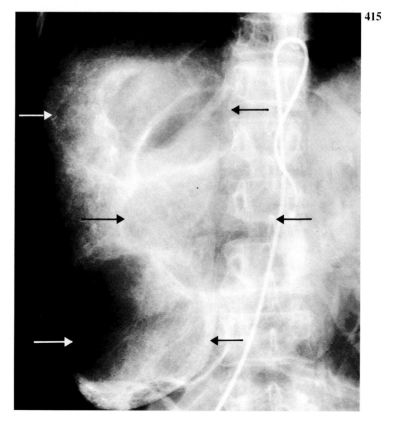

415

Schistosomiasis (bilharziasis)

Schistosomiasis of the liver usually results from infestation with *S. mansoni* or *S. japonicum*. The infection is prevalent in Africa, the Far East and South America. Ova are excreted in the faeces and in water to become free-swimming embryos. The embryos enter certain species of snails where they develop into cercariae. The cercariae leave the snails and gain access through the skin of bathers in infested water ('swimmer's itch'). The parasites migrate to the portal venous system where they develop into adult worms. The worms shed their eggs in the submucosal veins of the colon. Some of the eggs are carried in the portal venous blood back to the liver where they excite a hypersensitivity reaction with the formation of granulomas and fibrosis.

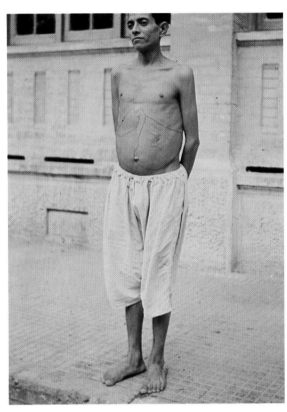

416 Schistosomiasis. The liver and spleen enlarge. Splenomegaly is due to portal hypertension. As the disease progresses, the liver shrinks and the spleen progressively enlarges. This Egyptian patient was infected with *S. mansoni*. He had a very large spleen and suffered repeated haematemeses from oesophageal varices.

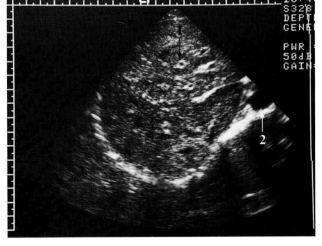

417 Schistosomiasis. Ultrasound scan in schistosomal liver disease shows bright portal tracts (1) and a thickened portal vein (2). This is due to the marked portal tract fibrosis (pipe-stem fibrosis) and is characteristic of hepatic schistosomiasis. Similar ultrasound changes may also be seen in the rare condition of congenital hepatic fibrosis.

418 Schistosomiasis. The portal vein can be greatly thickened. This ultrasound scan shows very thickened portal vein walls (arrowed).

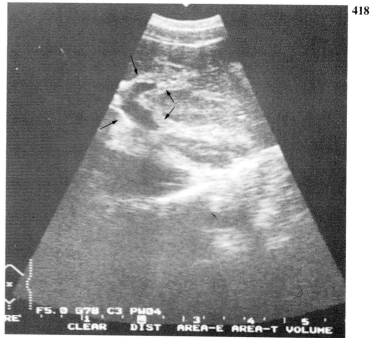

419 Schistosomiasis. An enormous spleen may develop in this condition due to portal hypertension. In a selective coeliac axis arteriogram the splenic artery (1) has filled a huge spleen (2). The hepatic artery (3) is also filled. The patient presented with splenomegaly and haematemeses.

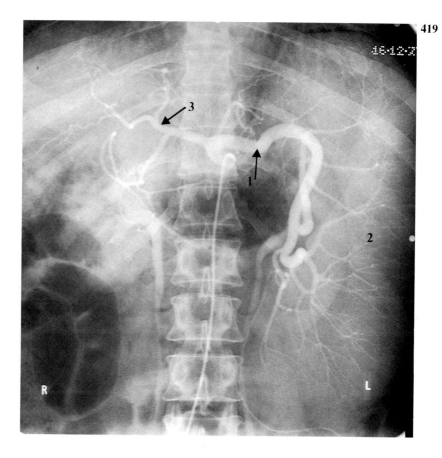

420

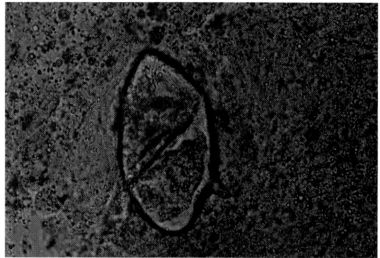

420 Schistosomiasis. A 'squash' preparation of part of a liver biopsy in glycerol may reveal the schistosomal eggs. This preparation showed a bluntly oval egg, measuring about $140 \times 60\mu m$ with a lateral spine. This is the ovum of *S. mansoni*.

421

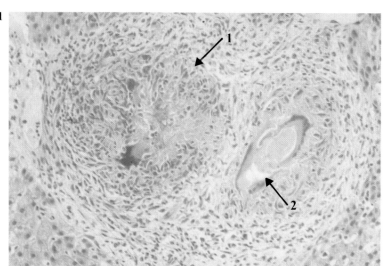

421 Schistosomiasis. The liver biopsy showed an enlarged portal tract containing a granuloma (1) and an ovum of *S. mansoni* (2). There is extensive fibrosis in the portal tract. Ova blocking the intrahepatic portal veins and the portal zone fibrosis lead to portal venous hypertension. *(H.&E. ×64)*

422

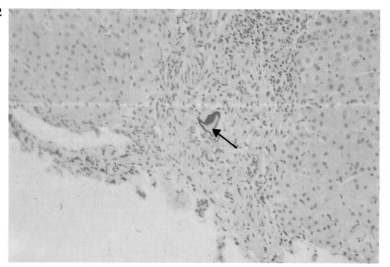

422 Schistosomiasis. The ova may be more readily identified by a Ziehl−Neelsen stain. In this liver biopsy the remnant of a schistosomal egg (arrowed) is stained deep pink in a fibrotic portal zone. *(×64)*

423 'Pipe stem' fibrosis of the portal tracts may develop in schistosomiasis. This is associated with a heavy infestation of the adult worms. Dense fibrous septa extend from the granulomas. There is sclerosis around the walls of the portal veins. Bile duct proliferation and regenerative nodules are usually insignificant. A reticulin stain of this liver biopsy shows dense portal zone (zone 1) fibrosis containing the portal veins (arrowed). The surrounding reticulin architecture is preserved. (×40).

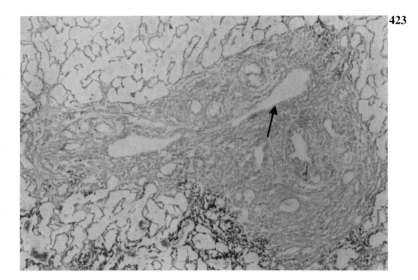

424 Schistosomiasis. Ova are often found in the rectum of patients with hepatic schistosomiasis. A Ziehl–Neelsen stain showed the dark pink staining walls of *S. mansoni* ova in this rectal biopsy. The patient's liver biopsy is shown in **420**.

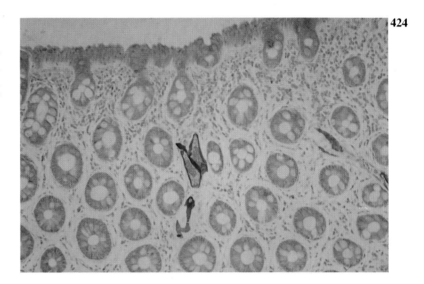

Miscellaneous infections

425 Tuberculosis of the liver. The liver is frequently involved in miliary tuberculosis. The commonest lesion is a caseating granuloma. This liver biopsy contains a large granuloma with lymphocytes, epithelioid cells and numerous giant cells (arrowed). The centre of the granuloma is caseating. Culture of the biopsy may yield tubercle bacilli. In some patients, extrahepatic signs of tuberculosis may not be obvious. (H.&E.×40)

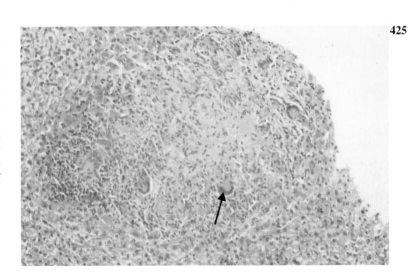

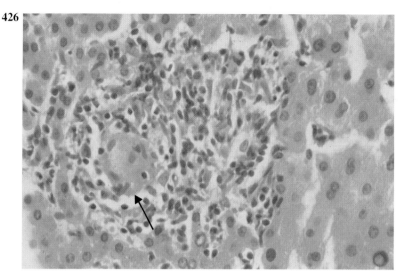

426 Sarcoidosis frequently involves the liver, causing widespread granuloma formation. The liver lesion is usually asymptomatic. An early sarcoid granuloma is a round, well-demarcated lesion commonly found in the portal tracts. The granuloma contains giant cells (arrowed) and pale staining epithelioid cells with a thin peripheral cuff of lymphocytes. In contrast to tuberculosis, there is no central caseation. *(H.&E.×160)*

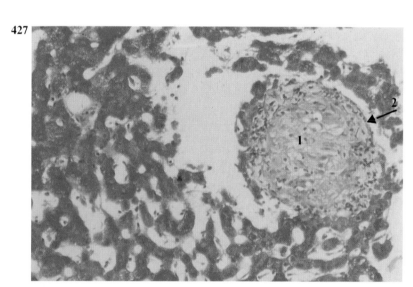

427 Sarcoidosis. Later in the course of the disease the granulomas develop a central area of acellular hyaline material (1) and a fibrous capsule. A peripheral ring of lymphocytes is present (2). The pallor of the granuloma is particularly marked in this biopsy stained for glycogen. *(Periodic acid Schiff ×64)*

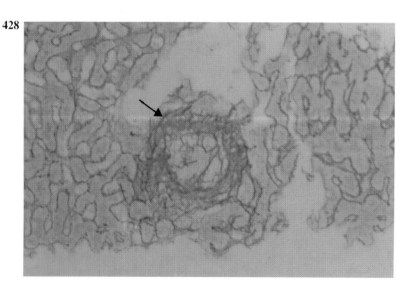

428 Sarcoidosis. A reticulin stain of the biopsy in **427** shows the fibrous capsule of a healing granuloma (arrowed). The surrounding reticulin architecture is preserved. Portal hypertension is a rare late complication. *(×64)*

429 Cholestatic sarcoidosis. Rarely, but particularly in black males, sarcoidosis can be associated with marked cholestasis. The clinical picture resembles primary biliary cirrhosis very closely. Liver biopsy of this young West Indian man with cholestasis of two years duration shows granulomas and cellular infiltration with grossly damaged interlobular bile ducts (arrowed). *(H.&E.×120)*

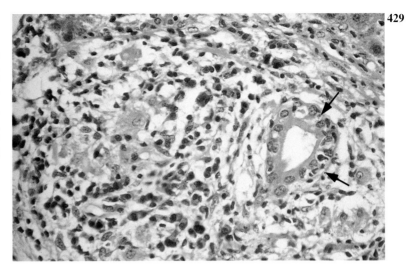

430 Brucellosis. Infection with *Brucella abortus* leads to widespread granuloma formation in the liver. The liver lesion is usually silent and hepatomegaly inconstant. The granulomas are indistinguishable from those of sarcoidosis. However, culture of part of the liver biopsy may yield the organism. In some patients, focal collections of lymphocytes, without granulomas, are seen. *(H.&E.×200)*

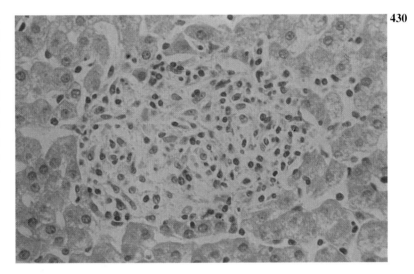

431 Syphilis. Occasionally hepatitis and jaundice complicate secondary syphilis. The clinical picture may simulate acute viral hepatitis. In some patients liver histology shows miliary granulomata. In others, portal tract inflammation is the principal lesion. In this biopsy syphilis has resulted in portal zone infiltration (arrowed) with neutrophils and lymphocytes, foci of liver cell necrosis and cell 'drop-out'. The liver is also involved in congenital syphilis and in tertiary syphilis, where gummas and a hepar lobatum may develop. *(H.&E. ×40)*

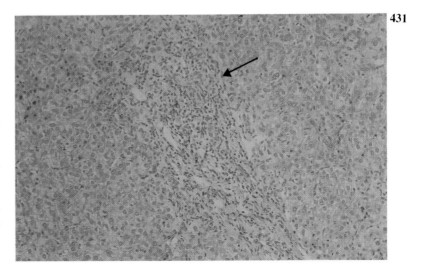

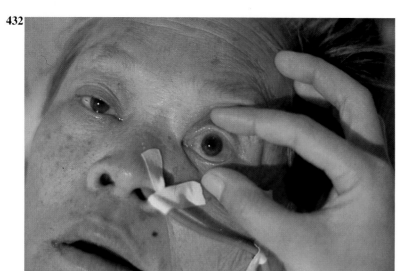

432 Leptospirosis. These infections are caused by a large group of leptospira, including *L. ictero-haemorrhagiae* (Weil's disease), and are usually spread by rats. The onset is abrupt with shivering followed by fever and marked prostration. Severe headaches, muscle and joint pains are common. Albuminuria is usual. This Thai patient shows the characteristic conjunctival suffusion of leptospirosis. There is great variation in the severity of the clinical course of these infections.

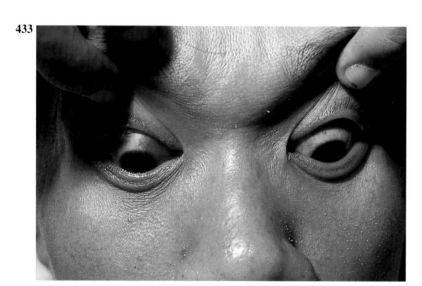

433 Leptospirosis. Jaundice appears between the fourth and seventh day in many patients and the liver is enlarged. The sub-conjunctival haemorrhage in this Thai patient is due to a bleeding tendency which usually accompanies severe attacks. Bleeding from the nose, gut and lungs, skin petechiae and ecchymoses may also develop.

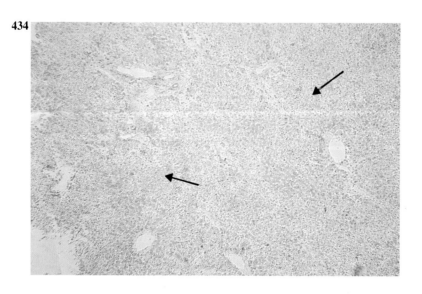

434 Yellow fever is caused by a Group B arbovirus. An incubation period of three to six days is followed by headache, backache and prostration. Hypotension, jaundice, albuminuria, widespread haemorrhages and vomiting of altered blood may develop. A liver biopsy shows severe liver cell necrosis particularly in the mid-zonal areas (arrowed) and Council-man bodies. Inflammatory cells are characteristically scanty. *(H.&E. ×8)*

435 Lassa fever is a viral disease encountered in West Africa which causes a 'haemorrhagic fever'. The patients develop headache, fever, muscle pains and pharyngitis. Vomiting, diarrhoea, proteinuria and a bleeding tendency may develop later. A liver biopsy shows widespread eosinophilic necrosis of liver cells without inflammatory cells. The liver changes may appear similar to yellow fever, except that in Lassa fever, necrosis develops in all areas of the lobule. *(H.&E.×8)*

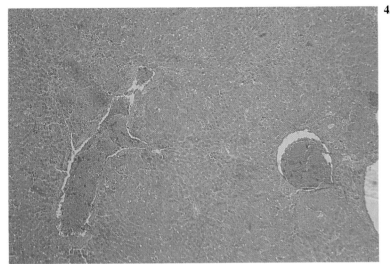

435

436 Infectious mononucleosis may involve the liver and mimic infectious hepatitis. A liver biopsy shows the portal tracts (arrowed) and sinusoids infiltrated with large mononuclear cells. Focal areas of liver cell necrosis develop, but unlike infective hepatitis, centrizonal necrosis is not present. *(H.&E.×64)*

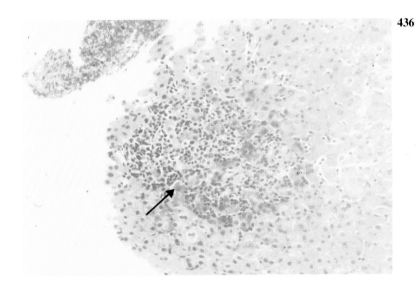

436

437 Marburg virus hepatitis has been contracted by laboratory workers from the Vervet (African Green Monkey). The incubation period is between four and seven days. Headache, pyrexia, vomiting, central nervous system involvement and a hepatitis develop. This rare disease is severe and a proportion of the patients have died. A liver biopsy shows areas of centrizonal necrosis containing numerous acidophilic bodies. Fatty change may also develop. *(H.&E.×64)*

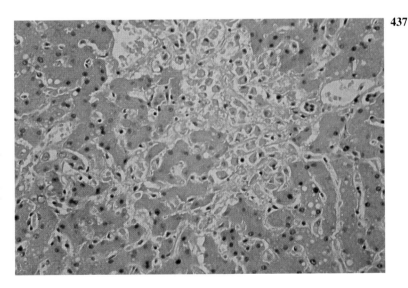

437

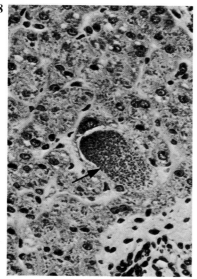

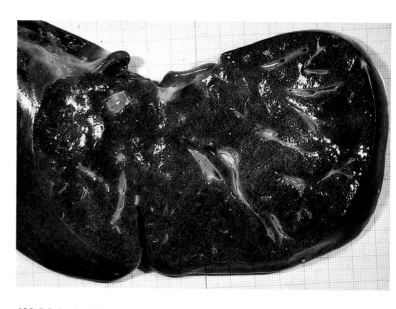

438 Malaria. The liver is infected during the preerythrocytic stage. Sporozoites from a mosquito invade liver cells where they divide to form a 'tissue' schizont (arrowed). The liver cell enlarges and finally ruptures liberating many merozoites which enter erythrocytes (erythrocytic stage). There are usually no specific signs of liver involvement in malaria. *(Giemsa-colophonium×350)*

439 Malaria. In chronic infections a brown pigment accumulates in the liver and spleen. This section of liver shows the typical dark brown appearance of chronic malaria. It is due to iron and haemofuscin in the Kupffer cells.

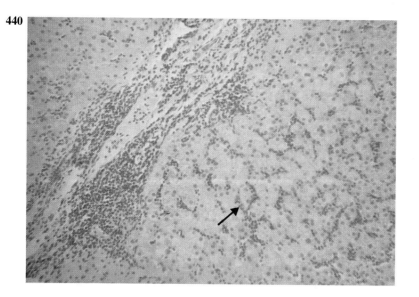

440 Tropical splenomegaly syndrome. An abnormal immune response to malarial infection may result in marked splenomegaly. The serum IgM concentration is always elevated. A liver biopsy shows dilated sinusoids (arrowed) heavily infiltrated with lymphocytes and hypertrophied Kupffer cells. *(H.&E.×40)*

441 Kala-azar (leishmaniasis) is a protozoan infection involving the reticulo-endothelial system, causing fevers and marked hepato-splenomegaly. A liver biopsy shows enlarged Kupffer cells (arrowed) distending the sinusoids. The Kupffer cells contain Leishman–Donovan bodies. The portal tracts are infiltrated with chronic inflammatory cells. *(H.&E.×100)*

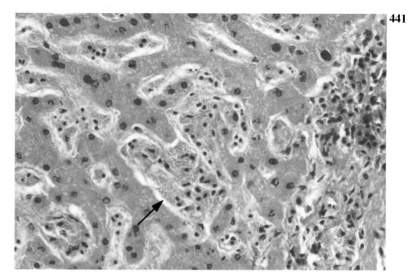

441

442 Ascariasis. The roundworm *Ascaris lumbricoides* may lodge in the common bile duct, causing partial biliary obstruction and cholangitis with liver abscesses. Haemobilia is a further complication. Biliary ascariasis is usually encountered in the Indian subcontinent and in the Far East. This endoscopic cholangiogram shows linear filling defects in the bile ducts (arrowed) due to *Ascaris* worms.

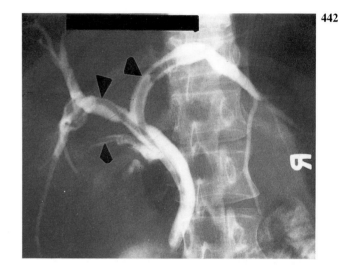

442

443 Toxocariasis. This worm, which is spread by dogs (*Toxocara canis*) and cats (*T. cati*), invades many tissues (visceral larva migrans). Infestation of the liver results in granuloma formation. The signs of liver involvement are non-specific. A marked blood eosinophilia is usual. *(×150)*

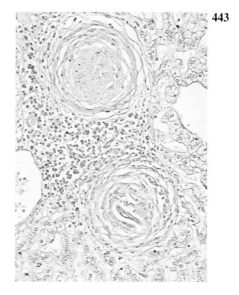

443

Liver flukes

444 *Clonorchis sinensis*. The Chinese liver fluke is found in eastern Asia. The mature fluke may reach 2cm in length. Man is infected by eating raw or partly cooked fish. The migration of the flukes to the biliary tree is usually accompanied by a pyrexia and a blood eosinophilia.

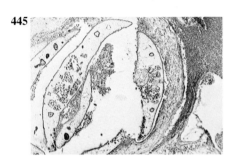

445 *Clonorchis sinensis*. This liver section shows the flukes in a bile duct where they cause severe fibrosis and adenomatous change *(×15)*. Bile duct obstruction, caused by these flukes, is frequently complicated by bacterial cholangitis, multiple liver abscesses and intrahepatic gallstone formation. *Bile duct carcinoma* and *primary liver cancer* may develop later.

446 *Opisthorchis viverrini*. These liver flukes are found in northeast Thailand, Laos and Cambodia. Uncooked fish is the usual source of infestation. *O. viverrini* causes similar biliary disease to *C. sinensis*.

447 Ecology of fasciola hepatica. Sheep and cattle are usually infected. The intermediate hosts, Lymnaea snails, thrive in wet pasture and excrete the encysted cercariae of the flukes. Man is usually infected by eating wild watercress. This picture shows the common British intermediate host *L. trunculata*, in a typical wet habitat.

448 Fasciola hepatica invade the biliary system, causing cholangitis with fever, pain and hepatomegaly. A blood eosinophilia usually develops. The clinical picture may simulate gallstones in the common bile duct. The spines of the fluke (arrowed) damage the biliary epithelium. *(×350)*

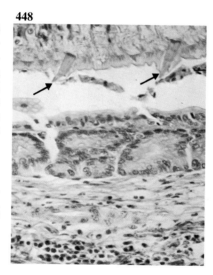

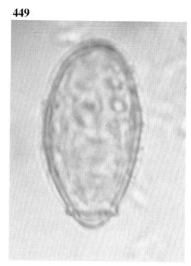

449 Liver flukes. The diagnosis can be confirmed by finding ova in the faeces. This is the ovum of *O. viverrini. (×500)*

Acquired Immunodeficiency Syndrome (AIDS)

Abnormal liver function tests are common in patients infected with the human immunodeficiency virus type 1 (HIV1). These patients can develop any liver disease but they are particularly susceptible to certain infections and malignancies. The cause of the liver dysfunction is usually related to the stage of the HIV1 infection. In the early stages (HIV antibody positive) the liver changes tend to be large droplet fatty infiltration and iron deposition. The excess iron follows blood transfusions given to treat the anaemia induced by azidothymidine (AZT) therapy. As the disease progresses and AIDS-related complex (ARC) and finally the acquired immunodeficiency syndrome (AIDS) develop, the liver may show the infections that these severely immunocompromised patients are susceptible to. These include atypical tuberculosis, *cryptococcosis, histoplasmosis, leishmaniasis* and *pneumocystis*. Chronic hepatitis due to hepatitis B virus infection is suppressed as the patient becomes immunocompromised and chronic active hepatitis regresses to chronic persistent hepatitis. Malignant lymphomas and Kaposi's sarcoma are the commonest malignant tumours that develop in AIDS and these may invade the liver.

Bile duct abnormalities develop in AIDS. The commonest are sclerosing cholangitis and ampullary stenosis. Extrahepatic bile duct strictures are also seen. An AIDS-associated pathogen can be identified in most patients. This is usually *cytomegalovirus* but *cryptosporidium*, atypical tuberculosis, Kaposi's sarcoma and Burkitt's lymphoma may be found in ampullary and biliary tissue.

450 Acquired immunodeficiency syndrome. These are the typical liver biopsy appearances from a patient with AIDS. The liver contains large droplet fat and a brown pigment which is iron. This 40-year-old male was HIV antibody positive and had mildly abnormal liver function tests. He was anaemic because of AZT therapy and consequently had 20 units of blood transfused. *(H.&E.×350)*

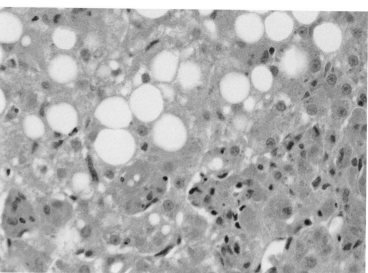

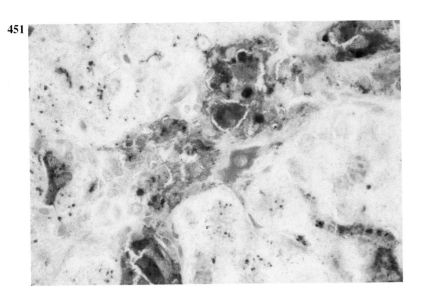

451 Iron deposition. A Perl's stain of the biopsy in **450** confirms that the brown pigment is iron. The iron is deposited mainly in the Kupffer cells lining the sinusoids and is a consequence of the blood transfusions. *(×350)*

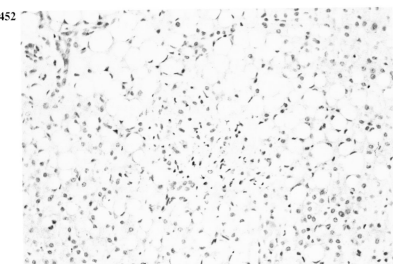

452 Atypical tuberculosis. This 37-year-old HIV antibody positive male had a *Mycobacterium avium intracellulare* infection of his terminal ileum. He now presented with abnormal liver function tests. The liver biopsy shows a fatty liver with a noncaseating granuloma. *(H.&E. ×150)*

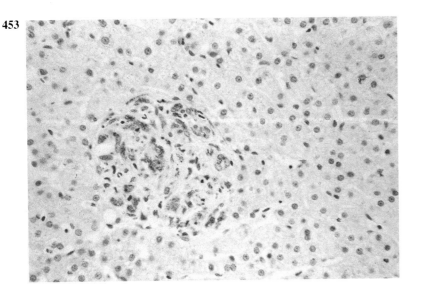

453 Atypical tuberculosis. A Zeihl−Neelsen stain of the granuloma in **452** shows a large load of *Mycobacterium avium intracellulare*. This is a typical finding in the immunocompromised AIDS patient. *(×150)*

454 Cryptococcus. This 45-year-old HIV antibody positive male presented with a temperature, the signs of meningitis and abnormal liver function tests. His liver biopsy shows the liver contains many yeast forms of *Cryptococcus neoformans*, stained black. *(Methenamine silver×350)*

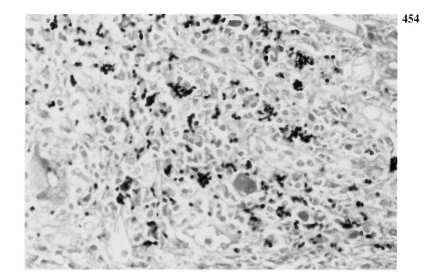

455 Histoplasmosis. This 39-year-old HIV antibody positive male presented with a temperature, weight loss, lung lesions and abnormal liver function tests. The liver biopsy shows many intracellular yeast forms of *Histoplasma capsulatum*, stained red. *(Periodic acid Schiff-diastase×500)*

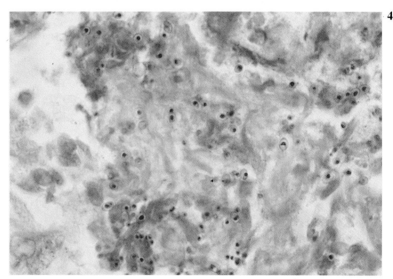

456 Leishmaniasis. A 45-year-old HIV antibody positive male from South America presented with temperatures, hepatosplenomegaly and abnormal liver function tests. The liver contains sheets of macrophages infected with *Leishmania donovani*. There is no granuloma formation. This presentation is common in endemic areas and contrasts with the presentation in immunocompetent patients, where the parasites are contained within granulomas. *(H.&E.×500)*

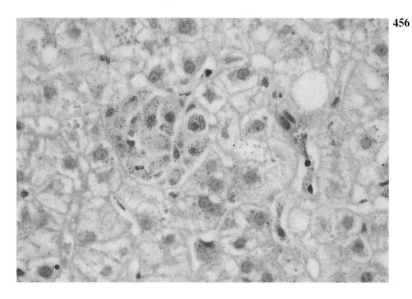

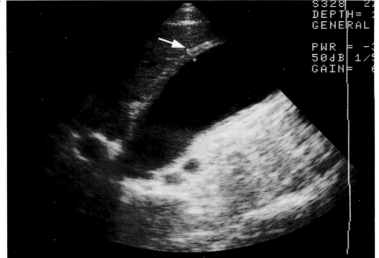

457 Sclerosing cholangitis related to cryptosporidiosis infection. Cryptosporidiosis usually causes diarrhoea, but may also affect the biliary system in AIDS. Symptoms include right upper quadrant pain, nausea and vomiting. Liver function tests are cholestatic. Ultrasound is a useful test to detect biliary infection with *Cryptosporidia sp*. This ultrasound scan in a HIV antibody positive patient shows marked thickening of the gallbladder wall (arrowed). The walls of the intrahepatic and extrahepatic biliary tree are also thickened. Cholangiography shows the changes of sclerosing cholangitis. *Cryptosporidia* oocytes were collected from the bile.

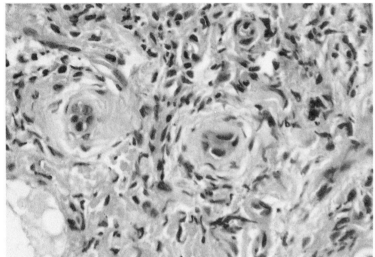

458 Sclerosing cholangitis in a 36-year-old HIV antibody positive male who presented with cholestatic (biliary obstructive) liver function tests. A liver biopsy shows the typical changes of sclerosing cholangitis. The portal tracts contain bile ducts with atrophic biliary epithelium and periductal fibrosis. *Cryptosporidia sp*. were isolated from the bile. *(H.&E.×350)*

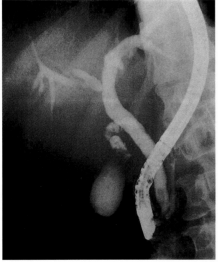

459 Ampullary stenosis and sclerosing cholangitis related to *cytomegalovirus* (CMV) infection. A 40-year-old HIV antibody positive male presented with cholestatic (biliary obstructive) liver function tests. His endoscopic cholangiogram shows a dilated biliary tree with an obstruction at the lower end of the bile duct caused by stenosis of the ampulla of Vater. The dilated common bile duct wall shows a fine irregularity due to an inflammatory reaction. The intrahepatic bile ducts are strictured due to sclerosing cholangitis.

460 Ampullary stenosis and sclerosing cholangitis related to CMV infection. An endoscopic biopsy of the ampulla from the patient in **459** shows the intranuclear and cytoplasmic inclusions of CMV. *(H.&E.×500)*

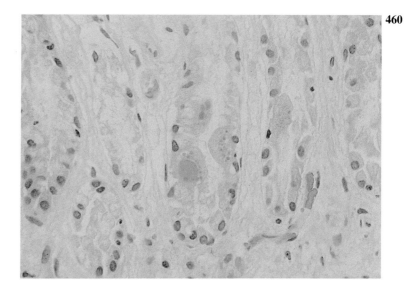

461 Pneumocystis. This 37-year-old HIV antibody positive male had previously had *Pneumocystis carinii* pneumonia. This was controlled by regular pentamidine aerosol inhalations. He then presented with abnormal liver function tests and this liver biopsy was performed. It shows a granular exudate and iron pigment. *(H.&E.×350)*

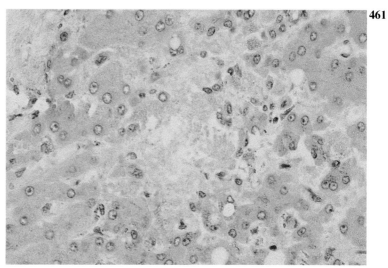

462 Pneumocystis. A methenamine silver stain of the liver biopsy in **461** shows the cysts of *Pneumocystis carinii* as the cause of the granular exudate. Hepatic pneumocystis is an increasing problem as pulmonary pneumocystis infection is controlled by inhaled chemotherapy. *(×500)*

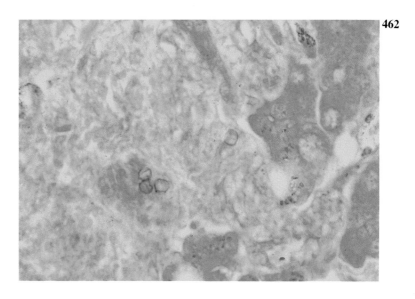

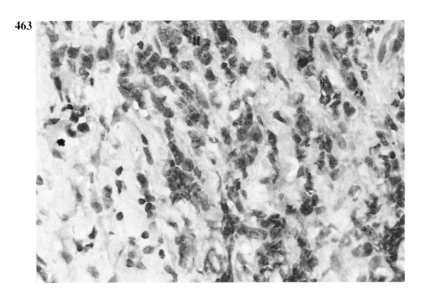

463 Lymphoma. This 36-year-old male had been HIV antibody positive for two years when he was found to have abnormal liver function tests. The hepatic sinusoids are infiltrated with large pleomorphic lymphoid cells of a B-cell lymphoma. The lymphomas that develop in AIDS are almost invariably of B-cell lineage. *(H. &E. ×350)*

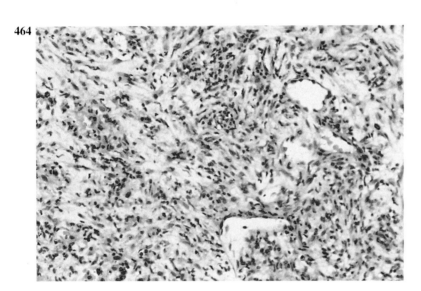

464 Kaposi's sarcoma. This 36-year-old male had been HIV antibody positive for one year and had developed widespread cutaneous and gastrointestinal Kaposi's sarcoma. The liver biopsy was performed when he developed abnormal liver function tests. The biopsy shows marked expansion of the portal tracts with a spindle cell tumour which is forming vascular clefts. These appearances are typical of Kaposi's sarcoma. *(H.&E.×150)*

10. *Fibropolycystic disease of the liver and biliary system*

Fibropolycystic disease encompasses a family of rare congenital hepato-biliary diseases. These include adult fibropolycystic disease (polycystic liver), congenital hepatic fibrosis, congenital intrahepatic biliary dilatation (Caroli's disease), choledochal cysts and microhamartomas (Von Meyenberg complexes). Many of the patients will have more than one of the diseases. The combination of both congenital hepatic fibrosis and Caroli's disease is most striking as the patients develop both variceal haemorrhage (due to congenital hepatic fibrosis) and cholangitis (due to Caroli's disease). Associated kidney defects are common. Malignant change may complicate congenital hepatic fibrosis, Caroli's disease and choledochal cysts. These diseases are of greatly differing severity and the prognosis in an individual patient is determined by the fibropolycystic diseases present.

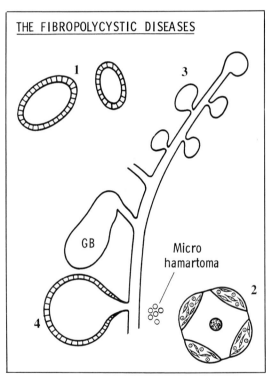

465 The family of fibropolycystic diseases affecting the liver and biliary system are depicted schematically. They include adult fibropolycystic disease (polycystic liver) (1), congenital hepatic fibrosis (2), congenital intrahepatic biliary dilatation (Caroli's disease) (3), choledochal cysts (4) and microhamartomas (Von Meyenberg complexes). (GB = Gallbladder.)

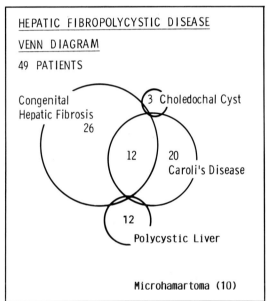

466 Association of fibropolycystic diseases. The Venn diagram shows that many fibropolycystic patients have more than one disease. In one series, congenital hepatic fibrosis alone was present in 14 patients, Caroli's disease alone in 8 and the combination of congenital hepatic fibrosis and Caroli's disease in 12 patients. Microhamartomas are underreported and so have been excluded from the diagram.

467

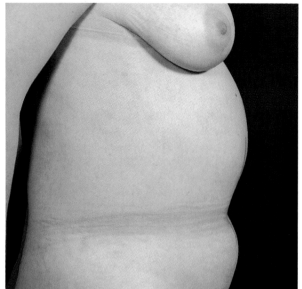

467 Polycystic liver disease affects women predominantly. Patients present with right upper quadrant pain and increasing girth. In this patient a large polycystic liver is the cause of the upper abdominal swelling. Liver function tests are normal. Provided no other fibropolycystic disease is present, polycystic liver disease has a benign course. The renal complications are much more important.

468

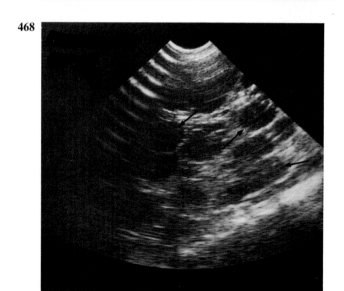

468 Polycystic liver disease. Ultrasound scanning is the most satisfactory non-invasive method of diagnosis. This ultrasound of the patient in **467** shows a liver containing many thin-walled cysts (arrowed). Percutaneous drainage of the cysts under ultrasound guidance was performed repeatedly in this patient to reduce the size of the liver.

469

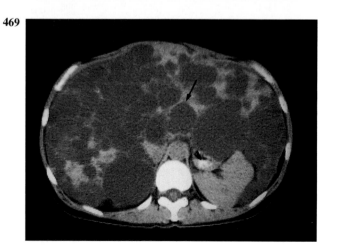

469 Polycystic liver disease. CT scanning of the patient in **467** clearly shows that the numerous liver cysts are of low density, indicating that they are fluid-filled (arrowed).

470 Polycystic liver disease. The liver contains many thin-walled cysts filled with a clear or brown-coloured fluid due to altered blood. The cysts vary in size from a pinhead to about 10cm in diameter. The remainder of the liver is normal. In many cases a polycystic liver is an incidental finding at autopsy.

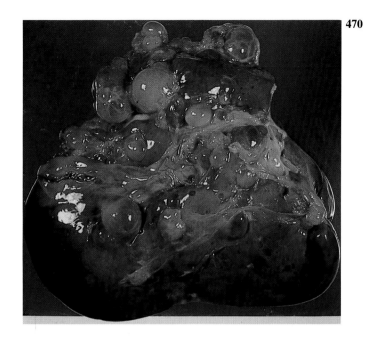
470

471 Polycystic liver disease. Cysts are lined by flattened epithelium of biliary type. Adjacent liver tissue shows fibrosis. The remaining liver parenchyma is normal. *(H.&.E×40)*

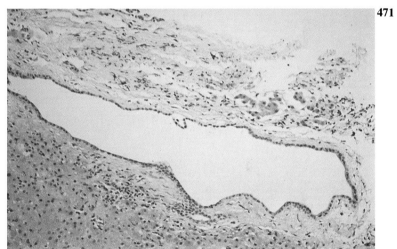
471

472 Polycystic kidneys. Patients with adult fibro-polycystic liver disease may also have polycystic kidneys. These may present with renal complications including renal failure. This abdominal CT scan (unenhanced by intravenous contrast) shows enlarged kidneys (arrowed) with multiple cysts, some of them with renal stones.

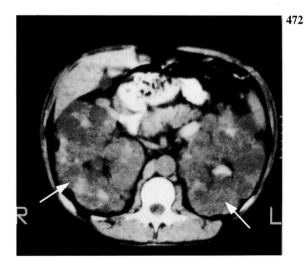
472

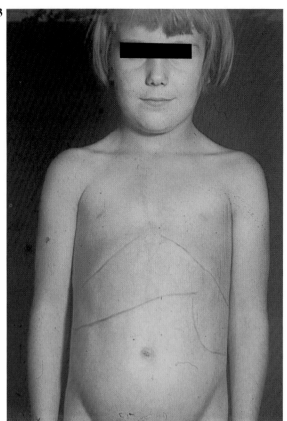

473 Congenital hepatic fibrosis. This rare condition is usually diagnosed before 10 years of age. Children present with a large, very hard liver, splenomegaly or bleeding from oesophageal varices. Note the hepato-splenomegaly in this child. The vein on the abdominal wall is a portal-systemic collateral caused by portal venous hypertension. Her development was normal. Congenital hepatic fibrosis may be misdiagnosed as cirrhosis. Abnormalities of the biliary system, such as Caroli's disease or choledochal cysts, may also be present.

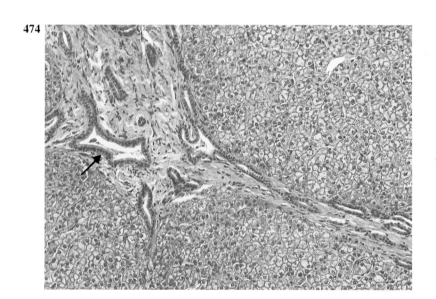

474 Congenital hepatic fibrosis. A liver biopsy reveals normal hepatic lobules encased by broad collagenous fibrous bands. Well developed bile ducts (arrowed) are present in the fibrous bands. (*H.&E.×40*)

475 Congenital hepatic fibrosis. The liver feels hard and the surface has a mottled white appearance due to the thick fibrous bands. The tough texture of the liver may make a percutaneous liver biopsy difficult.

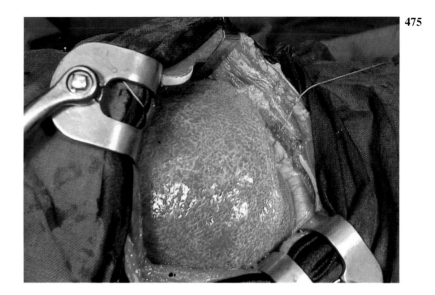

476 Medullary sponge kidney is the usual renal disease associated with congenital hepatic fibrosis Spotty areas of calcification (arrowed) develop in a medullary sponge kidney. These are small cysts adjacent to the renal calyces.

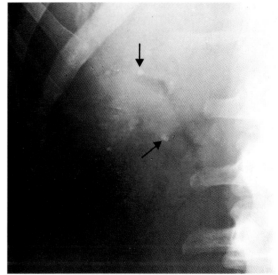

477 Congenital intrahepatic biliary dilatation (Caroli's disease). An endoscopic cholangiogram shows the bulbous dilatations of the intrahepatic bile ducts. The rest of the biliary tree is normal. Most patients are male and if the dilated intrahepatic ducts remain uninfected the patient will be symptom free. However most patients will eventually present with cholangitis, which can be intractable with gallstone and liver abscess formation. Bile duct cancer develops in about 7% of patients.

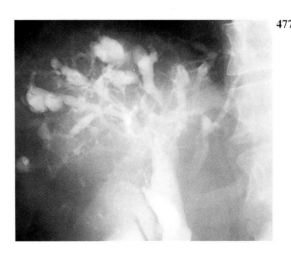

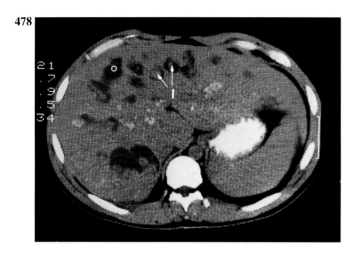

478 Congenital intrahepatic biliary dilatation (Caroli's disease). Intravenous contrast enhanced CT scan shows dilated intrahepatic bile ducts containing filling defects (the central dot sign in CT). These central dots (1), which appear after contrast enhancement, are portal vein radicles which are surrounded by dilated intrahepatic bile ducts. The adjacent radicles of the portal vein are also enhanced by the intravenous contrast (white dots) (2).

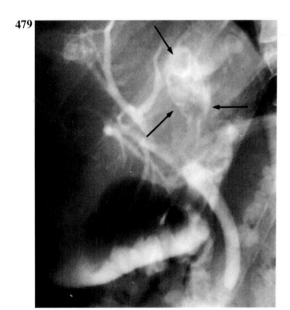

479 Congenital intrahepatic biliary dilatation (Caroli's disease). Rarely the disease is localized to one lobe of the liver, usually the left lobe. This endoscopic cholangiogram shows the bulbous dilatations of Caroli's disease restricted to the intrahepatic bile ducts of the left lobe of the liver (arrowed). The patient suffered recurrent bouts of cholangitis. The attacks of cholangitis ceased following a left partial hepatectomy.

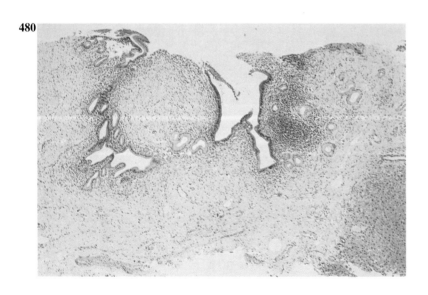

480 Congenital intrahepatic biliary dilatation (Caroli's disease). The liver biopsy shows cavernous ectasia of bile ducts in an oedematous, fibrotic portal tract. There is an acute and chronic inflammatory cell infiltrate around the cysts. The lining epithelium of the affected duct is partially ulcerated and focally hyperplastic with papillary projections. Since the disease is focal, liver biopsy may show normal liver tissue or simply the classic changes of biliary obstruction. *(H.&.E×16)*

481 Caroli's disease and congenital hepatic fibrosis.
This endoscopic cholangiogram shows the bulbous dilatations of the intrahepatic bile ducts that are typical of Caroli's disease (arrowed). In addition this patient had congenital hepatic fibrosis, as do approximately half the patients with Caroli's disease. These patients have a characteristic clinical presentation. They are usually male and first present in childhood with variceal haemorrhage from the portal hypertension caused by congenital hepatic fibrosis. In early adult life they then develop recurrent bouts of cholangitis due to infection of the Caroli's disease.

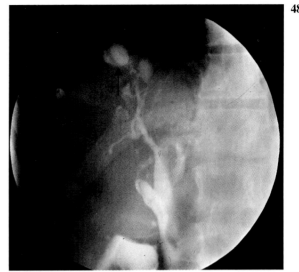

481

482 Caroli's disease and congenital hepatic fibrosis. Liver biopsy shows a combination of the changes of congenital hepatic fibrosis and Caroli's disease. Normal liver lobules are encased by broad collagenous fibrous bands. The fibrous bands contain cavernous ectatic bile ducts containing pus cells due to cholangitis. *(H.&.E×40)*

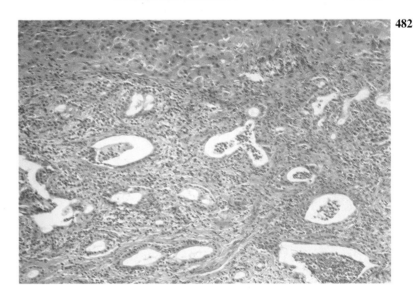

482

483 Choledochal cyst is a congenital dilatation of part or whole of the common bile duct. It is more common in girls and usually appears in childhood, but may present in early adulthood. Choledochal cysts classically cause a triad of intermittent pain, jaundice and a right hypochondrial mass. Choledochal cysts seem to be particularly common in Japanese and other oriental races. This 22-year-old woman presented with cholestatic (biliary obstructive) jaundice and an enlarged liver. An endoscopic cholangiogram shows a very large diverticulum of the common bile duct (arrowed) containing stones. This is a type II choledochal cyst. A nasobiliary tube has been inserted to provide biliary drainage.

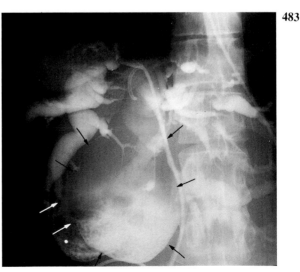

483

484

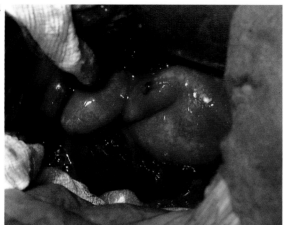

484 Choledochal cyst. At laparotomy in the patient shown in **483** the cystic common bile duct can be seen. Because of the risk of the development of adenocarcinoma or squamous cell carcinoma in choledochal cysts, excision is the treatment of choice. However the technical difficulty of excision is great and postoperative biliary stricture may follow.

485

485 Choledochal cyst. Black pigment gallstones commonly develop in choledochal cysts and cause biliary obstruction or pancreatitis. These stones were removed from the bile duct of the patient shown in **483**.

486

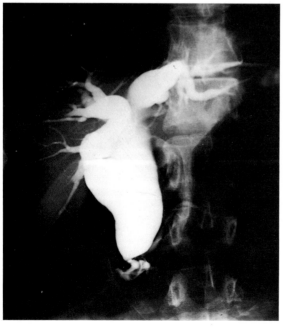

486 Choledochal cyst. This 20-year-old woman presented with recurrent acute pancreatitis due to stones in the cyst obstructing the pancreatic duct. She was never jaundiced. The endoscopic cholangiogram showed a massively dilated common bile duct. The gallbladder was normal, but obscured by the dilated bile duct. This is a type I choledochal cyst.

487 Microhamartoma (Von Meyenberg complexes). These are normally asymptomatic and diagnosed incidentally. Other fibropolycystic diseases may be associated. Rarely microhamartomas may be associated with portal hypertension. Histologically, microhamartomas consist of groups of rounded biliary channels lined by cuboidal epithelium and often containing inspissated bile. The biliary structures are embedded in a mature collagenous stroma. Microhamartomas are usually located in or near portal tracts. The appearances are often similar to congenital hepatic fibrosis, but in a localized form. *(H.&.E×40)*

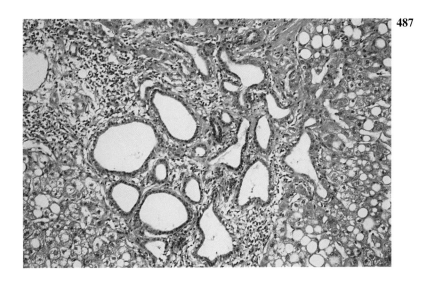

487

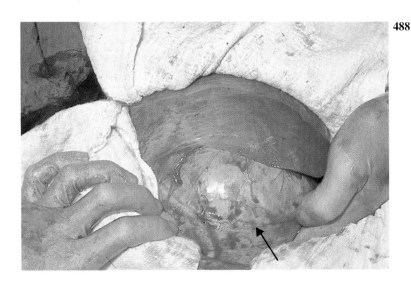

488

488 Solitary liver cyst. These are rare, presenting with abdominal distension, hepatomegaly or pressure effects on adjacent organs. They usually develop on the antero-inferior surface of the liver, as in this patient with a very large cyst weighing 4.5kg (arrowed). The cyst is multiloculated and contains a clear or brown-coloured fluid.

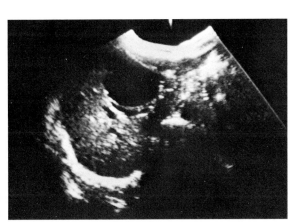

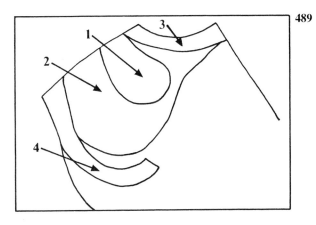

489

489 Solitary liver cyst. This patient presented with hepatomegaly. Grey-scale ultrasonography showed a solitary cyst (1) in the right lobe of the liver (2) under the anterior abdominal wall (3). The diaphragm is also shown (4). (Scanned 14cm above the umbilicus.)

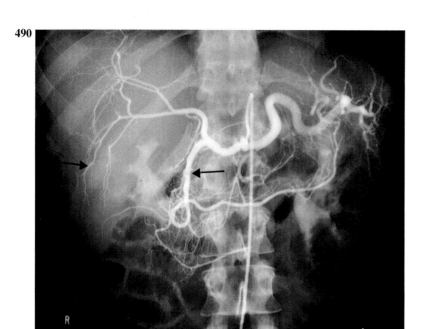

490 Solitary liver cyst. A selective coeliac axis arteriogram showed displacement and stretching of the intrahepatic vessels (arrowed) by the cyst shown in **489**.

11. *Tumours of the liver and biliary system*

Primary hepato-cellular carcinoma

The incidence of primary liver cancer shows wide geographical variations. It is a common cancer in Africa and south east Asia but rare in temperate climates. Predisposing factors include cirrhosis, type B and type C viral hepatitis, haemochromatosis and androgenic steroids, such as methyltestosterone and oxymethalone. Food carcinogens, such as aflatoxin, may be important in some areas.

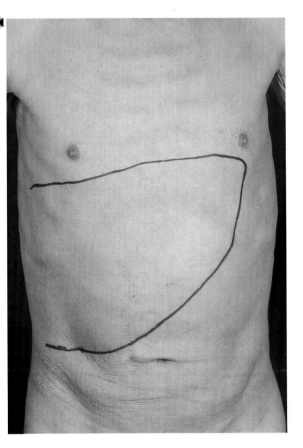 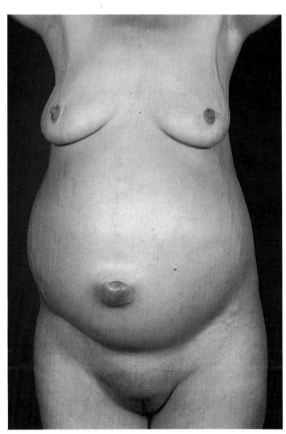

492

491 Primary liver cancer. This patient, with alcoholic cirrhosis, had stopped taking alcohol several years before. He presented with abdominal pain due to a rapidly enlarging liver. A primary liver cancer was present in the right lobe. Note the scanty body hair and muscle wasting.

492 Primary liver cancer may cause sudden clinical deterioration in a cirrhotic patient. The appearance of ascites in this woman with well compensated inactive cirrhosis heralded the diagnosis of a primary liver cancer. Note the scanty body hair, everted umbilicus and abdominal wall veins.

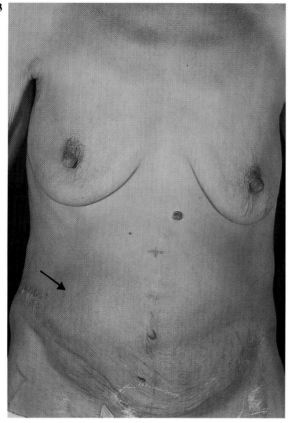

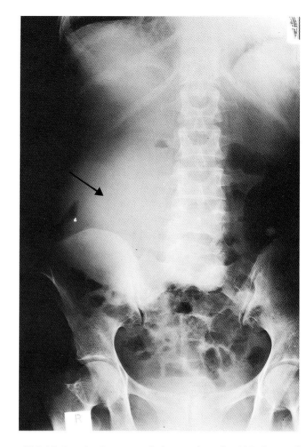

493 Primary liver cancer in a 40-year-old Arab woman presented as a mass in the right hypochondrium (arrowed). She had chronic type B viral hepatitis. An arterial bruit could be heard over the mass.

494 Abdominal x-ray of the patient in **493** showed a huge liver with a large round mass in the right lobe (arrowed).

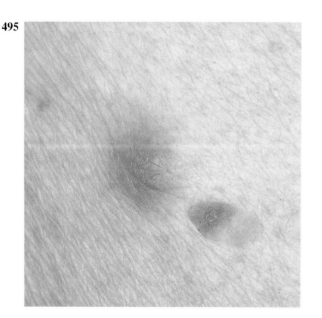

495 Primary liver cancer. Percutaneous biopsy of a primary liver cancer may result in seedling deposits developing along the biopsy track. In this patient the red skin nodule is a deposit of liver cancer at the site of a liver biopsy.

496 Primary liver cancer may rarely calcify. This abdominal x-ray shows 'sun burst' calcification in a primary liver cancer.

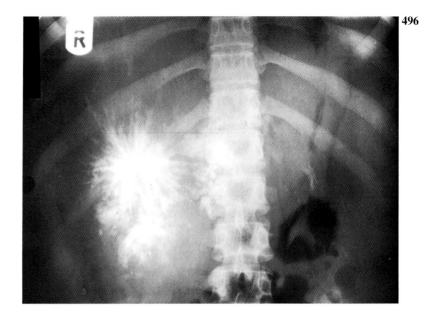

497

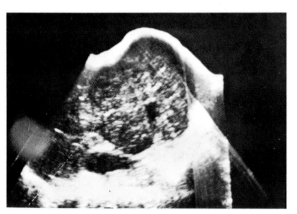

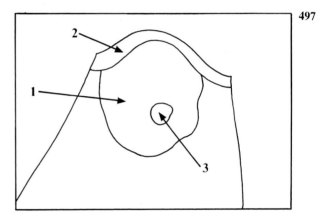

497 Grey-scale ultrasonography of the patient in **493** showed a large round primary liver cancer (1) pushing out the anterior abdominal wall (2). The cavity (3) in the centre of the tumour is due to necrosis. (Sagittal scan 6.5cm right of the umbilicus.)

498 Ultrasound is a powerful non-invasive technique for the early diagnosis of liver cancer. This small (2cm) lesion (crosses) was detected by ultrasound at a routine examination in a symptomless hepatitis B positive Chinese man aged 50 years.

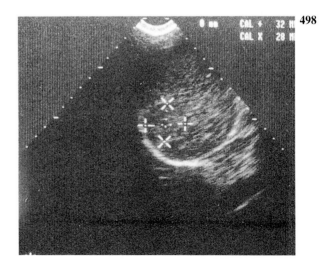

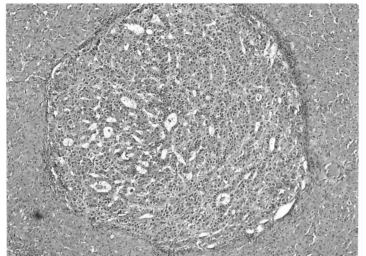

499 Primary liver cancer. The small space-occupying lesion detected by ultrasound examination in the patient shown in **498** was resected. Operative specimen confirmed that the lesion was primary hepato-cellular cancer. *(H.&E.×60)*

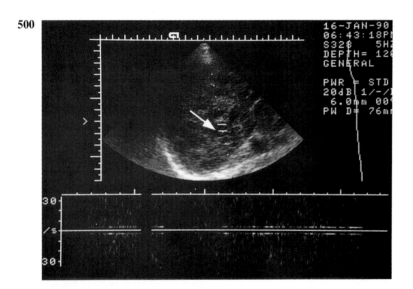

500

500 Doppler ultrasound can detect small primary liver cancers in a cirrhotic liver by their arterial supply. This cirrhotic patient had a rising serum alpha-fetoprotein level. The ultrasound scan showed a homogenous liver. Insonating the area arrowed gives a Doppler signal (lowest line) which is typical of low blood flow in a cirrhotic liver.

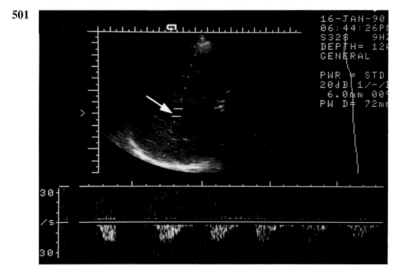

501

501 Doppler ultrasound. Insonating another part of the liver (arrowed) shows a strong Doppler signal indicating arterial blood flow (lowest line). This signal indicates a primary liver cancer.

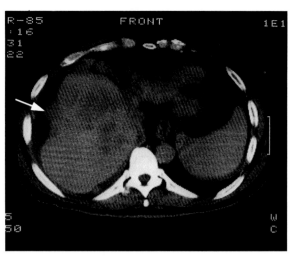

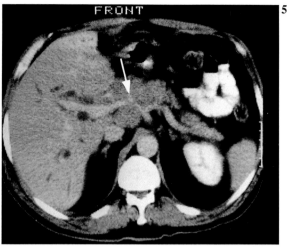

502 Primary liver cancer. CT scans are helpful in determining whether these tumours are operable. In assessing operability a liver biopsy is also necessary to determine whether the remainder of the liver is cirrhotic. This CT scan shows multi-focal space-occupying lesions in the right lobe of the liver. One tumour nodule is bursting through the capsule (arrowed). This patient developed bloody ascites and was dead within one week.

503 Primary liver cancer. Contrast enhanced CT shows encasement of the contrast-filled hepatic artery by the tumour (arrow). This is a contra-indication to resection or transplantation.

504 Coeliac axis arteriography is valuable in the diagnosis of these vascular cancers. The intrahepatic arteries are displaced and stretched (1) around the tumour. The vessels inside the tumour are irregular and fragmented (2). In contrast, secondary malignant deposits in the liver tend to be avascular. This is the arteriogram of the patient in **493.**

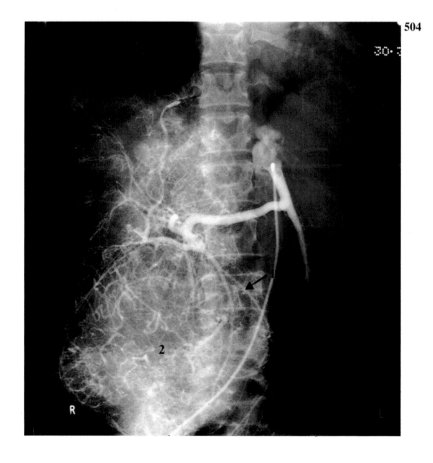

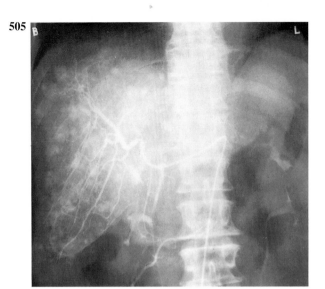

505 Primary liver cancer is often multifocal. This coeliac axis arteriogram shows multiple deposits of primary liver cancer as discrete pools of contrast medium throughout the liver.

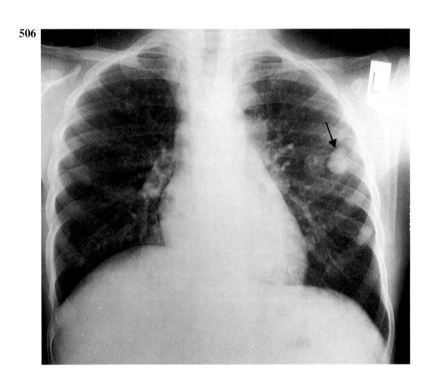

506 Primary liver cancer metastases caused the round shadows in the lungs of this six-year-old girl. Other sites for metastases are the supraclavicular fossae, bones and brain. The enlarged liver has elevated the right hemidiaphragm.

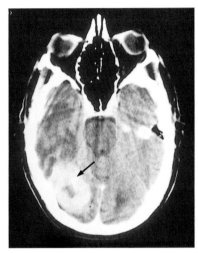

507 Primary liver cancer can be widely disseminated. In this patient a brain CT shows secondary deposits. A large occipital mass is arrowed.

508 Primary liver cancer has a predeliction for invading the portal vein. This patient with primary liver cancer had a variceal haemorrhage. The portal venogram showed deposits of liver cancer in the portal vein (1). Also shown are oesophageal varices (2) being fed by short gastric veins.

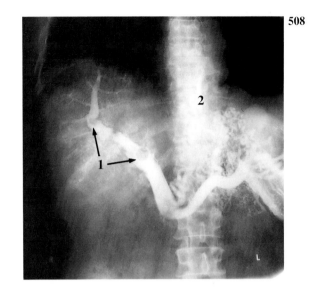

509 Primary liver cancer. This cirrhotic liver contained a large tumour (1) in the right lobe. The portal vein was thrombosed (2).

510 Primary liver cancer. A close-up view of the liver in **509** shows thrombus occluding the portal vein (arrowed). The surrounding liver is studded with pale nodules of primary liver cancer. Some of the nodules are haemorrhagic and necrotic. Portal vein thrombosis followed invasion of the portal vein by the tumour.

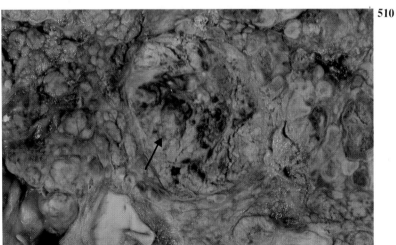

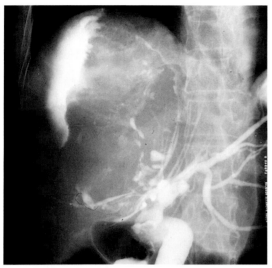

511 Primary liver cancer. An endoscopic cholangiogram in this patient shows a primary liver cancer displacing and invading the biliary system. Intrahepatic bile ducts are stretched around the tumour and the pooling of contrast medium along the margin of the tumour indicates that some bile ducts have been invaded.

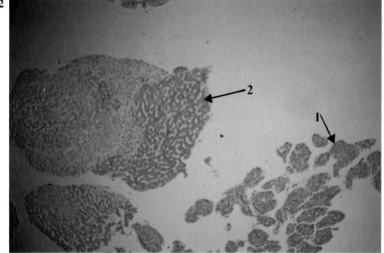

512 Liver biopsy in this patient yielded fragments of primary liver cancer (1) and nodules of cirrhotic liver (2). Fragmented biopsies are commonly encountered in cirrhotic patients. *(Best's carmine×50)*

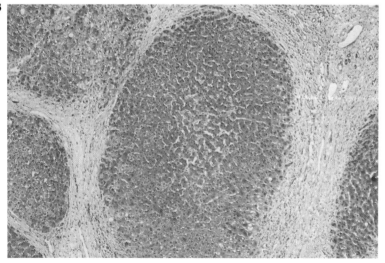

513 Primary liver cancer usually develops in an inactive cirrhosis. In another part of this cirrhotic liver, the tumour illustrated in **514** was found. *(H.&E.×40)*

514 Primary liver cancer cells resemble normal liver cells to a varying extent depending on the differentiation of the tumour. A higher magnification shows the tumour cells to be smaller than normal with large hyperchromatic nuclei. Mitoses are prominent. Some of the cells form pseudo-tubules. Between the cells are large blood-filled spaces, but little intercellular stroma. *(H.&E.×64)*

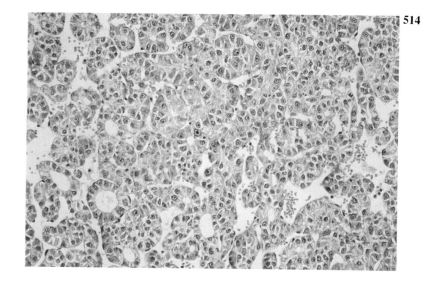

514

Adenomas of the liver

515 Liver adenomas are very rare tumours. In some patients there appears to be an association with oral contraceptive drugs. This 33-year-old American woman had taken oral contraceptives for 5 years when she developed pain and swelling in the right hypochondrium. Liver adenomas may rupture causing massive intraperitoneal haemorrhage.

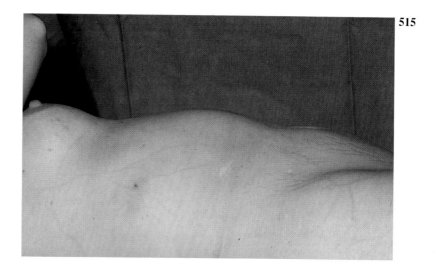

515

516 Computerized tomography of the abdomen of the patient in **515** showed a large lobulated tumour (arrowed) in the right lobe of the liver.

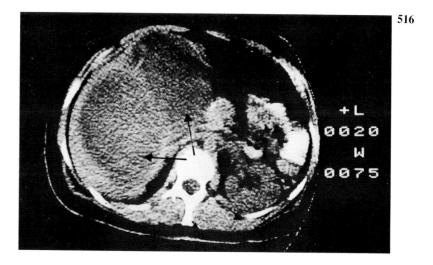

516

517

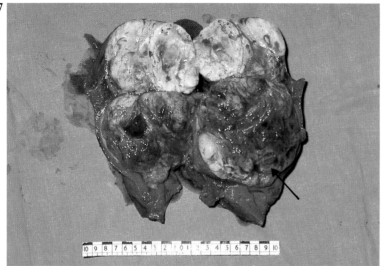

517 Liver adenoma removed surgically from the patient in **515**. Note the white lobulated tumour. Haemorrhage into one of the nodules (arrowed) has formed a blood-filled cavity.

518

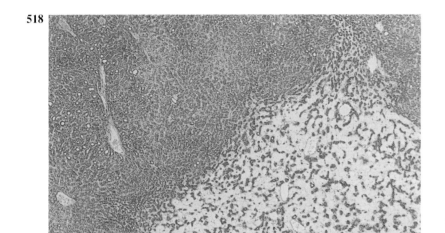

518 Liver adenomas. The liver cells and bile ducts appear normal but are not organized to form lobules. Note the necrotic centre (arrowed) of this tumour. *(H.& E.×10)*.

519

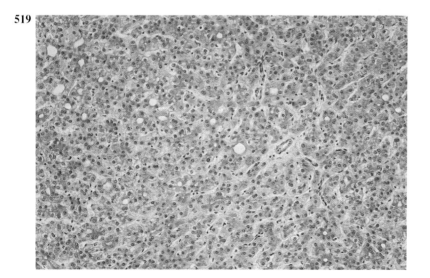

519 Liver adenoma. A higher magnification shows the normal liver cells but no normal liver lobules, i.e. absence of portal tracts. *(H.&E.×40)*

520 Peliosis hepatis may develop in a liver adenoma (1) causing large blood-filled spaces (2). A fibrous capsule (3) surrounds the adenoma separating it from the normal liver (4). This adenoma was associated with the oral contraceptive pill. *(H.&E.×10)*

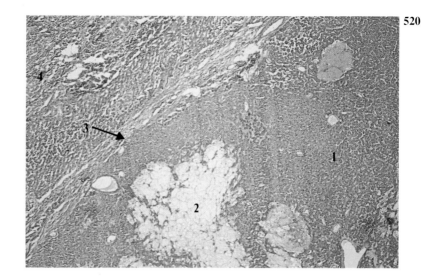

521 Focal nodular hyperplasia are firm solitary areas of liver usually found in women. They are commonly subcapsular. Fibrous septa radiate from a central core. Focal nodular hyperplasia must be distinguished from a liver adenoma. *(Picro-Mallory)*

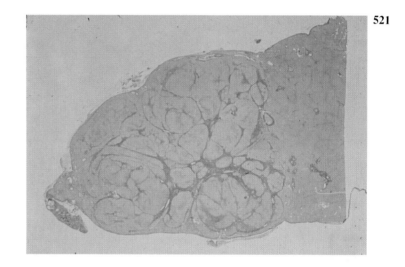

522 Focal nodular hyperplasia. A liver biopsy shows an encapsulated area of nodular hyperplasia containing prominent hyperplastic blood vessels and bile ducts. A focal stellate scar is arrowed. *(H.&E.×40)*

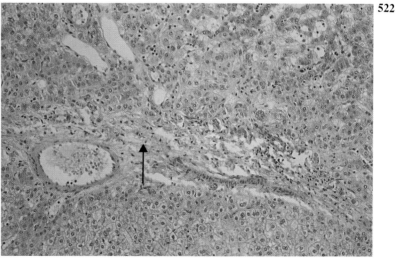

197

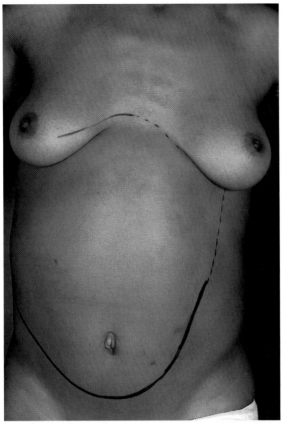

523 Cystadenomas of the liver are very rare tumours, derived either from bile duct cells (cholangioma) or both bile duct and hepatic cells (mixed tumours). Cystadenomas are multiloculated and may grow very large, as in this patient. They must be distinguished from fibropolycystic disease and solitary cysts of the liver.

524 Cystadenoma of the liver. A percutaneous catheter introduced into the cyst drained a greeny-brown fluid.

525

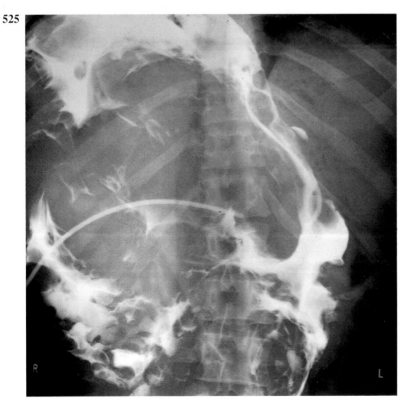

525 Cystadenoma of the liver. Contrast medium injected through the catheter shows the extent of this multiloculated cystic tumour.

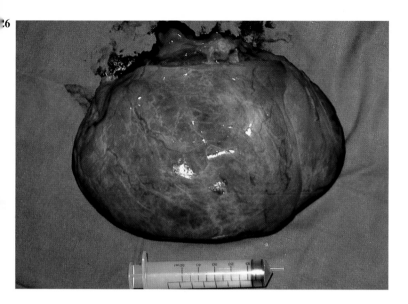

526 Cystadenoma of the liver. After drainage of the cyst, a large tumour was removed from the patient in **523**.

Tumours of blood vessels in the liver

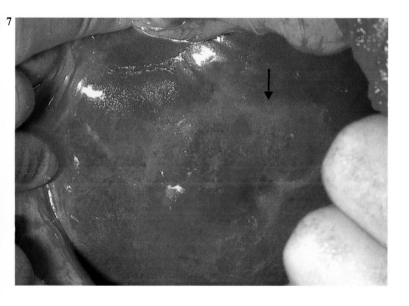

527 Haemangiomas are rare and often incidental findings at autopsy. Rarely they may cause hepatomegaly. Spontaneous rupture can occur. Haemangiomas of the liver usually appear as dark red subcapsular tumours on the convexity of the right lobe (arrowed).

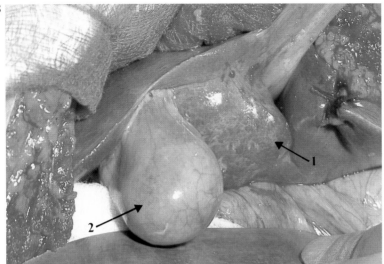

528 Haemangioma. On the inferior surface of the liver shown in **527** a pedunculated haemangioma (1) had developed adjacent to the gall bladder (2).

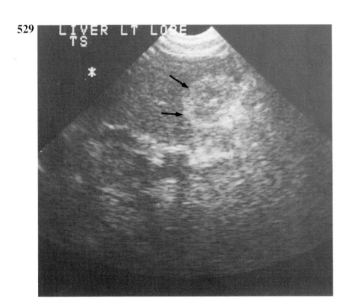

529 Haemangioma. Ultrasound shows well-defined echogenic masses (arrowed). However liver metastases may give similar appearances.

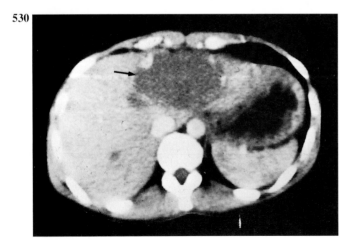

530 Haemangioma. Intravenous contrast enhanced CT scan shows a space-occupying lesion anteriorly (arrowed). Pools of contrast are present at the periphery of the lesion. In delayed films, the lesions fill in completely with contrast. These are characteristic CT features of haemangiomas.

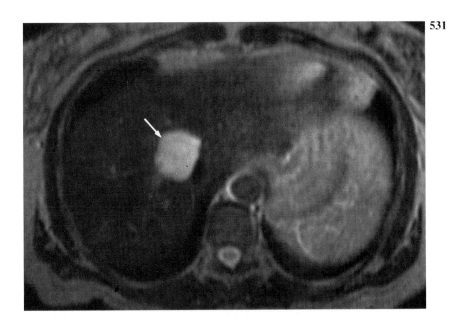

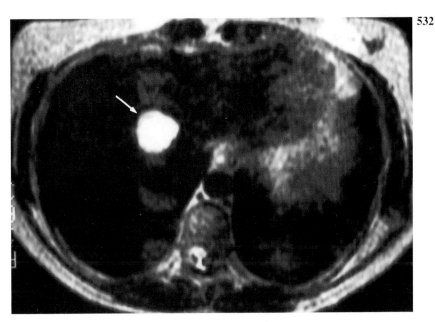

531,532 Haemangioma. Magnetic resonance imaging (MRI) will show characteristic features in haemangiomas without intravenous contrast. A T_2 weighted scan **531** shows a high signal lesion (arrowed) which in **532** becomes very bright (arrowed) when the patient is scanned with a longer TE time (echo time). These findings will occur in any lesion with a profuse and very sluggish blood circulation, but usually indicate a haemangioma.

533

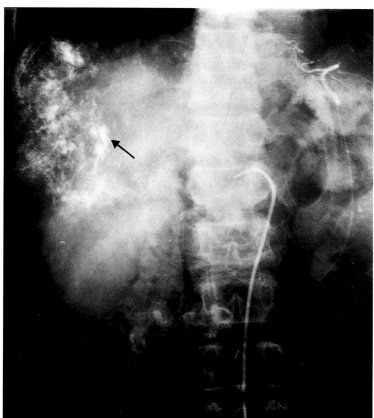

533 Haemangiomas in the liver are well demonstrated by selective coeliac axis arteriography. The vascular spaces of the haemangioma (arrowed) fill with contrast and remain opacified for a prolonged period after the injection.

534

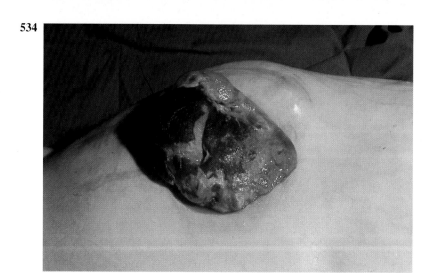

534 Haemangiosarcoma is a very rare and highly malignant tumour usually developing in childhood. The liver rapidly enlarges with nodular, cavernous growths. Bloodstained ascites usually develop. A vascular bruit may be heard over the liver. In this patient the dark vascular tumour had penetrated through the anterior abdominal wall. Exposure to *thorotrast* and *vinyl chloride monomers* have been associated with the development of haemangiosarcoma.

535 Haemangiosarcoma. A CT scan of the liver shows the multifocal nodular growths (arrowed) that develop with this tumour.

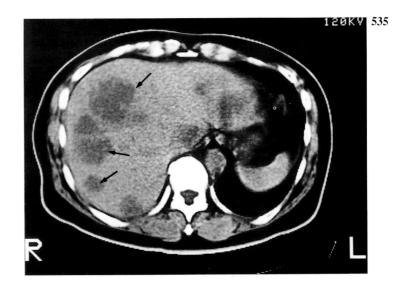

536 Haemangiosarcoma. A liver biopsy shows blood-filled spaces lined by layers of highly malignant anaplastic endothelial cells. (H.&E.×40)

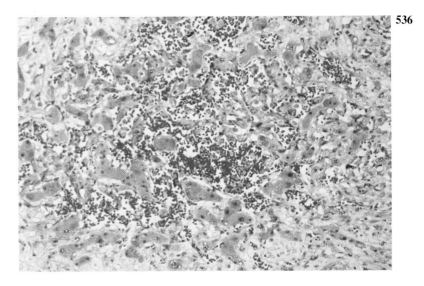

537 Thorotrast, a colloidal solution of the radioactive isotope thorium dioxide, was formerly used as a contrast agent in radiology. Thorotrast (arrowed) accumulates in the liver. Years later malignant tumours may develop including primary liver cancer, bile duct cancer and haemangiosarcoma. Thorotrast may also cause cirrhosis.

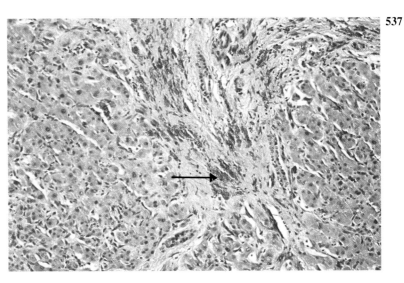

Secondary tumours of the liver

The liver is the commonest site for metastases from malignant tumours. Metastases usually spread to the liver via the blood. Deposits from cancer of the lung, breast, colon, stomach and pancreas are most frequently encountered.

538

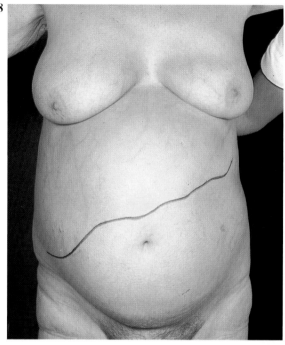

538 Secondary cancer of the liver usually presents with a very hard enlarged liver. This patient had metastases from carcinoma of stomach. The liver may become enormous, reaching the iliac crest. The liver surface often feels irregular. Patients frequently complain of fullness and swelling in the abdomen and a dragging sensation. General clinical deterioration and muscle wasting are usually rapid.

539

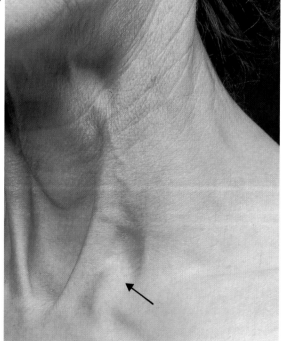

539 Secondary cancer. Metastatic deposits should be sought in other sites. In this patient, with carcinoma of the stomach, metastases (arrowed) were present in the lymph nodes of the left supraclavicular fossa (Virchow's node).

540 Secondary cancer. A metastasis from cancer of the pancreas in the umbilicus of this patient caused the painless, purple swelling.

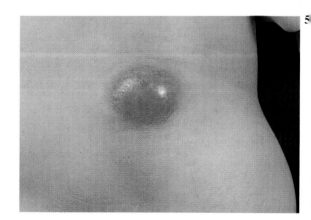

541 Secondary cancer. A ^{99}technetium isotope scan shows multiple filling defects in the liver. The primary tumour was cancer of the colon.

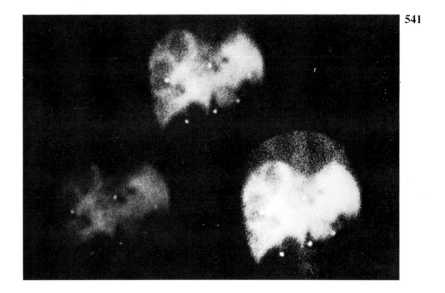

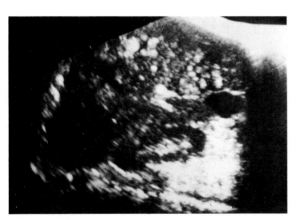
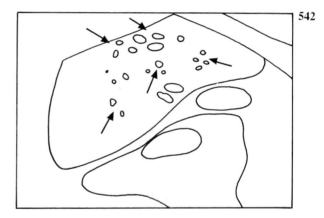

542 Secondary cancer. Grey-scale ultrasonography demonstrated multiple nodules (arrowed) in the liver of this patient. These were metastases from cancer of the pancreas.

543 Metastatic hepatic tumours. A CT scan from this jaundiced patient with secondary tumour from a primary colon cancer shows multiple space-occupying lesions (arrowed) throughout the liver.

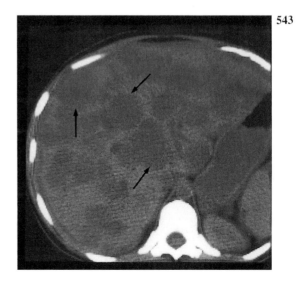

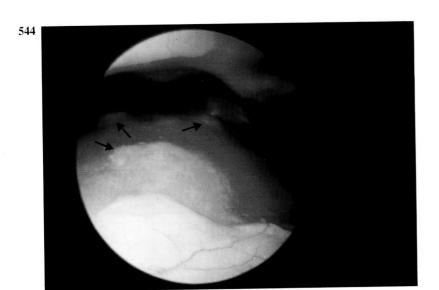

544 Secondary cancer. Laparoscopy in this patient showed the liver surface studded with metastases (arrowed). The primary tumour was cancer of the pancreas. This technique permits direct biopsy of the nodules.

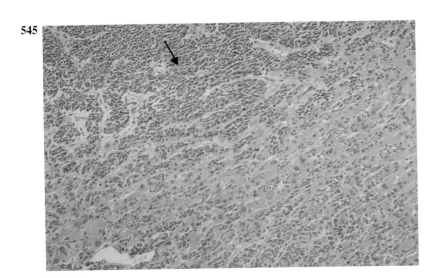

545 Secondary cancer. A percutaneous liver biopsy often reveals metastases in the liver. This patient presented with hepatomegaly. The liver biopsy showed a metastasis from a bronchial carcinoma (arrowed). Sheets of small dark malignant cells are invading the pale pink liver tissue. The primary tumour was not visible on a chest x-ray. *(H.&E.×40)*

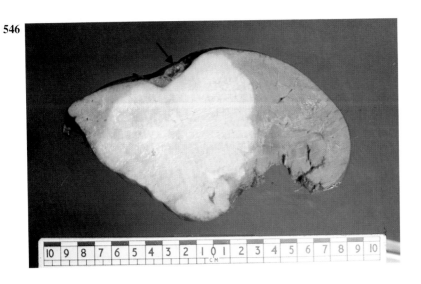

546 Secondary cancer. A large pale metastasis from adenocarcinoma of the colon is present in this section of the liver. The surface of the liver is umbilicated (arrowed). This is due to necrosis and subsequent shrinkage of the metastasis.

547 Carcinoid syndrome. Liver metastases from a gastrointestinal carcinoid tumour caused flushing attacks in this woman. Note the violaceous colour of her cheeks. The remainder of her face and the necklace area are also flushed. Diarrhoea and valvular lesions of the heart may develop. The primary tumour is usually found in the appendix, ileum or jejunum. Symptoms only develop when liver metastases are present.

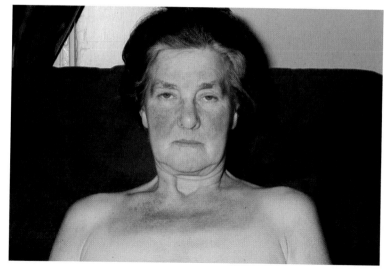

547

548 Carcinoid syndrome. In the venous phase of a coeliac axis arteriogram from the patient in **547**, the circular blushes (arrowed) are carcinoid metastases. Endocrine tumour metastases typically cause marked venous blushing.

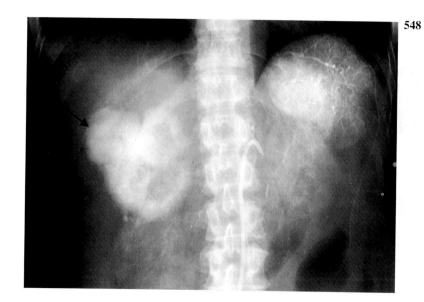

548

549 Carcinoid tumour metastases are the pale deposits in the liver of the patient shown in **547**.

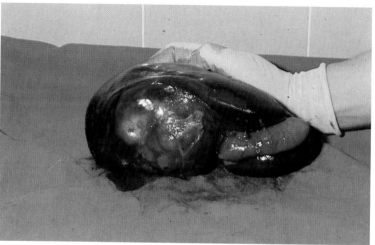

549

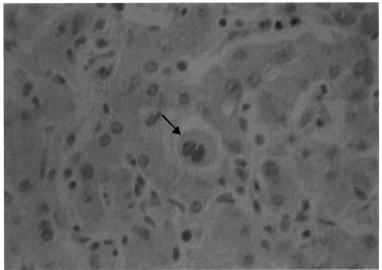

550 Myeloid metaplasia in the liver may follow irritation or replacement of the bone marrow by secondary carcinoma. It also develops in myelosclerosis, multiple myeloma and marble bone disease (Albers–Schönberg disease). A leuco-erythroblastic anaemia is commonly present. Liver biopsy shows increased cellularity in the sinusoids and portal tracts. These contain a variety of cells at different stages of maturation, including giant cells (arrowed) which resemble megakaryocytes. *(H.&E.×175)*

Tumours affecting the biliary system

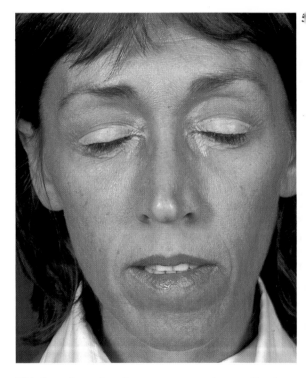

551 Carcinoma of the intrahepatic bile ducts usually affects older people and causes a cholestatic (obstructive type) jaundice. The level of icterus may fluctuate but eventually the patient becomes deeply jaundiced. Hepatomegaly is usual but the extra-hepatic biliary tree and gall bladder are collapsed. The serum bilirubin level in this patient was 35mg/100ml (595μmol/l).

552 Intrahepatic bile duct cancer is usually slow growing and patients may survive for years. This patient had been jaundiced for five years. The xanthelasmas around her eyes are the result of prolonged cholestasis.

553 Intrahepatic bile duct cancer. Ultrasound scan will often demonstrate the tumour. In this scan a bile duct cancer (between the marker crosses) of 1.62cm diameter is present at the hilum of the liver, obstructing the common bile duct (arrowed).

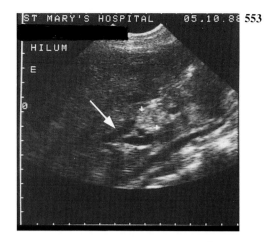

554 Intrahepatic bile duct cancer. An endoscopic retrograde cholangiogram may only fill the biliary system below the stricture. The common bile duct (1) is of normal calibre and terminates bluntly at the porta hepatis (2). The gall bladder (3) is not dilated. The pancreatic duct (4) has also been filled.

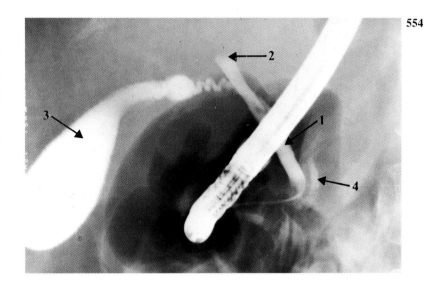

555 Intrahepatic bile duct cancer. A percutaneous cholangiogram from the patient in **554** shows a grossly dilated intrahepatic biliary tree above the malignant stricture (arrow).

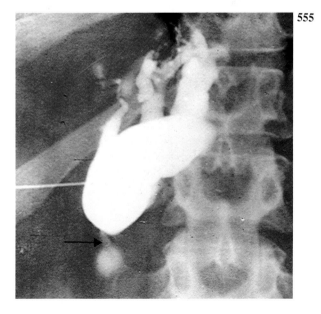

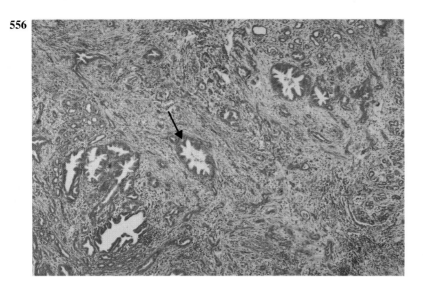

556 Intrahepatic bile duct cancers are usually firm, fibrous tumours. The malignant cells are arranged into tubules resembling bile ducts (arrowed) and are surrounded by dense fibrous tissue. Histologically, the tumours are scirrhous, mucus-secreting adenocarcinomas. *(H.&E.×13)*

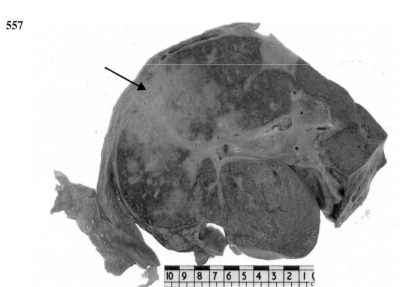

557 Intrahepatic bile duct cancer (arrowed) has spread along the bile ducts and into the liver parenchyma. This patient had survived for seven years. Note the dark green, nodular liver. Secondary biliary cirrhosis had developed.

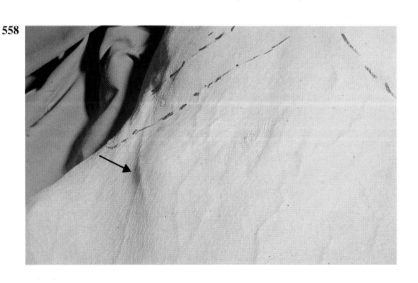

558 Cancer of the pancreas is a common tumour usually affecting the middle aged and elderly. Cancer of the head of the pancreas may obstruct the lower end of the common bile duct. A cholestatic (obstructive type) jaundice results. Prominent symptoms are jaundice, weight loss and dull abdominal pain. Hepatomegaly is usual. The extrahepatic biliary tree is dilated and in some patients the gall bladder (arrowed) is palpable or even visible (Courvoisier's law).

559 Cancer of the pancreas. Ultrasound scan shows a dilated common bile duct (1) obstructed at its lower end by a large pancreatic mass (2).

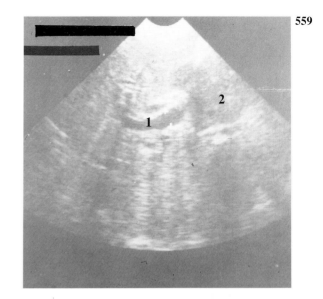

561

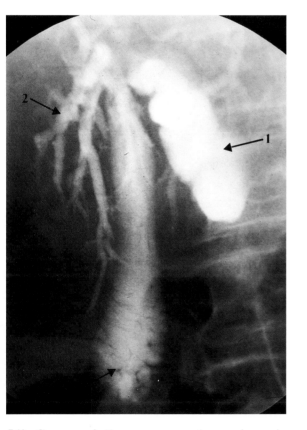

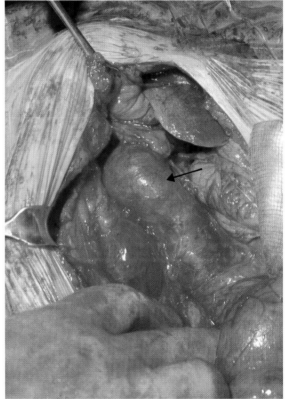

560 Cancer of the pancreas. An endoscopic retrograde cholangiogram reveals a grossly dilated common bile duct (1), intrahepatic biliary tree (2) and gall bladder (3). Note the blunt termination at the lower end of the bile duct caused by the pancreatic cancer. The prominent mucosal folds of the gall bladder are caused by oedema.

561 Cancer of the pancreas obstructing the lower end of the common bile duct caused this massive dilatation (arrowed).

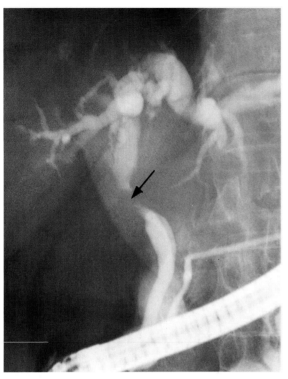

562

562 Carcinoma of the gall bladder. Gall bladder cancer is rare and pre-operative diagnosis is difficult. This endoscopic cholangiogram shows the characteristic changes in a patient who presented with obstructive jaundice. There is a tight stricture (arrowed) in the mid common bile duct and the intrahepatic ducts are dilated. Significantly the gall bladder does not fill with contrast because it is replaced by tumour.

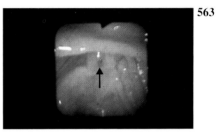

563

563 Ampulla of Vater (arrowed) is a nipple-like projection usually situated in the second part of the duodenum. The common bile duct and pancreatic duct drain via the ampulla of Vater into the duodenum. In this endoscopic picture bile is escaping from the ostium of the ampulla. A transverse fold of duodenal mucosa lies above it.

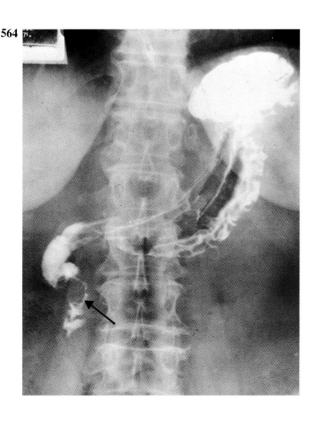

564

564 Cancer of the ampulla of Vater is an uncommon cause of common bile duct obstruction. Jaundice may be mild and intermittent. The tumour may bleed into the gastrointestinal tract causing anaemia and a 'silver' stool. This barium meal examination shows a filling defect (arrowed) in the second part of the duodenum caused by cancer of the ampulla of Vater.

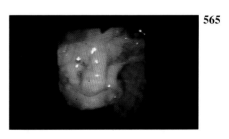

565

565 Cancer of the ampulla of Vater. The ampulla is usually enlarged with a necrotic surface which bleeds readily. This endoscopic picture shows a pale green slough covering an ampullary cancer. A cannula easily passed through this necrotic tissue to enter the common bile duct (**566**).

566 Cancer of the ampulla of Vater. An endoscopic retrograde cholangiogram from the patient illustrated in **565** shows a very dilated common bile duct (1) and intrahepatic biliary tree (2). Note the rounded obstruction (3) at the lower end of the common bile duct, due to the ampullary cancer.

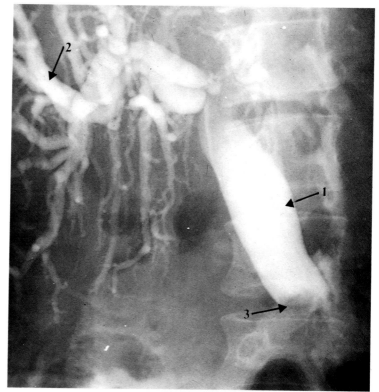

566

567 Pancreatic pseudocyst may obstruct the common bile duct. The appearance may be confused with a malignant bile duct stricture. However, extrinsic compression by a cyst (1) causes stretching and displacement of the common bile duct (2). The intrahepatic bile ducts are dilated (3).

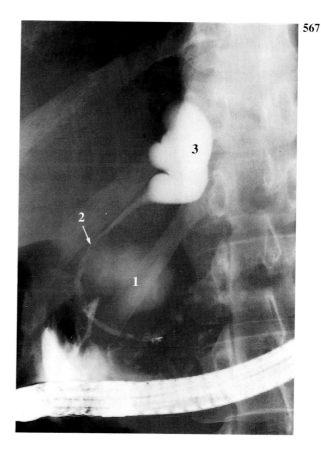

567

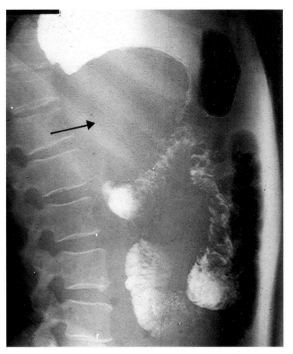

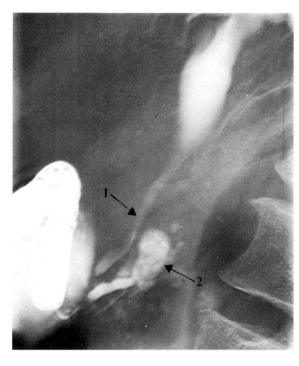

568 Pancreatic pseudocyst (arrowed) is revealed as a large retrogastric mass pushing the stomach forward in this barium meal examination.

569 Chronic pancreatitis may lead to a stricture of the lower end of the common bile duct and cholestasis. In contrast to a malignant obstruction, this stricture (1) is long and smoothly tapering. A short length of the pancreatic duct filled before the contrast entered a small pancreatic cyst (2). This x-ray of an endoscopic retrograde cholangiopancreatogram was taken in the lateral projection.

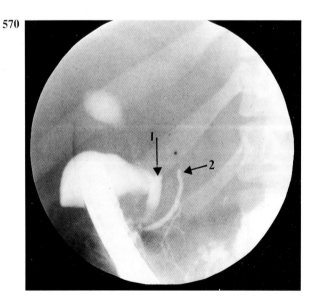

570 Hodgkin's disease may rarely involve the main bile ducts and cause jaundice. This endoscopic retrograde cholangiogram shows obstruction of both the common bile duct (1) and pancreatic duct (2) by Hodgkin's deposits. Other causes of jaundice in Hodgkin's disease include haemolysis and an obscure intrahepatic cholestasis.

Non-operative treatment of biliary tumours

Prostheses (stents) are used to relieve biliary obstruction caused by benign and malignant biliary strictures. Stents may be inserted endoscopically or by a percutaneous transhepatic approach. Endoscopic prostheses (endoprostheses) are preferred to percutaneous prostheses because their insertion carries a lower morbidity. In patients where it is not possible to insert an endoprosthesis a percutaneous prosthesis is used. Endoprostheses are as effective as bypass surgery in the relief of malignant biliary obstruction, but have lower morbidity and mortality rates. The prognosis is similar after either procedure. To facilitate insertion, a guide wire and catheter are passed through the biliary stricture, the endoprosthesis being passed into position along these. If the bile duct stricture cannot be cannulated endoscopically a combined approach is employed. Here the stricture is first cannulated during a percutaneous transhepatic cholangiogram by a guide wire, which is passed through the ampulla of Vater. The endoprosthesis is inserted endoscopically across the percutaneous guide wire. A combined approach exploits the ability of percutaneous cholangiography to pass guide wires through tight strictures, but avoids the morbidity associated with passing wide-bored prostheses through the liver.

Endoprostheses tend to block about every three months. The onset of cholangitis or jaundice indicates blockage of an endoprosthesis. Replacement is usually straightforward. Endoprostheses will also provide useful symptomatic relief in patients unfit for surgery who have multiple bile duct stones that cannot be removed by endoscopic sphincterotomy.

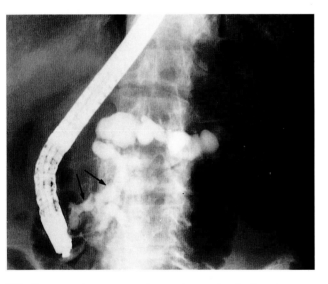

571 Pancreatic cancer. An endoscopic cholangiogram in this deeply jaundiced 73-year-old man shows a long stricture (arrowed) in the head of the pancreas. The distal pancreatic duct is dilated. The changes are typical of carcinoma of the pancreas.

572

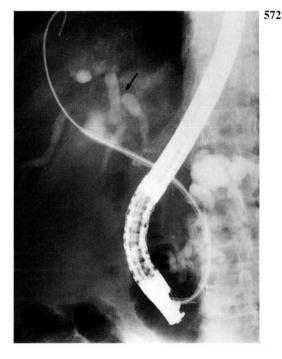

572 Pancreatic cancer. The cholangiogram in the patient shown in **571** reveals a dilated biliary tree (arrowed), caused by the pancreatic cancer obstructing the lower end of the common bile duct. A guide wire and catheter have been passed endoscopically through the stricture.

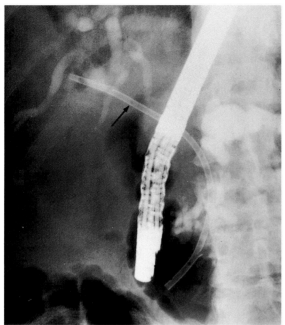

573 Biliary endoprosthesis. An endoprosthesis (arrowed) has been passed across the guide wire and catheter and through the stricture. The guide wire and catheter have been pulled back through the endoscope, leaving the endoprosthesis straddling the stricture. Bile flowed freely through the endoprosthesis and the patient's jaundice rapidly disappeared.

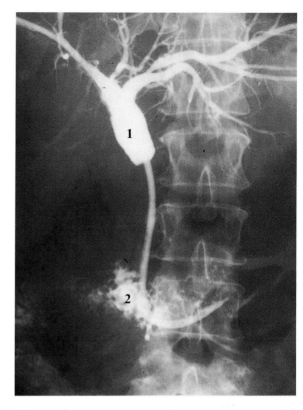

574 Percutaneous stent. In this patient with cancer of the pancreas obstructing the common bile duct (1) a Carey–Coons catheter has been passed through the malignant stricture across a percutaneous transhepatic guide wire. The catheter tip is placed in the duodenum (2) to permit endoscopic removal when it becomes blocked.

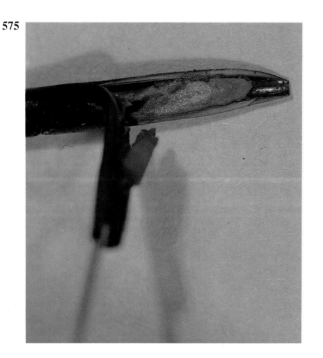

575 Endoprosthesis blockage. This endoprosthesis became blocked after four months. The patient presented with cholangitis. The lumen contains a yellow material which is composed of bilirubin and calcium salts deposited on a bacterial biofilm lining the walls of the prosthesis.

12. Liver transplantation

The complications following liver transplantation can be classified into problems affecting the liver, and problems with the bile ducts and infections. The clinical features of these complications are very similar and their diagnosis requires specialist investigations such as ultrasound and CT scanning, angiography, cholangiography and liver biopsy.

In the first five days the main problems are graft ischaemia and liver infarction. Both of these complications require re-transplantation. Graft ischaemia (or 'reperfusion injury') arises from poor graft preservation and is marked by elevated transaminases, deepening jaundice and scanty bile output.

Liver infarction results from hepatic artery thrombosis and is heralded by clinical deterioration, fever and elevated transaminases. The most serious consequence of hepatic artery thrombosis is infarction of the gall bladder and bile ducts. After five days acute cellular rejection may develop. The liver function tests deteriorate and the patient may feel unwell with a fever. Six weeks post-transplant, chronic rejection may develop in which the bile ducts are progressively damaged and ultimately disappear. Liver function tests show a steadily deteriorating cholestatic (biliary obstructive) pattern.

Each patient will have a mean of 2.5 infections after the transplant. These infections may be primary (e.g. bacteraemia and septicaemia), reactivation (e.g. hepatitis B or hepatitis C) or opportunistic due to the immunosuppression. Opportunistic infections may be due to *cytomegalovirus* (CMV), *Herpes simplex* virus, Epstein–Barr virus or fungi such as *Candida*, *Aspergillus* and *Cryptococcus*. Bile duct problems following liver transplantation fall into three types. In the immediate post-operative period, bile leaks may occur due to a faulty anastomosis. In the first two weeks, cholangitis and biliary obstruction are usually due to biliary sludge. After two months, cholangitis and biliary obstruction are usually due to biliary strictures at the site of the anastomosis. The biliary strictures are caused by a combination of an impaired arterial blood supply and chronic rejection directed against the biliary epithelium.

576 Graft ischaemia. This is also called 'reperfusion injury'. This biopsy is from a 39-year-old male two days post-transplant. The biopsy shows swelling of hepatocytes and rarefaction of the cytoplasm. These grafts have a poor prognosis. *(H.&E.×350)*

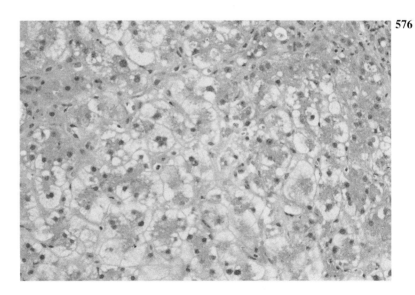
576

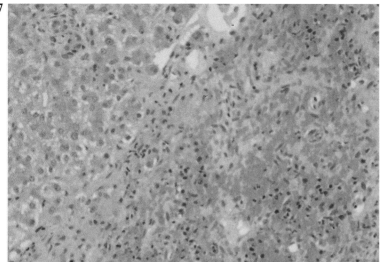

577 Liver infarction. This liver biopsy comes from a 36-year-old female who developed an hepatic artery thrombosis three days post-transplant. The biopsy shows an area of liver infarction with necrotic hepatocytes and haemorrhage adjacent to normal liver tissue. *(H.&E.×150)*

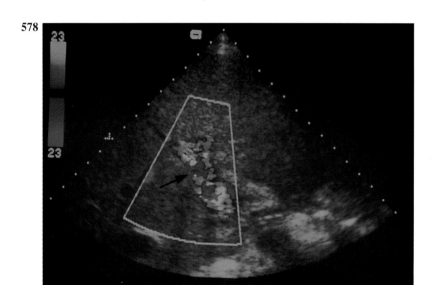

578 Liver infarction. Doppler colour ultrasound is a powerful non-invasive tool for determining the patency of blood vessels supplying the graft. In this patient, who developed abnormal liver function tests early in the post-operative period, the Doppler scan shows normal blood flow in the portal vein (arrowed).

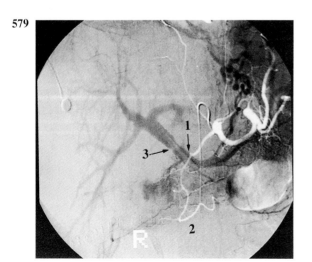

579 Liver infarction. This digital subtraction angiogram (DSA) was performed in a 60-year-old woman who deteriorated three days post-transplant. The DSA shows occlusion of the common hepatic artery (1) just distal to the origin of the gastroduodenal artery (2). The anastomosis between the patent donor and recipient portal veins is clearly visible (3). The donor liver showed infarction of the gall bladder and bile ducts.

580 Liver infarction. The appearances of an infarcted graft at the time of re-transplantation. The liver is swollen with blood and has a mottled surface due to alternating areas of normal and infarcted liver.

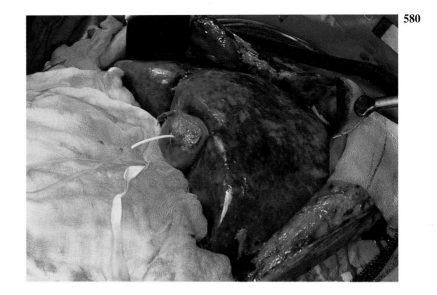

581 Liver infarction. This biopsy comes from the infarcted graft shown in **580**. It shows that the ischaemia has also led to transmural infarction of a large bile duct. The donor biliary tree depends on the hepatic artery for its blood supply. *(H.&E.×350)*

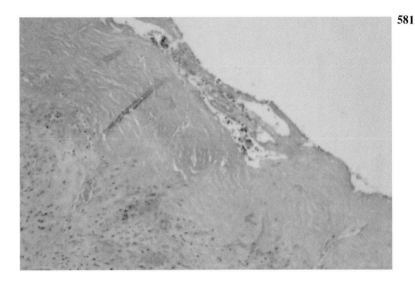

582 Acute cellular rejection. These are the typical histological features of acute rejection. The liver biopsy is from a 34-year-old female seven days post-transplant. The portal tracts are infiltrated with mononuclear cells and there is an endothelialitis of the cells lining the portal vein branch, as well as lymphocytic infiltration of the bile ducts. *(H.&E.×350)*

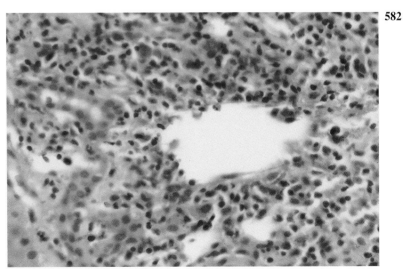

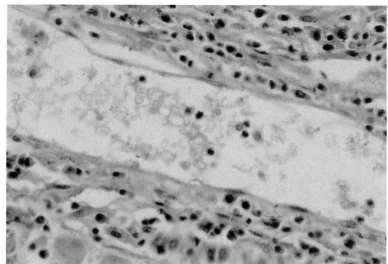

583 Acute cellular rejection. This biopsy is from a graft hepatectomy at the time of re-transplantation in a 47-year-old male and shows the characteristic endothelialitis in greater detail. Many of the endothelial cells lining the hepatic vein have been shed or are disrupted. *(H.&E. ×500)*

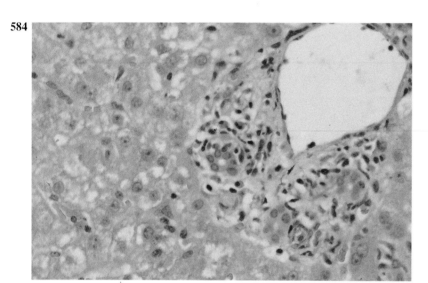

584 Acute cellular rejection. This biopsy was taken, following treatment, two days after the biopsy in **582** and shows the changes of mild acute cellular rejection. The lymphocytic infiltrate in the portal tract is less marked, but lymphocytic infiltration of the bile ducts and endothelialitis are still present. *(H.&E.×350)*

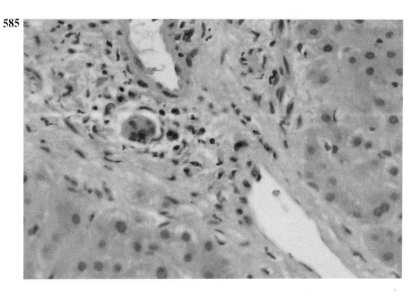

585 Early chronic rejection. This liver biopsy is from a 47-year-old male one year post-transplant. The biliary epithelium is atrophic and there is a sparse lymphocytic infiltrate. *(H.&E.×350)*

586 Chronic rejection. This liver biopsy comes from a 53-year-old male two years post-transplant. The bile ducts have disappeared from the portal tract. All that remains are portal vein and hepatic artery branches. This is one of the causes of the 'vanishing bile duct syndrome'. *(H.&E. ×350)*

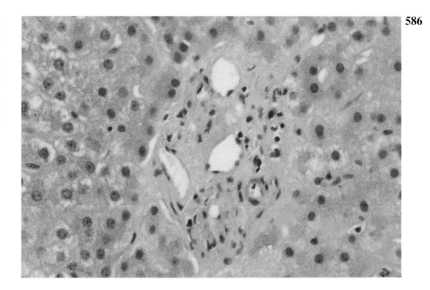

587 Cytomegalovirus. This 40-year-old male presented six weeks post-transplant with abnormal liver function tests. Liver biopsy shows that, adjacent to the portal tracts, the hepatocytes have enlarged nuclei containing inclusion bodies. This finding is very suggestive of CMV infection. *(H.&E. ×350)*

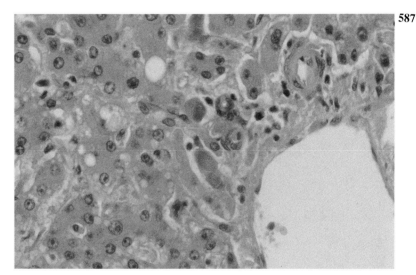

588 Cytomegalovirus. An immunoperoxidase stain, using anti-CMV antibody, of the biopsy shown in **587** confirms the presence of CMV as brown intranuclear deposits. *(×350)*

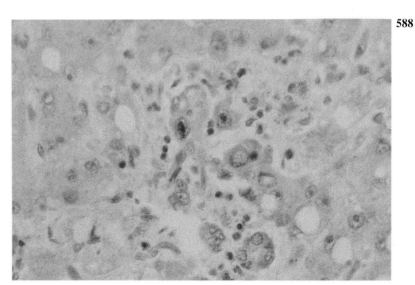

589

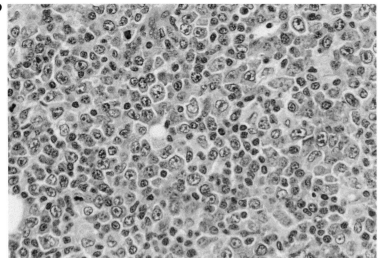

589 Epstein–Barr virus (EBV) associated lymphoproliferative lesion. This lymph node was taken from the porta hepatis of a 39-year-old male nine months post-transplant. The biopsy shows sheets of lymphocytes replacing the normal lymph node architecture. EBV-associated lymphocytic proliferation is related to immunosuppression and disappears when the dose of cyclosporin is reduced. *(H.&.E×300)*

590

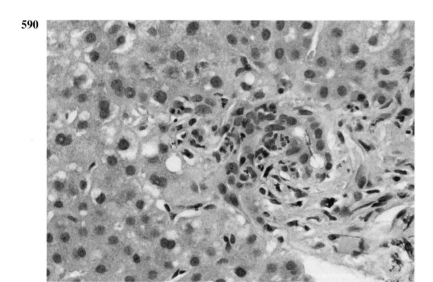

590 Cholangitis. This biopsy comes from a 26-year-old female who developed bile duct obstruction of the transplant. The biopsy shows an enlarged portal tract containing bile ductules infiltrated with polymorphonuclear leucocytes. Identical histological changes occur in transplant patients who develop septicaemia. Bile duct obstruction after transplantation may be due to biliary sludge or strictures at the site of the biliary anastomosis. *(H.&E.×350)*

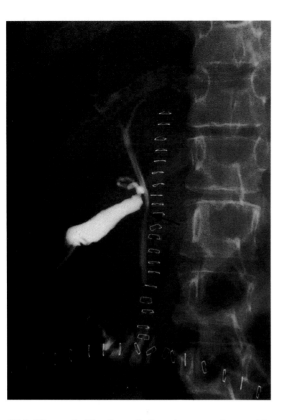

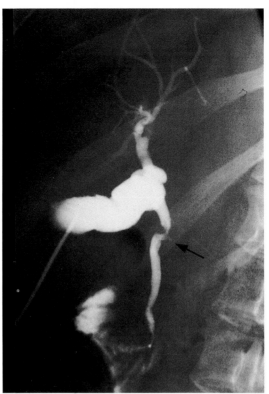

591 Normal T-tube cholangiogram in a 19-year-old woman seven days post-transplant. The anastomosis between the donor and recipient bile ducts is barely visible (arrowed). The donor biliary tree is of normal calibre.

592 Biliary stricture. A T-tube cholangiogram of the patient shown in **591** two months post-transplant. A stricture has developed at the site of the biliary anastomosis (arrowed) and the intrahepatic bile ducts are dilated. These biliary strictures are best treated by repeated endoscopic dilatation, and in some patients by stenting.

13. Trauma of the liver and biliary system

Damage to the liver and biliary system may follow either open trauma (e.g. gunshot wounds) or closed trauma (e.g. road traffic accidents) and lead to rupture and bleeding. Sepsis is a complication of open trauma.

Bile duct injury usually follows cholecystectomy. Major catastrophes, such as section or ligation of the common bile duct, present in the immediate post-operative period. Section of the bile duct leads to a continuous large leakage of bile through the wound drains. The patient may become jaundiced. Ligation of the bile duct causes a steadily deepening cholestatic (biliary obstructive) jaundice in the post-operative period. Post-traumatic bile duct strictures present as jaundice or cholangitis several months or even a year after the surgery. These strictures are caused by damage to the blood supply of the bile duct which results in fibrosis and stricture formation. The repair of damaged bile ducts is complicated. Post-traumatic bile strictures can also be treated by endoscopic balloon dilatation and stents.

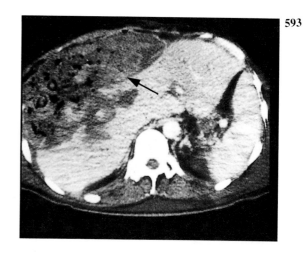

593 Liver trauma. CT is particularly useful in the investigation of patients with trauma. This scan comes from a young soldier who suffered a severe gunshot wound to the anterior abdomen. CT (intravenous contrast enhanced) shows a low attenuation haematoma with disorganized liver tissue and gas, indicating infection (arrow). The patient was successfully treated by surgical drainage of pus, debridement and angiographic embolization of a feeding hepatic artery branch.

593

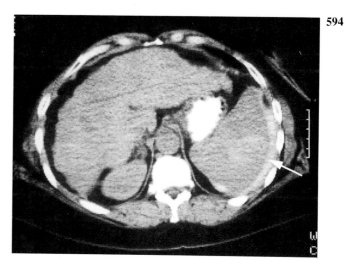

594 Splenic rupture. This middle-aged woman with primary biliary cirrhosis and portal hypertension had a splenic venogram. Three hours later, she complained of upper abdominal pain but was not shocked. CT (intravenous contrast enhanced) shows a perisplenic haematoma (arrowed). Treatment was conservative and symptoms subsided.

594

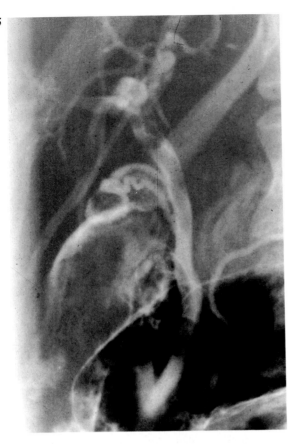

595

595 Haemobilia. Twelve hours after a percutaneous liver biopsy this patient developed biliary colic, enlargement of the liver and jaundice. ERCP shows linear filling defects in the common bile duct, representing blood clots.

596

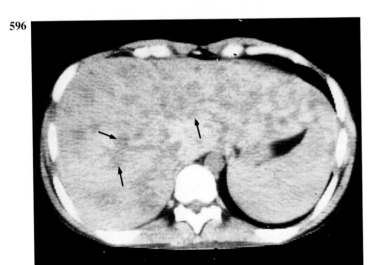

596 Multiple pyogenic liver abscesses. This 25-year-old man suffered extremely severe burning when an oil burner exploded. Skin sepsis with many organisms, including *staphylococci*, was followed by multiple liver abscesses. These are shown in this CT scan as small space-occupying lesions (arrowed). The spleen is enlarged.

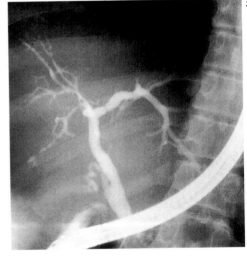

597 Multiple pyogenic liver abscesses. The patient shown in **596** recovered from the multiple liver abscesses, but developed persistent cholestatic (biliary obstructive) liver function tests. This endoscopic cholangiogram shows that the widespread hepatic sepsis had resulted in diffuse secondary sclerosing cholangitis.

598 Rupture of the gall bladder. This alcoholic cirrhotic developed bile-stained ascites after hitting the steering wheel in a minor accident. The endoscopic cholangiogram shows contrast medium escaping from the gall bladder (1) into the peritoneal cavity (2). Gall bladder rupture may occur after only moderate trauma in cirrhotic patients. This is probably due to the distended gall bladder that develops in cirrhosis.

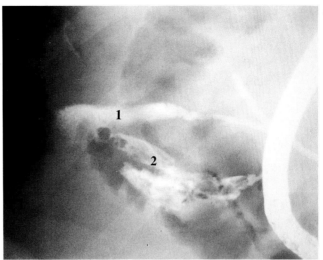

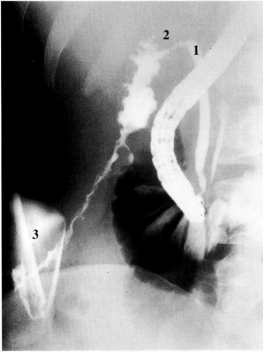

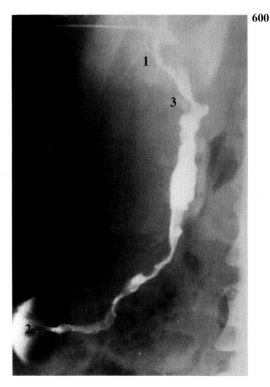

599 Section of the common bile duct. This patient developed jaundice immediately after a cholecystectomy and there was copious bile flow through the wound drain. An endoscopic cholangiogram showed the lower end of the common bile duct (1) and contrast escaping from the bile duct at the level of the cystic duct (2) into the wound drain (3). No contrast entered the intrahepatic ducts.

600 Section of the common bile duct. A percutaneous cholangiogram in the patient in **599** shows contrast medium entering the intrahepatic ducts (1) and escaping into the wound drain (2) at the level of the cystic duct (3). No contrast medium enters the common bile duct. These studies demonstrate a complete section of the bile duct.

601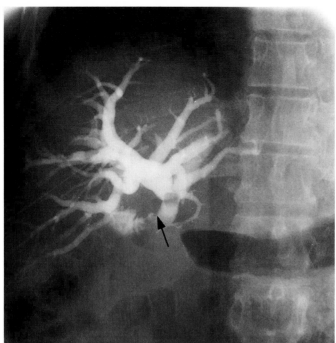

601 Biliary stricture. This 70-year-old man in poor general condition had a cholecystectomy and for the subsequent two years suffered episodes of cholangitis and jaundice. Percutaneous cholangiography shows a benign high biliary stricture (arrowed). The intrahepatic bile ducts are dilated.

602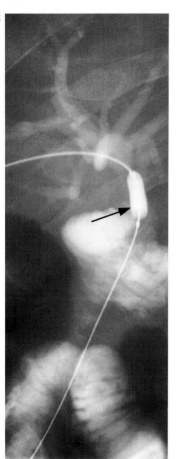

602 Biliary stricture. A balloon catheter (arrowed) has been introduced by a percutaneous transhepatic approach through the stricture of the patient in **601**. Inflation of the balloon has dilated the stricture.

603 Stricture of surgical anastomosis.
A biliary stricture may develop at the
site of a choledochojejunostomy. In
this patient a tight stricture of the
anastomosis has led to dilatation of the
intrahepatic ducts and formation of a
stone (arrowed) above the stricture.
These strictures cannot be reached
with an endoscope and a percutaneous
transhepatic approach is necessary.

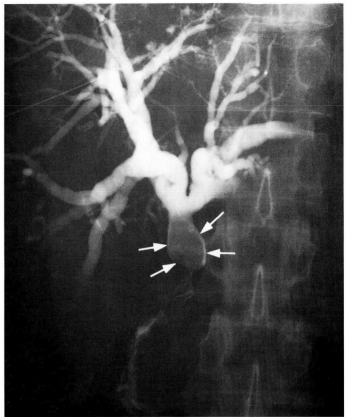

604 An expandable metal stent was
passed across the stricture shown in
603 by a percutaneous transhepatic
catheter. The metal stent was expanded *in situ* by a dilating balloon
catheter. The expanded metal stent
(arrowed) keeps the anastomosis
widely patent.

14. Gallstones

Gallstones are classified according to their predominant component as either *cholesterol* stones or *pigment* stones. Cholesterol gallstones are the commonest type encountered in the Western world. A small proportion are pigment gallstones. Pigment stones also develop in chronic haemolytic states, cirrhosis, recurrent biliary infections and, in the Far East, are associated with *Clonorchis sinensis* infestations.

605 Cholesterol gallstones are usually multiple, faceted and a greeny-yellow colour. They may contain varying amounts of calcium salts. Occasionally a single large gallstone is found in the gall bladder.

605

606 Pigment gallstones are generally small, round and a dark green or black colour. The gall bladder may contain hundreds of calculi. These pigment stones were removed from a patient with thalassaemia major (see **621–623**).

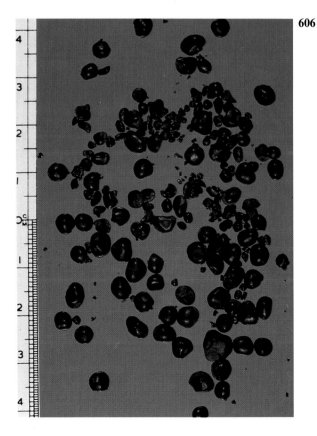

606

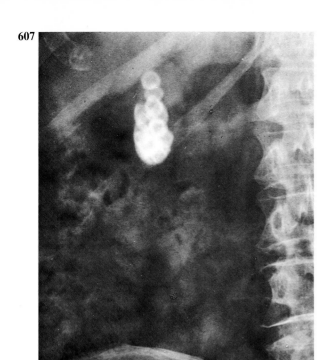

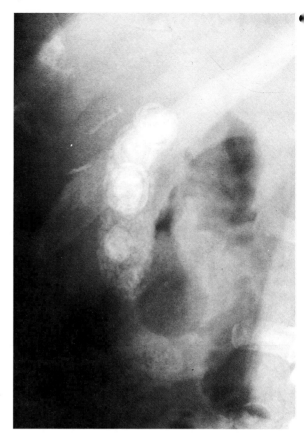

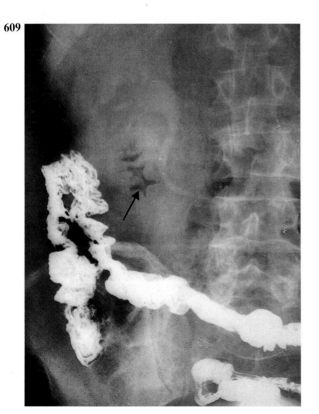

607 Calcified gallstones. A small proportion of gallstones contain sufficient calcium to make them radio-opaque in an abdominal x-ray. This plain x-ray (flat plate) shows the gall bladder full of stones with a peripheral ring of calcium.

608 Calcified gallstones are occasionally laminated due to alternate deposition of layers of cholesterol and calcium salts.

609 'Mercedes Benz' sign. Rarely, the centre of a gallstone contains gas which shows as a stellate translucent pattern (arrowed) in an abdominal x-ray. In the search for the cause of this patient's abdominal pain a barium enema and intravenous pyelogram had been performed.

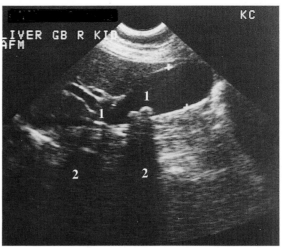

611 Ultrasound scan of the gall bladder is the preferred first test for the diagnosis of gallstones. This scan shows a gall bladder containing at least three stones (1). The acoustic shadows (2) cast by the stones are typical.

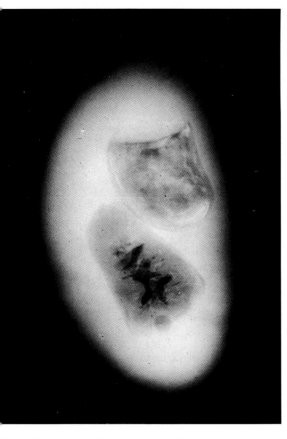

610 'Mercedes Benz' sign. After cholecystectomy, an x-ray of the gall bladder specimen confirmed that the translucent stellate pattern seen in **609** was due to gallstones.

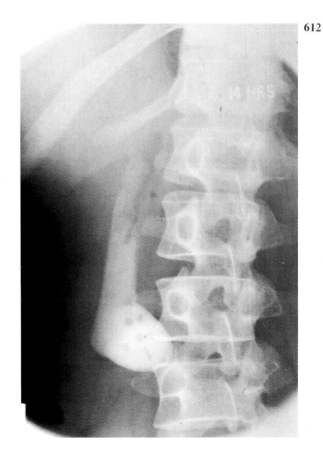

612 An oral cholecystogram will demonstrate radiolucent gallstones provided there is sufficient gall bladder function to concentrate the radio-opaque contrast medium. Tomography may be necessary. This cholecystogram shows at least five stones as lucent filling defects in the gall bladder.

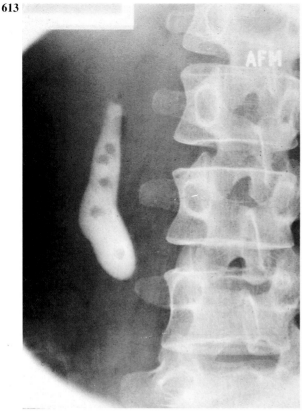

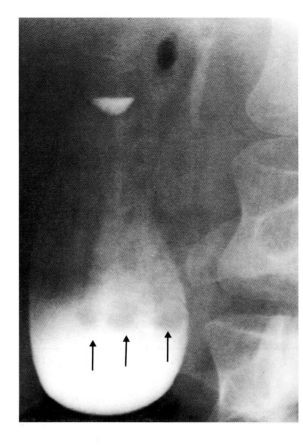

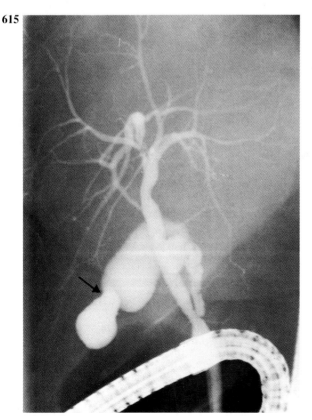

613 Oral cholecystogram. A fatty meal caused the gall bladder shown in **612** to contract. This is a sign of good gall bladder function. The calculi are seen more clearly.

614 Floating gallstones (arrowed) are lying on the surface of a dense layer of contrast medium in the gall bladder. These calculi were only seen when the patient stood erect. Most stones are sufficiently dense to sink through the contrast medium.

615 'Phrygian cap' is a congenital malformation causing folding between the body and fundus (arrowed) of the gall bladder. Gall bladder function is normal. A 'phrygian cap' is of no significance, but in cholangiograms must not be confused with disease of the gall bladder.

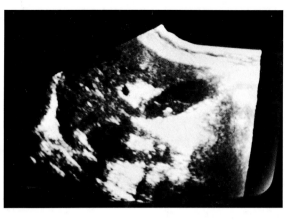

616 Acute cholecystitis usually follows impaction of a stone in the cystic duct. This grey-scale ultrasonogram shows a distended gall bladder (1) containing stones (2). A stone is impacted in the cystic duct (3). The inflamed and distended gall bladder causes abdominal pain and tenderness on palpation of the liver edge (Murphy's sign). Infection may develop, causing a pyrexia. In severe cases the gall bladder is filled with pus (empyema of the gall bladder).

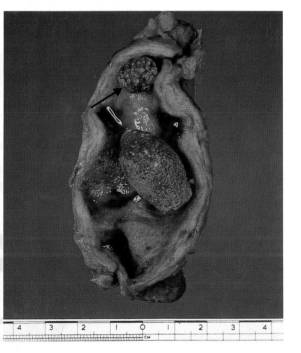

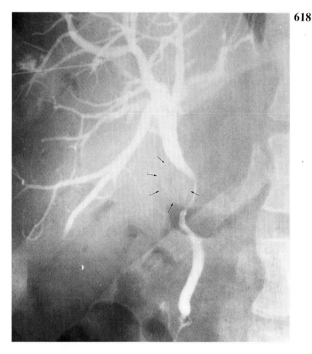

617 Chronic cholecystitis follows recurrent attacks of inflammation. The gall bladder wall is thickened and chronically inflamed. Several stones are present, one obstructing the cystic duct (arrowed).

618 Mirizzi's syndrome. Percutaneous cholangiography shows a large gallstone impacted in the cystic duct (arrowed). This has caused partial obstruction to the common hepatic duct. The patient presented with recurrent cholangitis. In such cases a stone may have eroded into the common hepatic duct creating a single cavity. Patients may also present with obstructive jaundice.

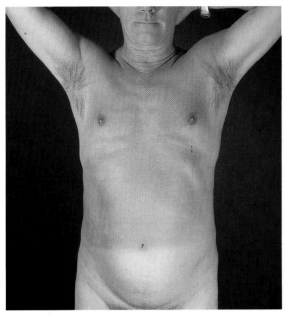

619 Gallstones in the common bile duct have usually migrated from the gall bladder. Biliary colic, cholangitis and cholestatic jaundice may develop. This patient became jaundiced after an attack of biliary colic while on holiday (he is suntanned). The serum bilirubin level was 11mg/100ml (187μmol/l).

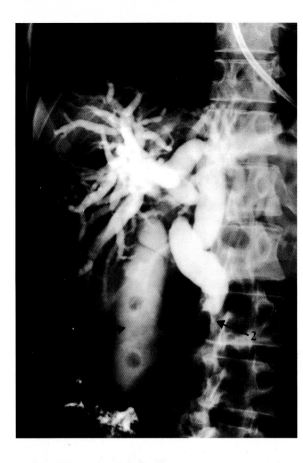

620 Percutaneous cholangiogram from the patient in **619** shows stones in the gall bladder (1) and a stone (2) obstructing the lower end of a dilated bile duct.

621 Chronic haemolysis is associated with pigment gallstones, which may obstruct the common bile duct. This patient with thalassaemia major suddenly developed jaundice, itching, pale stools and dark urine. The serum bilirubin concentration was 19mg/100ml (323μmol/l). Note the prominent malar bones, which are enlarged with erythropoietic tissue.

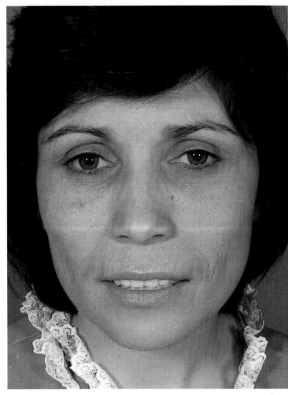

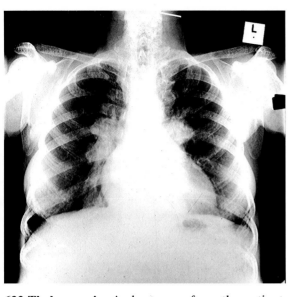

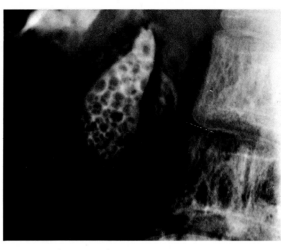

622 Thalassaemia. A chest x-ray from the patient in **621** shows circular shadows at the hila of both lungs. These are masses of erythropoietic tissue at the posterior ends of the ribs. The ribs show coarse trabeculation. The enlarged heart is due to iron overload in the myocardium.

623 Thalassaemia. A percutaneous cholangiogram from the patient in **622** shows the gall bladder full of stones. The coarse trabeculation of the vertebral bones is due to the excessive erythropoiesis of a chronic haemolytic state. This is the clue that the calculi are probably pigment stones. The stones are shown in **606.**

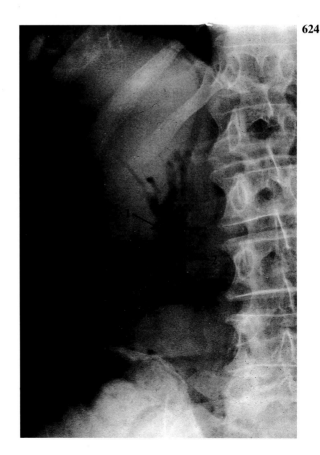

624 Air in the biliary tree (1) is usually a consequence of biliary tract surgery, either a sphincterotomy or an anastomosis between the bile duct and the small intestine. Rarely, it is caused by infection with gas-producing organisms such as *Clostridium welchii.* Air in the biliary tree may also follow the spontaneous passage of gallstones from the biliary tract into the gut. In this patient, the round shadow at the lower end of the air-filled common bile duct is a gallstone (2). The patient was suffering from biliary colic when the x-ray was taken. Note the fluid levels (3) in the surrounding 'sentinel' loops of the bowel. Rarely, the passage of a large gallstone may cause intestinal obstruction ('gallstone ileus').

625

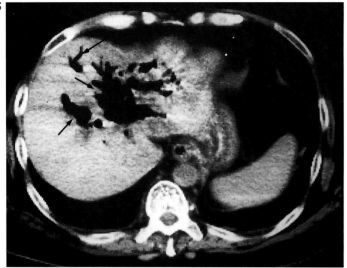

625 Air in the bile duct. This intravenous contrast enhanced CT scan was taken two years after a choledochojejunostomy was performed to treat a post-cholecystectomy biliary stricture. The bile ducts are dilated and contain air (arrowed).

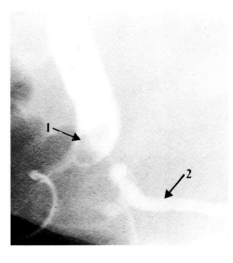

626 Pancreatitis may be caused by a gallstone (1) at the ampulla of Vater obstructing the pancreatic duct (2). This endoscopic retrograde cholangiogram was performed soon after an attack of acute pancreatitis.

627

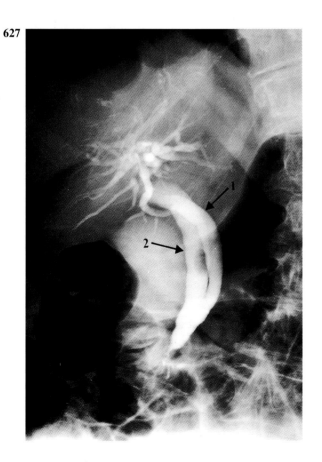

627 The cystic duct remnant (1) after cholecystectomy may be very long if the cystic duct is inserted low down the common bile duct (2). Symptoms are uncommon. However, stones may develop in a long cystic duct stump and result in recurrent attacks of cholangitis.

628 Retained bile duct stone removed by endoscopic sphincterotomy. Cholesterol was the principal component of this oval calculus.

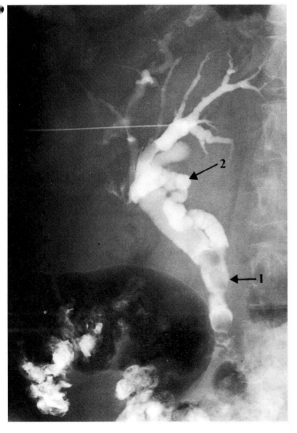

629 Retained bile duct stones. This patient became jaundiced after a cholecystectomy. A percutaneous cholangiogram shows three stones (1) obstructing the lower end of a dilated common bile duct. A long cystic duct remnant (2) was present.

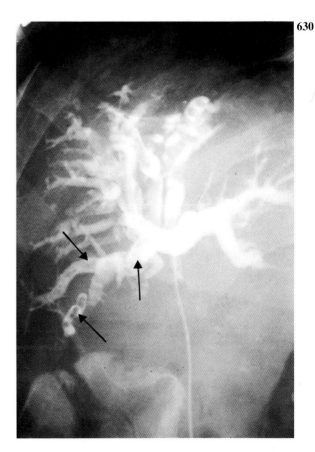

630 Intrahepatic gallstones usually follow prolonged biliary obstruction due to a bile duct stricture or sclerosing cholangitis. In the Far East they are associated with *Clonorchis sinensis* infestation. Small, gutty, dark-green or black pigment gallstones are the usual finding. This operative cholangiogram from a patient with a benign post-cholecystectomy biliary stricture shows multiple intrahepatic gallstones (arrowed).

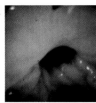

631 Solitary duodenal diverticulum at the ampulla of Vater is associated with gallstones. In this patient the ampulla of Vater was hidden inside the diverticulum. The endoscopic picture shows bile escaping from the mouth of the diverticulum.

632

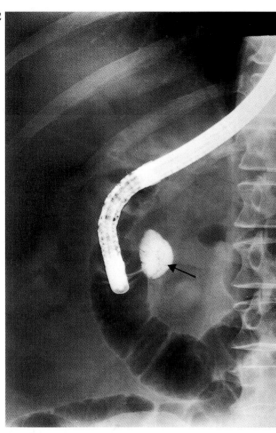

632 Solitary duodenal diverticulum in **631** has been filled with contrast medium (arrowed). It is situated in the second part of the duodenum which is filled with air.

Non-surgical management of gallstones

Endoscopic sphincterotomy is employed for the removal of stones in the bile duct. The usual indications are retained bile duct stones overlooked at surgery and the removal of bile duct stones in patients who are unfit for surgery. The ampulla of Vater is cut open at endoscopy by a diathermy cannula. In a small proportion of patients this will be complicated by haemorrhage or pancreatitis. After sphincterotomy, small stones may be left to pass spontaneously. The bile duct may be cleared of stones up to 2cm in diameter by a dormia basket or balloon catheter. Larger stones are first reduced by *in situ* dissolution with solvents or by extracorporeal shock wave lithotripsy. Where a large T-tube has been placed in the bile duct, stones may be removed by percutaneous extraction with a steerable basket catheter passed through the T-tube track. In patients with numerous biliary calculi, which cannot be removed by sphincterotomy, symptomatic relief may be obtained by inserting an endoprosthesis.

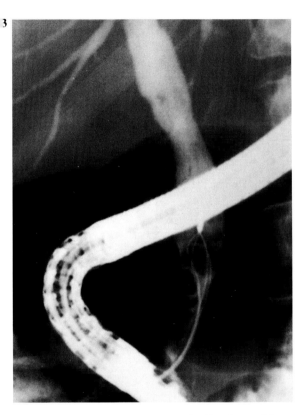

633 Dormia basket extraction. Following sphincterotomy this stone was snared by a dormia basket (arrowed) and is being extracted from the bile duct.

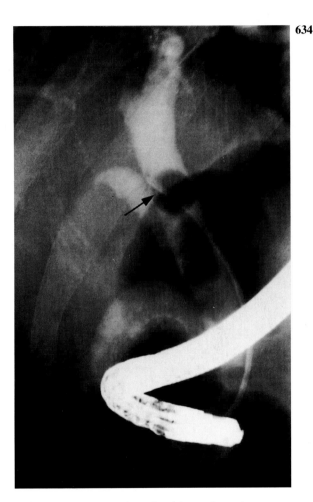

634 Balloon extraction. In this patient the stone was too large to be snared by a dormia basket. A balloon catheter (arrowed) has been passed above the stone and inflated. The stone was removed by withdrawing the balloon catheter.

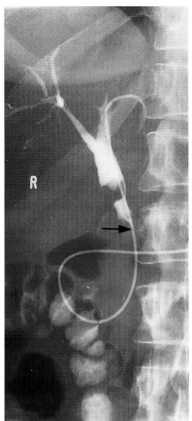

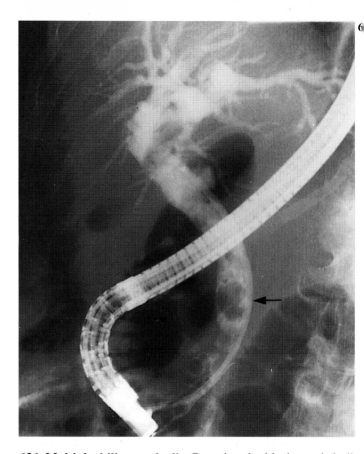

635 Acute cholangitis due to gallstones may cause a fulminating illness with septicaemia. An endoscopically inserted nasobiliary drain (arrowed), as in this patient, provides emergency biliary drainage and relieves the symptoms.

636 Multiple biliary calculi. Occasional elderly and frail patients who are unfit for surgery have bile ducts which contain so many large stones that they cannot be removed by endoscopic sphincterotomy. This 92-year-old man had recurrent bouts of cholangitis caused by a bile duct which was full of large stones. An endoprosthesis (arrowed) was passed into the bile duct of the patient shown after performing a sphincterotomy. The endoprosthesis disrupted the aggregates of stones and provided drainage of the biliary system. The patient's attacks of cholangitis ceased after this endoprosthesis was inserted.

Index

Numbers in bold type are caption numbers; those in normal type are page numbers.